A Consequentialist Defense
of Libertarianism

A Consequentialist Defense of Libertarianism

Richard Fumerton

LEXINGTON BOOKS
Lanham • Boulder • New York • London

Published by Lexington Books
An imprint of The Rowman & Littlefield Publishing Group, Inc.
4501 Forbes Boulevard, Suite 200, Lanham, Maryland 20706
www.rowman.com

6 Tinworth Street, London SE11 5AL, United Kingdom

British Library Cataloguing in Publication Information Available

Library of Congress Cataloging-in-Publication Data

Names: Fumerton, Richard A., 1949– author.
Title: A consequentialist defense of libertarianism / Richard Fumerton.
Description: Lanham : Lexington Books, [2021] | Includes bibliographical
references and index. | Summary: "In defending freedom, most
libertarians have appealed to a moral framework that puts an emphasis on
the concept of moral rights. Rejecting that approach, Richard Fumerton
offers a fresh, nuanced, and balanced "consequentialist" perspective on
the importance of defending liberty"— Provided by publisher.
Identifiers: LCCN 2020057356 (print) | LCCN 2020057357 (ebook) | ISBN
9781793632043 (cloth) | ISBN 9781793632067(pbk) |
ISBN 9781793632050 (epub)
Subjects: LCSH: Libertarianism—United States. | Libertarianism—Moral and
ethical aspects. | Consequentialism (Ethics)
Classification: LCC JC599.U5 F835 2021 (print) | LCC JC599.U5 (ebook) |
DDC 320.51/2—-dc23
LC record available at https://lccn.loc.gov/2020057356
LC ebook record available at https://lccn.loc.gov/2020057357

For Alex and Charlie

Contents

Preface

For those of us who genuinely love this country, one of its greatest virtues, we often think, is that it really is the land of the free. To be sure, we sometimes describe democratic rule as the primary political value to which we subscribe. But de Tocqueville was surely right to warn us that majorities can behave very badly, and there is no guarantee that democratically elected governments and democratically supported laws will prevent deplorable tyranny. In many Middle Eastern countries, the so-called Arab "Spring," a Spring that included the occasional much-celebrated election, turned very quickly into a nightmarish winter. Democracy doesn't ensure even a decent way of life for many of the people who live under democratic rule. It certainly doesn't guarantee the kind of liberty that most of us value so much.[1]

The framers of the U.S. Constitution understood all of this. They tried to ensure that the United States was founded on principles dedicated to the importance of freedom, and Americans have fought and died to preserve those freedoms. But there is also an ongoing debate about which sorts of freedoms we ought to protect and which we ought to be prepared to sacrifice for what some will take to be greater goods, like security and prosperity.

Since virtually the beginning of philosophy, philosophers have been arguing about the extent to which people ought to be free to do as they choose. In the *Republic*, Plato clearly thought that unbridled freedom was the road to ruin. Just as parents should be permitted and, indeed, required to restrict the behavior of their children, so also, Plato thought, appropriate rulers ought to restrict the behavior of the people whose welfare they are supposed to supervise. Without the paternalistic intervention of "gold-souled" rulers, Plato argued, the worst instincts of people will drive them to engage in behavior that is not only self-destructive, but destructive to the well-being, indeed the very survival, of their state.

In the eighteenth century, John Stuart Mill, in his classic work, *On Liberty*, predicted that controversies concerning freedom are likely to become the "vital" questions of the future (1956). We are living in that future to which Mill refers and are, therefore, ideally situated to evaluate the accuracy of his prediction. With increasing controversies over the wisdom of allowing a state more access to e-mail and phone records, calls for censorship of the internet, restrictions on immigration, the never-ending abortion controversy, calls for relaxation of drug laws, and a host of controversies concerning the role of government in controlling the economy, it is difficult to argue that Mill missed the mark with his prediction.

While it is a bit of an understatement to suggest that it is difficult to predict political trends, many Americans do seem hungry for a political movement that stresses the importance of both economic and personal freedom, a movement that is often called libertarianism. One might expect at this point a definition of libertarianism. Certainly, the official Libertarian Party of the United States has a platform (Libertarian National Committee, Inc. 2018). The planks of that platform are couched mainly in terms of rights, and as we will see later, I'm not that comfortable with a rights-based conception of ethics. The rhetoric of the platform (as one might expect from such a document) is not precise or careful—sometimes it is extraordinarily vague. And in any event, not all self-proclaimed libertarians will support all of the planks in that platform. In this work, I'm interested in the more general question of what sorts of liberties one *ought* to defend. The difficulty, to put it bluntly, is in finding a *sane* form of libertarianism. Many of libertarianism's proponents seem dangerously *impractical*. Most versions of libertarianism come across as extreme, I will argue, primarily because they presuppose a correspondingly extreme deontological or "rights-based" conception of rationality and morality.[2]

There are at least two fundamentally different approaches to answering ethical questions: one is consequentialist, the other is deontological.[3] The consequentialist starts with the intuitively appealing idea that what one ought to do is entirely a function of the *consequences* of what one does (compared to the consequences of alternatives open to one). Even more crudely, the consequentialist is committed to the view that the right thing to do is whatever makes the world the best place possible. The crude idea needs to be made much more sophisticated. The view needs to specify what counts as having positive and negative value, what counts as a genuine alternative, and what consequences (actual, probable, or possible) are relevant to the rightness or wrongness of an action. The view I have defended in the past takes the relevant consequences to be those that are possible (even if their probability is very low). But if one embraces such a view one also needs an account that allows one to factor in the *probability* of a consequence in "adjusting" its value prior to "summing" the positive and negative values that results from an act in order to compare that sum with the sum one gets from adding the adjusted values of the possible consequences of alternatives. One also needs an account of the relevant concept of *probability* at play.

Despite its initial plausibility, consequentialism of the sort I just described has come under relentless attack throughout the history of philosophy. Perhaps the most common form of criticism focuses on what philosophers call counterexamples. We've all heard people (often politicians) being *criticized* for thinking that the ends justify the means. The consequentialist, of course, should respond with irritation at such a criticism. What else, after all, would justify taking some means but some end one was trying to accomplish? How can taking appropriate means to achieve some end be a moral failing of some sort? The answer is supposed to be that it is part of a plausible conception of morality that there are certain *constraints* on how to accomplish goals, even goals that are very good.[4] The consequentialist is committed to the view that given odd enough circumstances just about *anything* might be morally required—we might be morally required to torture, lie, steal, kill innocent children, or target civilians in war, to take just a few examples. All this and more might be required if we find ourselves in circumstances in which such acts maximize value. The deontologist typically finds all of this wildly implausible and, as suggested above, seeks to place certain constraints on what one may reasonably or morally do in order to achieve even valuable ends. This book will argue that consequentialism of the right sort can respond effectively to the deontologist's criticisms.

As I suggested above, libertarian arguments for freedom have classically been *deontological* in nature and have appealed to certain *rights* people have—rights that cannot legitimately be trumped for the sake of making the world a better place. There are at least two sorts of rights that political philosophers distinguish: positive and negative. Crudely, one has a positive right to something, X, when some person or group has a moral obligation to see that you get X. One has a negative right to do X, when others have an obligation not to use their power to prevent you from doing X. The liberties so dear to libertarians are often construed as negative rights. According to the libertarian, our right to free speech, to religious association, and to own firearms, to take just a few familiar examples, involves the kind of actions that both morality and the law protects. We think it would be wrong for others to prevent us from speaking our political minds, from endorsing a given religion, or, much more controversially, of course, to own at least certain sorts of weapons.

A critical philosophical question concerns just how to understand all this talk of rights. In the realm of law, the concept of a negative right is relatively straightforward. At least it is as straightforward as is the concept of law itself. One has a negative *legal* right in Society X to do something, Y, just in case there is no law in Society X prohibiting one from doing Y. Most (though not all) ethical philosophers would want to distinguish between questions of law and morality. A society might legally prohibit behavior that it morally shouldn't prohibit. And most philosophers would allow that it might be morally wrong to behave in ways that are legally permitted. But can one make sense of all this talk about *moral* rights?

Back when so-called natural law theories of morality were relatively common, it might not have been that hard-to-find analyses of moral rights that paralleled those of legal rights. The basic idea was that there are moral *rules* just as there are legal *rules*. Just as human-made laws permit, require, and prohibit certain sorts of behavior, so also moral "laws" permit, require, and prohibit certain sorts of behavior. But some are decidedly skeptical of this notion of natural law, as illustrated by this quote from the famous political philosopher Jeremy Bentham:

> Natural rights is simple nonsense: natural and imprescriptible rights, rhetorical nonsense—nonsense upon stilts. (2019, 53)

I am frankly quite sympathetic with Bentham, and the consequentialism I defend in this book rejects the very idea that one can make sense of *laws* of morality.[5] Consequentialists can, however, acknowledge the need for people to use what are sometimes called rules of thumbs—rough and ready guidelines learned primarily from past experience concerning the tendencies of certain kinds of actions to have good and bad consequences. And these "rules" of morality can form the basis for at least some laws that are written in such a way that they (unlike the rules of thumb) do not admit to exceptions.

Part I of this book deals with the theoretical issues roughly sketched above. Part II examines the consequentialist case for formulating "libertarian" laws—laws that respect the importance of social and economic freedom. It is in the very nature of the consequentialist argument that the relevant empirical facts will be highly controversial. A philosopher can, of course, appeal to experts in other fields to support empirical claims, but everyone knows that the "experts" in the relevant social "sciences" disagree profoundly with one another. But a philosopher can usefully contribute this much—a philosopher can make the relevant distinctions, ask the relevant questions, and discuss conclusions one should reach *given* certain possible answers to the empirical questions. Framing the debate correctly is a critical part of knowing how to go about resolving it.

There are many people I should thank for their contributions to the evolution of my thought on these matters. While she certainly disagrees with many of my conclusions, my colleague, Diane Jeske, has been an invaluable critic. When I need to talk through an idea or get a reaction to an argument, she is the person whose views I most value. The many roundtables I attended on law and philosophy organized by Michael Moore and Heidi Hurd have always been thought-provoking and just plain fun. And Michael and Heidi, in particular, are among the best philosophers with whom one could hope to interact. I received helpful advice from anonymous referees. Jan Narveson gave me valuable critical (sometimes *highly* critical!) feedback on an earlier draft of the manuscript, and I hope that the book is better as a result. John Kirchner read and commented on an early draft of the manuscript, and Brady Hoback was extremely helpful giving input that worked its way into further significant revisions. Finally, I want to thank the University of Iowa, the Iowa Board of Regents, and the State of Iowa for the developmental assignment whose support allowed me a semester to concentrate on research and writing.

NOTES

1. Throughout the book we'll talk much more about what kind of liberty that is.

2. I do not mean to imply that any "rights-based" libertarianism will be extreme. Vallentyne (2007) argues that even within the constraints of rights that are consistent with some versions of libertarianism, one can defend a robust role for government. He calls this version of libertarianism "left libertarianism." In his well-known defense of libertarianism, Narveson (1988) has no patience for a libertarianism based on absolute rights, but even he builds the foundation of the libertarianism with which he is most sympathetic on the idea of property rights that is not parasitic upon the idea of law. I'll have much more to say about the key notion of property rights later in the book.

3. As we will discuss later, there is a third approach, virtue theory, that is making a bit of a comeback. I'll talk briefly about the role of virtue in ethical theory later.

4. See Gaus (2001) for an extended discussion of different ways in which one might try to distinguish a deontological ethics from a consequentialist ethics.

5. To be contrasted, of course, with moral laws in the sense of human-made laws that we ought to have.

Part I

Theoretical Controversies: The Importance of Consequentialist Reasoning

ONE

Level Distinctions and a Philosophical Dilemma

As I indicated in the preface, I think that this country wants and needs a really careful, reasoned evaluation of libertarian principles. Indeed, I suspect that people may be ready to vote for the right kind of libertarian candidate, either as a candidate representing one of the two mainstream political parties, or as a candidate running for a third party. But while I have always been interested in highly *theoretical* questions concerning the content of moral claims and claims about rationality, I have also always endorsed a very "old-school" approach to philosophy. On that approach, one insists on carefully distinguishing "meta" questions from "first-level" questions. Furthermore, I used to think that the philosopher, *qua* philosopher, was equipped only to answer the meta-questions. At the same time, as I shall explain in a moment, many of the most difficult political questions concerning freedom are "first-level" questions. Specifically, the questions concerning how we ought to structure a state and what laws we ought to enact to preserve freedoms are paradigmatically first-level questions.

Though it is not the approach taken by most defenders of freedom, I will try to convince you that in debating fundamental questions concerning what freedoms we should protect, we should argue from within a framework that stresses that what one morally and rationally ought to do is a function of facts about the *consequences* of what we do. Such a view is sometimes simply called consequentialism, but, as we shall see, there are fundamentally different versions of consequentialism. While I try to convince you in part I that consequentialism is the correct approach to debating the issues that will concern us in part II, I will also try to convince you that any plausible alternative to consequentialism will also need to stress

3

the *relevance* of consequences in deciding what policies we ought to adopt.

THE DISTINCTION BETWEEN META-QUESTIONS AND FIRST-LEVEL QUESTIONS AND A PROBLEM FOR PHILOSOPHERS

Let me explain the distinctions between meta-questions and first-level questions and illustrate them with a few examples. In metaethics, philosophers are concerned primarily with answering questions of the form: What does it *mean* to say of something that it is morally good/valuable, or that an action is morally permissible, morally required, morally forbidden? There are still more abstract disputes lurking in the background, and some philosophers will object to the characterization of metaethics in terms of an investigation into "meaning." Our interest, they might suggest, is the nature of moral *properties*. They might prefer to put the relevant meta-questions this way: What makes something morally good or bad; what makes a morally right action right and a wrong action wrong? When we say of some alternative open to us that we ought to take it, what, if anything, would make it true that the act is such that it ought to be taken? Those who prefer thinking of the meta-questions in terms of meaning may worry that the proposed investigation into the nature of moral *properties* or *facts* already begs important questions by assuming that there are such properties as being good or being morally required, for examples, that enter into moral facts.[1] But however one understands precisely the meta-questions, philosophers trying to answer them will typically distinguish these questions from the substantive, first-level questions about what *is* good and bad, what we should and shouldn't do, what we are permitted to do, if not required to do, and so on. You and I could agree with each other completely on what makes an act such that it ought to be done (agree with each other on the meta-position), but nevertheless reach dramatically different conclusions concerning what we ought to do.

One can draw this sort of meta- versus first-level distinction with respect to just about any topic. And there is no end to the interesting philosophical disputes that arise at these meta-levels. We learn how to recognize colors at a very early age, but if you get four philosophers in a room arguing about what makes something red, you are likely to get four very different answers. One might tell you that being red is a simple, indefinable property of which you are directly aware; another might identify the redness of an object with the capacity of that object to affect normal humans under normal conditions with that familiar sensation of looking at red.[2] Yet another might insist that the redness of an object should be understood in terms of the way in which the surface of that object reflects or absorbs light. And yet another might tell you that there is no such thing as being red—we confusedly *mistake* something subjective in us for something objective "out" in the world. But all four of these philosophers, and for that matter any child, will be able to follow instructions to go to the grocery store and pick out a nice red tomato.

The connection between morality and *rationality* is a topic of much dispute. Some argue that what one morally ought to do cannot come apart from what one rationally ought to do. Others argue that the concepts should be kept quite distinct, and that it is a completely open question as to whether a rational person will pay any attention to what morality requires. We'll talk more about that issue later in the book (chapter 3). In any event, one can again distinguish questions of meta-rationality from questions about what course of conduct would be rational for a person or a state to take. If we put the meta-question in terms of meaning, at least one fundamental question of meta-rationality would be the following: What does it mean to say of some person (or group, or society, or country), X, that X rationally ought to take some course of action, Y?

It is tempting, though controversial, to argue that meta-questions are, in some sense, more fundamental than first-level questions. Put another way, it is tempting to think that in an *ideal* world one should have answers to meta-questions before one even attempts to find answers to the first-level questions. How can one try to figure out which items are good or bad, for example, without knowing what would make something good or bad? How can one determine what action is rational for one to take without knowing what makes an action rational? It would be like going on a hunt for elephants without knowing what an elephant is. I suppose if you shoot everything in sight you might succeed in your goal of bagging an elephant, but it would surely be more rational to figure out what you are looking for before you try to find it.

As I said, the above (rather cryptic) argument is more than a little controversial. We earlier noted that a child can pick out a red tomato at the grocery store without ever considering, let alone answering, the meta-question concerning what makes something red. But there is still some force to the argument concerning the priority of meta-questions, I think, if one emphasizes that meta-questions should be answered first in an *ideal* investigation. And the more complex the concept one is interested in applying, the more obvious it is that one would be well-advised to figure out precisely what the concept is before one tries to apply it. Furthermore, as I shall argue shortly, confusion at the meta-levels can create no end of confusion in arguing for or against various sorts of freedom.

One might suppose that a philosopher working in an ideal way would write a book like this with the goal of answering *both* meta-questions *and* first-order questions. One should answer the meta-questions first and put into action one's theoretical conclusions in addressing first-order questions. This is precisely the approach I will take, but not before acknowledging that there is a very real difficulty for a philosopher proceeding in this way.

The potential problem is that almost all interesting first-level questions—particularly questions about what one morally ought to do, or what it is rational to do—require extensive *empirical* knowledge to answer.[3] The empirical knowledge required is of a sort typically investigated by the various "hard" and "soft" sciences, including, but not restricted to physics, astronomy, biology, chemistry, geography, geology, climatology, psychology, sociology, economics, political science, and demographics. And most philosophers, at least philosophers *qua* philosophers, don't have the relevant empirical expertise. The reverse is also true. Most of those who have the relevant empirical knowledge (or, at least, who participate in the relevant empirical investigations)[4] lack the relevant philosophical sophistication to engage, seriously and intelligently, the relevant meta-questions.

Let me illustrate the point with the most obvious example of a meta-theory in ethics or practical rationality that would render first-level questions very complex empirical questions. As I mentioned in the preface, one of the oldest, and perhaps initially most plausible, theories of morality is known as consequentialism (a theory that we will be examining in much more detail in chapter 3). Again, on the crudest (not the most plausible) version of the view, one identifies the right action (of the alternatives open to one) with the action that "maximizes" value.[5] The *rough* idea is that there are facts about what the world would be like as a result of taking various actions—let's call these the consequences of taking a given alternative. Some of the consequences that would occur would be good; some, bad. Most would be neither good nor bad. If I shoot you, your pain and suffering, the anguish of your family and friends—those consequences of my action would all be bad. If you were hated by at least some people, perhaps the pleasure they would get from having you removed from their lives would be good. The shooting itself has, indefinitely, many other consequences, however. The bullet leaving the gun displaces air molecules that, for all we know, will forever continue in a slightly different spatial location. If I am caught and punished, my life will be different for years to come—some aspects of life will be better, some worse, some more or less the same. One can introduce the idea of the *net* value that would result from taking an action as the "sum" of the positive and negative values that attaches to the various consequences that would result from that action. One can then define the right action as the action that would result in the greatest "net" value (allowing of course that there might be "ties" and thus that there might be alternatives that are equally acceptable). Life being what it is, the right thing to do might yield net negative value. The man pinned under a rock who had to amputate his own arm in order to avoid death was hardly thinking his day was going well as he hacked away with his pocket knife.[6] Nevertheless, his choice could still have been the right action to take in virtue of the fact that the net value yielded by every alternative would be even lower.

As I indicated, we'll talk much more about consequentialism later. The point here is just to illustrate that if anything *like* this view were correct, one would need extensive knowledge of the world in order to reach rational conclusions about what one ought to do. In particular, one would need to know a great deal about what causes what. And when it comes to the decisions people argue most about—decisions about whether to go to war, how to structure an economy, what liberties to allow people—the causal questions are *exceedingly* difficult to answer.

As we shall see, consequentialism is a decidedly controversial view, and is rejected particularly by many who engage in the kind of disputes that will be the central focus of Part II of this book. But as we shall also see, the need for empirical data hardly gets less critical on alternative views about metaethics and meta-rationality. The *deontologist*, for example, rejects the idea that one can *define* what one ought to do in terms of the goodness and badness of consequences. Deontologists argue that the right action to take may not yield the greatest net value. Perhaps the most well-known (and, I think, one of the best) deontologists, W. D. Ross, took certain action *types* to be prima facie right and prima facie wrong,[7] and further thought that one couldn't *define* these critical notions of being *prima facie* right and wrong, though we can identify kinds of actions that have this moral character (1988, 19–20).[8] As we shall see, one can have a prima facie duty to act in a certain way, even if, all things considered, one ought to reject that action. That's because the same particular action can be prima facie right in virtue of having one characteristic, but prima facie wrong in virtue of having another. But difficulties arise even if we focus on prima facie obligation. To figure out whether a given action is *in fact* prima facie right or wrong, one needs to determine whether the action *is* of the relevant *sort*. So, for example, suppose that one thinks that everyone has a prima facie moral reason to be kind to other people. Would it be straightforward, then, to determine whether or not a given action taken by someone has the relevant feature of being kind that makes it prima facie right in this way? Hardly. Children don't think that their parents are being kind when they are punished by those parents. Yet we all know that a good, *kind*, and loving parent must punish a child occasionally, not only for the well-being of others, but also for the well-being of the child. Teachers sometimes need to grade harshly a student's work, but a good teacher might do so hoping that the student learns from the evaluation—the good teacher might view himself or herself as acting in a way that is actually *kind* (by being beneficial) toward the student. But it is the rare student who views the teacher's assignment of the low grade as an act of kindness.

We talked about the consequentialist's view that the rightness or wrongness of an action is a function of the goodness and badness of consequences (suitably understood). Even the staunchest of deontologists virtually always feel the force of the suggestion that consequences matter. Kant might genuinely have believed that morality always requires you to tell the truth, *no matter what*.[9] But almost no one else adheres to a deontology that strong. We lie (and should lie) to our hosts about how pleasant the meal was even if the meat was sadly overcooked. We tell guest lecturers that we enjoyed their talks even when we didn't. But it is not just the permissibility of "white" lies that is at issue. The protectors of Anne Frank were not only morally permitted, but morally required, to lie about her whereabouts should they be questioned by Nazis trying to round up Jews. If someone working for the CIA gets captured by an enemy country, the president of the United States is not just morally permitted, but morally required to lie about the person's real occupation. And what is true of lying is true of just about any other kind of action of which one can think. The permissibility of torture has come under considerable scrutiny in the last decade, and there are those who righteously proclaim that torture is unacceptable under *any* circumstances. But there are few moralists who won't fold their tent when faced with the most extreme of hypothetical situations where millions of lives are at stake and it is *stipulated* in the thought experiment that the torture has a high probability of success.[10]

So, is the almost painfully obvious relevance of consequences to moral conclusions (or more generally conclusions about what one ought to do) a nail in the coffin of deontology? Hardly. You will recall that the kind of subtle deontology endorsed by Ross specifically begins only with the idea of a prima facie reason (duty, obligation) to act in a *certain* way. One must distinguish one's prima facie duties from one's "all things considered" reasons to act. As we saw, prima facie obligations, if such exist, can obviously conflict. On a view like Ross's one might have a prima facie duty to tell the truth that is trumped by a prima facie duty of care to a loved one. And, importantly, Ross himself also recognized what he called a prima facie duty of *beneficence* and a prima facie duty to avoid *maleficence* (1988, 21–22). Stripped of the terminology, Ross agrees with this much of consequentialism: if there are no other duties at play, one ought to do whatever maximizes value.

Some deontologists like to talk about so-called threshold deontology.[11] The idea is that one embraces deontological views while recognizing that if the consequences of an act become momentous enough (either really good or really bad), those consequences might trump deontological considerations. But this way of looking at things is decidedly confused. If you are going to be a deontologist, be a deontologist. If one thinks that one needs to acknowledge the relevance of consequences, then, like Ross, include in one's deontology prima facie duties to bring about the best consequences. As always, when taking such an approach, one will need to acknowledge that in reaching a conclusion about what one ought to do, *all things considered*, one will need to weigh prima facie reasons both for and against acting in various ways. [12]

Again, we will need to look at the consequentialism/deontology debate much more carefully, but for now I just want to stress again, that once a deontologist includes among the action kinds that generate prima facie obligations something like an action that maximizes value, one is every bit as committed to the critical relevance of empirical investigation into consequences as is the consequentialist. It is almost always only empirical research that will enable us to tell if an action is of the relevant kind.

I haven't said anything yet about how the deontologist balances all of these prima facie reasons to act so as to generate a truth about what one ought to do, all things considered. We'll look at that question later. It may be that *this* question could, in principle, be decided without *further* recourse to empirical investigation. But the information necessary to settle it, as we saw above, is thoroughly infused with the answers to empirical questions.

There is a third approach to ethical theory that we haven't yet discussed. Virtue theory is making a bit of a comeback these days. [13] That we have the concept of virtue seems almost obvious. Providing a successful philosophical analysis of what makes a given character trait a virtue is, however, difficult. It is tempting to think that having certain properties makes one virtuous just insofar as people with those characteristics are more likely to do what they ought to do in life. Consequentialists and deontologists could both embrace such an account of virtue (though, of course, they offer different accounts of what makes it true that one is doing what one ought to do). One might, however, argue that the concept of virtue has a more *fundamental* role to play in ethical theory. Roughly, one might argue that one should understand the concept of what one ought to do relying on the concept of virtue. More specifically, if one could *independently* grasp what makes a character trait a virtue, one might try to define what one ought to do in terms of what a virtuous person would do. In such a view, virtue becomes the conceptual lynch pin in understanding other ethical concepts.

This book isn't the place to provide an extensive evaluation of virtue theory. I can't figure out how one could ever get a grasp on the concept of virtue without *first* having some grasp of what makes an action the right action to take. Understanding virtue seems to me almost obviously parasitic upon understanding the role virtues play in leading one to act as one ought to act. That is not to deny that we have the concept of a virtue. Nor is it to deny that both consequentialists and those deontologists who include among prima facie duties the duty of beneficence will stress the importance of taking into account the consequences of one's actions on one's *character traits* (one's dispositions to behave in certain ways). One can, through one's actions, affect the kind of person one is, and changes of this sort can result in further morally significant consequences. But how and when this might happen as a result of choices one makes is yet another empirical question that is very difficult to answer.

If all the above is true, then there really does appear to be a bit of a dilemma for a philosopher who is interested (as most of us are) in substantive questions about how we should live our lives. In the context of this book, the dilemma arises for a philosopher trying to reach substantive conclusions about how to decide the plausibility of various versions of libertarianism. If such conclusions require extensive empirical knowledge, and the philosophers, acting as philosophers, haven't been trained in such matters, why shouldn't we conclude that the philosophers are just out of their depths when it comes to answering the relevant questions?

There are at least two approaches one might take to answering this question. One, of course, is to partner up with those who should have the relevant expertise in the critical fields. So, if we are arguing as libertarians for various forms of economic freedom, we might be able to engage the help of an economist. If we are worried about the costs and benefits of various social freedoms, we might need to partner up with psychologists and sociologists. Such cross-disciplinary work is all the rage these days, and only a troglodyte would shy away from forging the relevant partnerships.

But let me say a word or two for the troglodytes. In political and social philosophy (and in ethics more generally), there is no getting around the need to answer the difficult meta-questions that are the purview of philosophers. Just as philosophers may not have the expertise to answer certain empirical questions, so also, intellectuals in other fields usually don't have the expertise to answer the critical philosophical questions. Because of the nature of philosophy, this sometimes isn't as obvious as it should be to those who jump right into a philosophical controversy without the relevant training. There is no shortage of academics outside of philosophy who fancy themselves capable of dealing with abstract philosophical questions. But they tend to be really bad at philosophizing, and, of course, that should be no surprise given that philosophy is hard and requires its own specialized training.

But so what? The whole point of a cross-disciplinary approach is that one relies on the expertise of those trained in different fields. Here, however, one must face the unavoidable fact that there is simply no consensus within philosophy on what the correct answers are to the fundamental meta-questions with which the philosopher grapples. So, if you are an economist, or a doctor, or a sociologist, or a psychologist, hoping to work on a problem with a philosopher, what are you supposed to do? Spin the wheel of philosophical positions and engage with a philosopher who endorses the view indicated by the needle? Given the number of radically different, and mutually exclusive, philosophical positions taken by prominent philosophers, you are *likely* to end up partnering with someone who has a false position.[14] After all, if there are more than two positions and if you have no more reason to accept one over the others, then relative to your evidence, each position is unlikely to be true.

One might quickly conclude that philosophers are the "weak siblings" of intellectual partnerships. If only our cross-disciplinary endeavors required nothing more than the expertise of those well-versed in empirical sciences, we could proceed more efficiently. But when it comes to answering the sorts of questions that will be raised in this book, such a view is itself wildly implausible. To be sure, philosophers might be among the most obvious examples of academics who fail to reach consensus on the questions that define their subject. But to answer questions concerning what freedoms we ought to guarantee in our society, we will need the help of specialists in economics, psychology, and sociology, to name just a few disciplines. One doesn't need to know much about the academic study of economics to realize that there is almost as much disagreement among economists as there is among philosophers. Confirmed Keynesians will try to convince you that huge state debt matters little. Many conservative economists will try to convince you that debt will stifle economic growth and ultimately crush an economy. Some sociologists will argue that the legalization of most recreational drugs will have little or no effect on the behavior of most individuals. Others predict that the legalization of "heavy-duty" drugs will spell the end of a well-functioning society. One only needs to sample books on "best practices" concerning child rearing to realize that psychologists disagree with each other almost as much as philosophers. So, the philosophers looking for the right empirical scientists with whom to partner in a cross-disciplinary investigation are almost in as bad a position as are the empirical scientists pondering the philosophical positions on which they should place their bets.

I do have philosophical positions on the kinds of meta-questions I sketched above. And I fancy that I am as well-qualified as any other philosopher to answer the relevant questions. There is the problem of how one takes account of the disagreement one finds among one's "peers."[15] But that is a question that will lead us far astray in the present context. I also do have views about many of the empirical questions, answers to which I think are critical in determining the plausibility of libertarian policies. I would admit, however, that there is no particular reason for others to trust my views on these matters, given that most of what I believe is based on "intuitions" concerning the plausibility of various empirical positions about which I read. Given that I want to discuss libertarian positions in this book, how should I proceed?

Well, I'll start with the theoretical, abstract questions that are clearly the province of philosophers. If we are going to discuss intelligently controversies concerning freedom, we need to be clear about how to frame the debate. We need to make careful distinctions of a sort that are characteristically philosophical. If we do our work well, we will be able to think carefully and critically about the strength and weaknesses of various critical meta-positions. I'll try to convince the reader that my meta-views are correct, but I'll also try to get as clear as we can about how reaching alternative meta-positions would affect the way in which we should go about trying to settle the critical questions concerning freedom. Once we have the meta-positions out on the table, we can think clearly about the empirical information we will need to reach ultimate conclusions about what we ought to do—in particular, how we ought to structure society in such a way as to maximize protection of relevant freedoms.

But without the relevant empirical information, or, at best, with empirical information that is a matter of considerable dispute even among "experts" in the relevant empirical fields of investigation, what kind of conclusions can we rationally reach? It is at this point that the philosopher can always turn an empirical question into one that is genuinely philosophical, by relying on one of the philosopher's best friends—the conditional. Even if I am not sure what the relevant truths are in economics, I can still reach conclusions about what one ought to do *if* such and such were the truth. And it seems to me that I can settle this sort of question from the armchair. Conditional truths, of course, don't get you unconditional conclusions. Even if I convince you that if the empirical facts are F then one ought to endorse laws of form L, you won't know whether to support such laws until you know (or have at least a reasonable belief) that the facts are F. But that doesn't make the conditional useless. It tells you where you ought to direct your efforts in trying to decide what to do.

THE STRUCTURE OF THIS BOOK

If there is one contribution philosophy can make to a discussion of political issues, it is its ability to make clear, useful distinctions, and to make explicit the theoretical presuppositions that underlie various sorts of claims. As we noted earlier, much discussion of political libertarianism, and, indeed, much discussion of political views more generally, is heavily infused with talk about rights, and corresponding (perhaps equivalent) talk about what it would be wrong for others to do. We have the right, it is often argued, to act in certain ways free from government intrusion. It would be wrong for people to prevent us from acting in accordance with certain choices we make. In chapter 2, we will begin trying to make progress on all this talk about rights by distinguishing carefully morality and legality. I will argue that talk about what we have a right to do, and a right to get, is relatively harmless in the context of a legal system, but that it is far from obvious that these legal notions have a parallel in the context of morality. Chapter 3 will continue this theme by arguing more polemically for the "right" way to talk about rights and wrongs. After critically evaluating the divide between consequentialists and deontologists, I will defend consequentialism in morality against many of the strongest objections that have been leveled against it. Having made clear some of the critical background theoretical issues, we will be ready to address some of the important issues concerning freedom that have risen to the fore of political thought here in the United States and elsewhere. There is probably no more influential historical figure writing on freedom than John Stuart Mill, and it seems appropriate to begin, in chapter 4, with a critical evaluation of Mill's approach. For reasons that will become apparent, in part through our discussion of consequentialism in chapter 3, we will need to reject Mill's harm principle (and, indeed, any principle like it), as a useful ethical underpinning of a principled libertarian position. In chapters 5 and 6 we will try to defend arguments sometimes hinted at by Mill (though inconsistently) for libertarian positions in both the realm of freedom of expression and "lifestyle." In chapter 7, we'll address in an admittedly superficial way some thorny issues concerning economic freedom. And in chapter 8, we'll make some brief concluding remarks, including an appeal for more humility when it comes to the political positions one takes on controversial issues concerning freedom.

NOTES

1. Some moral philosophers (called non-cognitivists) argue that ethical sentences don't make *assertions* that are either true or false. Prescriptivists, for example, think we should understand certain ethical utterances as having a meaning more like that of an imperative. To say that we ought to be generous is something like saying, "be generous." See, for example, Hare (1965).
2. This approach initially appears to be circular. We are trying to explain what makes the surface of a physical object red and we appeal to the idea of something looking *red*. But circularity can be avoided if (and this is a significant "if") we can distinguish physical redness from what is sometimes called phenomenal redness. The latter involves that familiar, but probably indefinable, "what it is like" to have a certain sort of color experience. See Fumerton (2013) for more detailed discussion of these and related metaphysical issues.
3. For our purposes here, we can understand an empirical question as one that can only be answered through an extensive investigation into how the world happens to be (as opposed to how the world is necessarily). A more precise historical characterization of empirical knowledge characterizes such knowledge as relying ultimately on sense experience and introspection (looking into one's own mental state). Here I am mainly interested in a more vague distinction between what one can discover "from the armchair" and what one can only discover by getting out into the world and employing the methods of the sciences sketched above.
4. As we shall see, the relevant empirical knowledge is decidedly hard to come by. Economists, sociologists, and political scientists who spend their lives studying these matters have hardly reached any sort of consensus.
5. Of course, we will need to get clear about what all this talk of value means.

6. A reference to Aron Lee Ralston who did precisely that when, in 2003, his arm was pinned while hiking through a canyon in Utah.

7. Very roughly, to say that X is prima facie right is to say that X would be the right thing to do if there were no other moral considerations relevant to whether or not one ought to do X. Alternatively, one might say that X is prima facie right if one always has at least a moral reason to do X (even though there may be other reasons against doing X).

8. This claim is not uncontroversial. Narveson has suggested to me in correspondence that Ross would define the concept of prima facie right in terms of the concept of being right simpliciter. The rough idea is this: Some feature R of action X makes X prima facie right if were X the only morally relevant feature of X, X would be the right thing to do. This principle might be true, even necessarily true, but I don't think that it *defines* being prima facie rightness. First, reference to the absence of other morally relevant features clearly includes the absence of other kinds of features that would make the act prima facie right or wrong. Understanding this involves, once again, understanding the concept of something being prima facie right or wrong. Second, Ross is clear that what one ought to do, all things being considered (what is right, all things considered), is a function of the various prima facie reasons for and against acting a certain way. The relation of this dependence suggests that the idea of being all things considered right is built upon the ideas of being prima facie right and prima facie wrong.

9. Kant really does seem to hold the strongest of deontological views—one that holds that certain "imperatives" of morality admit of no exception. See Kant (1993, 30–38). A clear statement of the view seems to me a reductio of it. It is not difficult to think of a promise, for example, that would be utterly absurd to keep.

10. Obviously, the real world is rarely like this. As always, there will be complex empirical questions about the likelihood of torture extracting useful information that will prevent calamity. And there are additional important questions about immediate, but particularly long-term consequences of engaging in such practices (assuming that one gets caught). Even so, I don't really think it is that controversial to suppose that torture is sometimes morally permitted and morally required. Such a position, as we shall see later, is perfectly consistent with the position that a state should make torture illegal and punish those who break the law.

11. For a discussion of threshold deontology, objections to the view, and possible responses, see Zamir and Medina (2010).

12. And as Ross makes clear, the process of weighing prima facie duties would be exceedingly complex. Indeed, Ross denies that there is any sort of algorithm one can apply. It is less, clear, however, whether the unavailability of an algorithm is due to the complexity of identifying (for purposes of calculation) the *strength* of such prima facie duties as the duty of beneficence, or it is, instead, something that is, "in principle," impossible to do.

13. For an excellent anthology of articles on virtue theory, see Russell (2013).

14. For a collection of essays discussing the question of what belief one ought to hold in the face of such disagreement, see Feldman and Warfield (2010).

15. See Feldman and Warfield (2010).

TWO

Law, Rationality, and Morality

We have already had occasion to note in the preface that the quality of a state is determined not just by how its government is chosen, but by the content of the laws that state passes. Majorities can, indeed, problematically tyrannize some of its citizens. They can even behave inappropriately, one might argue, toward the very people who support that state and its laws. We can summarize the point this way: A democratically elected government can behave badly toward its people. And many would be happy to say that a democratically elected government can fail to respect the rights of its people.

There is no doubt that we are addicted to talk about rights. In the context of political debate, people talk about our right to free speech, our right to bear firearms, our right to adequate health care, our right to choose abortion, and our right to life, liberty, and the pursuit of happiness. But there is no consensus on how to understand all this talk of rights. Indeed, in some views about the meaning of fundamental ethical expressions, talk of rights is nothing more than a needlessly confusing distraction. The earlier quote from Bentham is worth repeating:

> Natural rights is simple nonsense: natural and imprescriptible rights, rhetorical nonsense—nonsense upon stilts. (2019, 53)

Before we get involved in a prolonged debate about what freedoms people have a right to, we had better think carefully about clearly defining the terms we employ in our argument.

THE DISTINCTION BETWEEN LEGAL AND MORAL RIGHTS

The first step in clearly defining a controversy about rights is to make a distinction between legal rights and moral rights.[1] While there are scholars who insist that, necessarily, moral truths partly determine what the law is (or determine how to interpret the law), on the face of it such views aren't very plausible.[2] The ordinary concept of law allows that a given nation might be governed by very bad laws indeed. If one allows that there can be evil laws, then the fact that one has a legal right to do something seems to have nothing much to do with the question of whether one has a moral right to do it (and, similarly, that one lacks a legal right has nothing much to do with whether one lacks a moral right). So, in Nazi Germany, for example, the state had a legal right to imprison Jews for having sexual relations with people of the "Aryan" race. It surely had no moral right to behave in such an atrocious manner. (And Jews had almost no legal rights whatsoever, but, surely, they had exactly the same moral rights as any "Aryan.")

The issue might not be quite this straightforward. As I have already had occasion to note, some deontologists make a distinction between what one is prima facie obligated to do and what one ought to do, *all things considered*. At a first stab, we might identify prima facie obligation in terms of the hypothetical absence of other morally relevant considerations. One has a prima facie obligation or duty to keep a promise, one might suggest, if one ought to keep a promise absent of any other morally relevant feature of that act of keeping a promise. If keeping the promise involves harming another person, for example, one needs to think carefully about whether one ought to keep the promise (assuming, of course, that producing harm is something that is morally relevant to whether one ought to act in a certain way). As we shall see in chapter 3's more detailed discussion of these issues concerning morality and rationality, even the consequentialist can develop a *very* weak counterpart to a prima facie obligation. Consequentialists, you will recall, are committed (roughly) to the view that one can define what one ought to do in terms of facts about the consequences of alternative actions open to one and the value of those consequences. But they can also introduce the concept of having *a* reason to act in a certain way. One might be said to have *a* reason to do X (one that might *easily* be trumped by other reasons), just insofar as X will (or might) result in at least some positive value (or prevent some negative value). Either the deontologist working with the conceptual building blocks of prima facie obligations, or the consequentialist (working with the concept of having a reason to act) might insist that even when a law is deplorably bad, one still has a prima facie obligation (the deontological way of putting it), or *a* reason (one among many—the consequentialist way of putting it) to obey said law. They can then both quickly emphasize that, in the case of Nazi law, whatever reasons there are to obey the law are overwhelmed by countervailing reasons to break it. We'll return to these issues later in this book.

As we noted earlier, in the context of discussing both legal rights and moral rights, it is useful to distinguish negative and positive rights.

Roughly, negative rights have to do with what it would be wrong for other people to prevent you from doing. To say that someone has a legal right in country Y to do X is roughly to say that there is no law in country Y that prohibits a person from doing X. So, for example, in the United States, I have a legal right to buy a red car, to own certain sorts of firearms, to give to charity, and to refuse to give to charity.[3]

Positive legal rights concern what *other* people are legally required to provide for you. To say that someone has a legal right to get something, X, is to say that the law requires someone or other to provide X to that person. So, for example, in this country, if (under certain circumstances) I have paid you to provide me with services and you have contractually committed to do so, then I have a legal right either to get from you those services or, should you fail to provide them, to receive appropriate compensation—you are legally obliged to either provide those services or compensate me for the damages I suffer from failing to obtain those services. If I pay too much in federal income taxes (more than the law requires me to pay), then I have a legal right to a refund—the federal government is legally obligated to pay me the relevant amount.

Controversies will arise, of course, concerning what one has a legal right to do and get. Laws require interpretation. And as we saw in chapter 1, even if we are clear about what the law requires of people in certain situations, it can be very difficult to determine whether the relevant situation obtains. There are conditions that define the making of a legally binding contract. If you enter a quid pro quo contractual arrangement *and* are of sound mind at the time you enter the agreement, understood the agreement, are of the appropriate age, and so on (the list is actually rather long), the law requires you to live up to your end of the agreement or compensate the other party appropriately for your lack of performance. The terms of the agreement itself might be perfectly clear, but it might be entirely unclear whether the other relevant conditions for making a legally binding contract were met. You might argue, for example, that you had a rather large number of martinis before you entered into the agreement, or that you didn't understand the terms of the agreement (that there was no meeting of the minds). The law itself won't settle the question of how many martinis consumed precludes an appropriate meeting of the minds.

The above controversies arise even assuming that the terms of the proposed agreement *are* clear. But lawyers make a great deal of money as a result of the fact that agreements themselves are often unclear or ambiguous. The lack of clarity or ambiguity is sometimes due to less than careful drafting of the relevant contract (or in the case of the state, the legislation), but often the vagueness and ambiguity are by design. Both parties may have wanted the contract to leave room for alternative interpretations, each anticipating possible circumstances in which it would be advantageous for it to argue for one of a number of possible readings.

Just as this is true of agreements reached among non-state actors, so also laws that legislators pass at the federal and state level often bring with them notorious vagueness and ambiguity. If we view the Bill of Rights and its amendments as a kind of meta-law limiting what other laws there can be in the United States, it is by now perfectly obvious to everyone that the language used to describe freedoms that cannot legally be abridged is often extremely vague—subject to a wide range of interpretations. The Second Amendment seems to make clear that *someone* has the right to own and bear arms. Some will argue that the surrounding language makes clear that the freedom in question was restricted to members of militia—others insist that the introductory remarks refer only to the need for *possible* militias and offer only a *justification* of the right described subsequently. But even putting aside that question of interpretation, we need to figure out what a reasonable interpretation of "arms" might be. Almost everyone agrees that it covers bolt-action rifles and pump-action shotguns. Some think that it obviously covers more sophisticated semi-automatic and automatic weapons. Only a few, however, think that it allows me to have my own nuclear-tipped ballistic missile in my back yard.

There is often another serious issue concerning particularly the interpretation of positive rights. As we explained the idea, you have a positive legal right to something just insofar as someone else is legally required to provide you with that thing. In the case of specific contractual agreements, it often isn't that hard to identify the relevant person, entity (in the case of a corporation), or institution that has the legal obligation that in turn defines the positive legal right. But just as in the case of morality (more about this later), where one often hears talk of the right to have such-and-such provided, so also in the case of law one can legally require that such-and-such be provided, without the law making it clear either who is supposed to do the providing, or (what, for all practical purposes, may amount to the same thing) who is supposed to bear the relevant costs involved.

In the above discussion of legal rights, I have mainly been proceeding with the unstated presupposition that where there are controversies about what the law requires, they concern empirical questions concerning circumstances, or hermeneutical questions concerning interpretation. The latter, in turn, might suggest that there is at least some "black letter" law that requires interpretation. But as anyone who has been to law school will tell you, in Britain and the United States (as well as a number of other countries), much of what we call law is so-called common law. While more and more of common law is evolving into law written down in books, there remains a great deal of law that hasn't made it to the status of "black letter." And one could write a whole book (many have) trying to figure out just what makes a set of principles part of the *common* law. Most think it has something to do with trying to piece together various specific decisions judges have made in an effort to come up with some plausible principle or principles that would unify and explain those decisions. When writing their decisions, the judges in question might have helped by explicitly stating the principles upon which they were relying. But not all judges explain their decisions in any sort of detail. Some are also inarticulate when they do. And, of course, some are stupid—their explanations make little or no sense and are sometimes internally inconsistent. Moreover, there is no reason to suppose that even if different judges over time were tried to be consistent with each other and prior decisions that they would be successful. It is small wonder that the meta-question, "What makes something a law?" is extremely difficult to answer.

The desire to come up with a unified set of principles that are consistent and allow us to make sense of the common law drives some to bring morality into the meta-question of how to understand the law of a given country. Earlier, we noted that on the face of it there is no tight connection between what the law requires and what morality tells us that we ought to do. But even if that is true, one can find intelligible the suggestion that when piecing together precedents in the search for underlying unifying principles, one might turn, particularly in unclear circumstances, to some sense of morality to find the relevant principles (or to choose from among equally plausible suggestions as to what the underlying principles might have been).[4] Such a concession, however, leaves intact the point made earlier. However, much morality creeps into interpretations concerning the law, there will be circumstances in which relatively unambiguous laws legally require people to act in ways that are morally abhorrent.

Before leaving the domain of legal rights, obligations, and requirements to investigate that same sort of language when used in the context of morality, it is worth talking a bit more about the connection between law and morality, not just in actual societies but in *ideal* societies. As we shall see, there are serious issues about which we must be clear if we are to avoid confusion in our search for legal principles that morally and rationally ought to govern an ideal state.

THE CONNECTION BETWEEN LAW, MORALITY, AND RATIONALITY IN AN IDEAL WORLD

We have already had occasion to note that there seems to be no strong connection between what the law requires us to do and what we morally or rationally ought to do, at least all things considered. Even if we were to talk ourselves into the idea that there is always *a* reason to obey a law or a prima facie duty to obey a law (perhaps conditional on whether the government in question has been chosen in a certain way—say democratically), almost everyone will admit that there are circumstances in which morality and rationality might not only permit but require one to break the law of one's land. Still, one might suppose, surely in an *ideal* society the law will mirror morality and rationality.[5] In an ideal society the law will permit, forbid, and require precisely what morality and rationality will permit, forbid, and require. If that were so, then we might argue that questions of morality and rationality are straightforwardly more funda- mental than questions of legality. Once we figure out what morality and rationality require of us independently of law, we need only follow Mo- ses's lead and write down the moral commandments delivering them to the people in the form of law.

Laws of Coordination and Definition

It doesn't take much thought to realize that this initial idea must be significantly modified. There are many laws whose primary purpose is to solve co-ordination problems. To take a much-used example, any place that deals with high volumes of car traffic, needs laws to coordinate the movement of that traffic. In the United States, we (legally) require people to drive on the right side of an otherwise unmarked two-lane road. Brit- ain (legally) requires people to drive on the left side. We are obviously missing the point if we start debating the question of which of these two traffic laws occupies the moral high ground. Still, even here, it is not as if questions of morality and rationality have no place. It is *rationality* that tells us we have a coordination problem and need to solve it—the collec- tive has a strong reason to pass laws of this sort. The neutrality enters in only after we realize that there are many different but equally rational ways of accomplishing the same end.

Similar things might be said about other obvious functions of the law—including that of legally defining terms, usually for the purpose of formulating other laws. So, the expression "taxable income" has a rela- tively precise definition. It was important to define the term clearly, once we (collectively) decided that a certain percentage of that income was going to the state (local and federal) to pay for various services and projects. We legally define terms like "marriage," "divorce," "contract," "client," "agent," "guardian," and "executor" primarily because we want to use the terms in a precise way when formulating laws. Again, there are alternative ways of defining the relevant expressions and often one defi- nition will do just as well as another provided that all are equally clear and unambiguous. That doesn't mean that there aren't issues of morality and/or rationality that undergird the need for the definitions. The feeling that this has nothing to do with morality/rationality is just the realization that for some of the terms that receive legal definition it doesn't matter much if we define them one way rather than another. What matters is if we fail to define them at all.

Law and Societal Encoding of Morality

Leaving aside those laws that solve coordination problems and define terms that will be useful to use in formulating other laws, isn't it still clear that *one* purpose of law is to encode, as well as it is practically possible, certain truths about how people should (morally and rationally) behave even in the absence of law? Once we legally define property, we have laws preventing people from taking (without permission) the property of others, and we have laws prohibiting killing, raping, torturing, blackmail, and indefinitely many other kinds of acts. It is tempting to suppose that insofar as we think these are good laws to have, it is because we also think that people shouldn't behave in the ways that are prohibited by these laws, even were the laws not to exist.

Before developing any such view much further, its proponents would probably be quick to point out that even in an ideal system, laws wouldn't attempt to make illegal *everything* that is immoral. If I promise to read my colleague's paper by Monday and renege on that promise (for no particularly good reason), most people will conclude that I have done something wrong. But almost no one would argue that we should pass and enforce *laws* prohibiting such conduct.[6] While lying certainly isn't always wrong, most of us engage in relatively harmless lies more often than we should. But again, it would probably be a huge mistake for society to attempt to make such conduct illegal. People should say "please" and "thank you," should hold the door open for others, should be, in general, kind and generous, but we would be making an almost comical mistake if we tried to enforce various sorts of etiquette with law and its accompanying sanctions.

But why do we think it foolish to require and prohibit with law certain kinds of actions that we nevertheless think people should and shouldn't take? There are a variety of perfectly good answers. One sort of consideration is practical. It costs money, time, and effort to put laws on the books, and it takes even more money, time, and effort to enforce such laws. If we tried to enforce all of morality (even were we to restrict ourselves to the morality upon which there is consensus), the justice system would be absolutely overwhelmed. The "thank you" police unit required to enforce etiquette would itself bankrupt many a city government.

In *On Liberty*, Mill unequivocally allows that a legitimate state might legally require people not only to refrain from harming others in various ways, but it might also require people to benefit others. He then cryptically suggests that the latter would be the exception rather than the rule (1956, 14–15). He doesn't explain any further, but one might suppose that, here again, the concerns would be practical. The last *Seinfeld* episodes aside,[7] so-called Good Samaritan laws are rare. And even where they exist, there is very little attempt to enforce them. It would not only be wrong, but morally egregious for me to watch a small child drown in the river outside my office without trying to do something about it. I'm a strong swimmer, the current out there isn't that strong. My failure to act might not be as bad as pushing the child into the river with the specific purpose of watching a child drown, but doing nothing when it wouldn't be difficult to save a life is heinous. Yet there is almost no jurisdiction that has laws that would allow me to be formally punished for my inaction. The explanation surely has something to do with the difficulty of crafting such laws. Would we try to write a law that requires anyone in a position to save a life to do so? That would be obviously far too broad. We don't want to legally mandate acts of saintly heroism. Should we legally require anyone to benefit another when that person can do so at relatively little risk to himself or herself? But what if there are hundreds of people in a position to save the drowning child, none of whom do so? Are we going to arrest them all? And harm that results from failure to act isn't limited to those who die because others haven't jumped in the river to save a child. As I look outside my window right now, I see people working on their tans, talking excitedly on their cell phones, sitting on benches listening to music through earphones. They could be patrolling the river, or at least be paying close attention to their surroundings so that they might be poised to save someone who is in danger. The cost to them of being alert is hardly that burdensome, though the cost of trying to *prove* that someone was less than mandatorily alert would be high indeed.

So, there are countless examples of moral conclusions we reach that most of us also realize we shouldn't try to mirror with laws, if for no other reason than that the practical obstacles to doing so are severe. But there is another obvious reason that as a society we decide not to translate all of morality into law. And that is the lack of consensus. Part of classical liberal political theory demands (or at least pretends to demand) a certain sort of societal neutrality when it comes to different visions of the good life. I add the cynical "pretends" language, as it becomes obvious to almost everyone that we aren't going to remain neutral with respect to *all* moral conclusions. Thus Rawls, who talks a great deal about the importance of neutrality, also concedes that the law can enforce values when they are "overlapping" values that any "rational" person would accept (2005, 144–172). A great deal more would need to be said, of course, about how exactly we are to understand "overlapping"—it would clearly be too strong to understand it in terms of universal consent. And even more would need to be said about what makes acceptance of a value claim rational. A great many liberal philosophers justify their rejection of enforcing morality, in part, because they believe that there are no objective truths concerning how people ought to live their lives. The closest substitute for objectivity is consensus with respect to what most people subjectively value. But without objective value, it is not clear how to understand *rational* valuing. On one view, one can rationally value X for its own sake only if X is intrinsically good (or, perhaps, rationally believed to be intrinsically good). But that appeal to goodness in understanding rational valuing isn't available to the subjectivist and relativist when it comes to understanding rationality. We'll talk much more about these critical issues in the next chapter.

However, we understand agreement and disagreement concerning issues of morality; society, particularly a democratic society, is obviously confronted by serious problems when faced with a citizenry who are sharply divided on the morality of various sorts of actions. To take a well-worn example, the people of the United States still seem more or less deadlocked on the question of whether various sorts of abortion are morally permissible. There are many pro-lifers who consider abortion murder (morally wrongful killing). Pro-choicers may attach some disvalue to the killing of a fetus, or may even think that it is prima facie wrong, but, by definition,[8] don't think that it is wrong (in all situations), all things considered. Both sides are likely to concede that the moral controversy is significant. If we refuse to legally prohibit abortion, it is not because we think that the matter is too trivial to translate into law. Rather, some are understandably reluctant to force people to act or refrain from acting in certain ways when there are sharp disagreements on the morality of doing so.

The matter isn't as straightforward as the preceding remarks might suggest. When there are sharp moral divisions, it is not as if by refusing to encode a moral position in law we thereby refuse to take a state-sanctioned moral stance. By not making abortion illegal, we are allowing people to act in ways that one side of the controversy thinks are morally egregious. The pro-lifers didn't get what they wanted when it comes to legality. The pro-choicers did. It may be that we think that there is a kind of default position when it comes to controversy that we legally allow people to do what they want—that actually passing a law *prohibiting* behavior of a certain sort requires much more justification and much more consensus than does failing to pass such a law. We'll look more at the potential significance of action/inaction distinctions in chapter 3. In any event, if we are relying on something like the above principle in the case of abortion, we certainly don't seem to be consistent. When it comes to moral controversies concerning whether to legalize recreational drug use, prostitution, or gambling, for example, there is significant disagreement, but we haven't hesitated (though matters might be changing as I write) to pass legislation prohibiting the controversial behavior.

I have discussed the problem of encoding morality in law when the morality is a matter of considerable dispute as though it were unlike the practical problems we discussed earlier. In the end, however, perhaps it is just another species of practical difficulty. Consider again abortion. When abortion was illegal in most states, abortions obviously didn't stop. All sorts of people, some well-trained, some not, were perfectly willing to perform abortions. And one common argument against making abortion illegal is that you wouldn't really cut down significantly on the frequency with which women choose the procedure. You would just virtually ensure that many of the women who get abortions did so under unsafe conditions. Similar arguments were made about the relatively short-lived U.S. prohibition laws. There were enough people who wanted to drink and few enough people who felt like supporting, with time and money, the effort it would take to sharply reduce the amount of alcohol consumption, that it became obvious that the cost of enforcing the prohibition law simply wasn't worth any potential gain.

Both arguments are problematic. It is a bit of a myth, for example, that prohibition didn't significantly reduce the consumption of alcohol, or that strict laws prohibiting abortion didn't reduce the number of abortions women had. To be sure, people will often violate laws, particularly laws with which they disagree, but that can hardly be, in itself, a reason not to have those laws on the books. There is virtually no law that isn't violated by relatively large numbers of people. Laws, in general, are costly to enforce and very difficult to enforce equitably. But the gain is surely significant enough in a wide range of cases to justify the law. A society without laws, after all, couldn't function. But there is a continuum of cases and a continuum of relevant factors all of which need to be considered carefully before trying to legally prohibit people from acting in a certain way. One (though *only* one) factor is the number of people who will be likely to violate the law and the corresponding cost that enforcement of that law will consequently involve.

Blunt Law and Nuanced Morality/Rationality

There is yet another commonly recognized reason why we should not expect the laws of even an ideal society simply to encode truths about what we morally and rationally ought to do even in the absence of law. The reason is that to be at all practical, laws must be relatively blunt. Though a full discussion of this issue will involve controversies discussed in the next chapter, I will argue that truths about what we morally and rationally ought to do are often highly nuanced. We talked a bit about consequentialism and its fundamental idea that we ought to do depends on the net value of consequences that would result from alternatives open to us. Just as is true of everything else, a specific action can be characterized in indefinitely many ways. Put more cryptically, an individual act is simultaneously an act of many different kinds. So, when I break my promise to you in order to help a friend, we might be able to truly describe what I did as breaking a promise, as helping a friend, as breaking a promise to help a friend, as maximizing well-being, as doing what God would have wanted me to do, as doing what I wanted to do all things considered, as acting the way a consequentialist would act, and so on. However, we choose to characterize the act, it has indefinitely many consequences that don't have anything to do with how we characterize it. There is a view that is sometimes called "situational ethics." Joseph Fletcher (1966), in a book of the same name, raised a fair bit of interest by arguing that there are unusual circumstances (situations) that would morally permit us to perform acts that we normally think of as very wrong. If the thesis is that certain kinds of actions are almost always wrong (perhaps even obviously so) but are sometimes permissible (perhaps even obligatory) under unusual circumstances, the thesis really isn't all that controversial. Certainly, the consequentialist will be fully on board. After all, the consequences of one's actions vary depending on the circumstances.

Consider again the ongoing debate over the use of torture. When we torture someone for information, that act has all sorts of significant consequences. But the consequences vary dramatically, and are *likely* to vary dramatically, based on the circumstances. If the situation resembled one of the classic plot lines of 24 (e.g., season 3, "Day 3: 6:00 a.m.–7:00 a.m.") and there were good reasons to think that torture would be effective at extracting useful information—when millions of innocent lives are at stake—it is really hard to resist the conclusion that those in a position to do so should go ahead and engage in torture (and probably also try not to get caught doing so). It is not that our actions won't be risking a great many bad consequences as well. The desire for revenge seems to be a deep-seated characteristic of human beings, and the groups to whom the victim of torture belong are almost certainly more likely than ever to react in kind. People who engage in violent behavior can easily become calloused and more likely to do so again, even in situations that don't call for it. In the case of our country, the United States, our engagement in torture violates various agreements that we have made with other countries, and the more one gets a reputation for violating agreements, the harder it will be to secure agreements, often useful agreements to have in place, in the future. But if the stakes on the other side of things are great enough, the calculations will still come down in favor of violating the international agreements. Or so it seems to me.

What is true of torture is true of virtually any kind of action, at least if the kind is defined in terms of something other than the consequences of the action.[9] Again, I'm not presupposing consequentialism here—only that consequences are going to be at least *relevant* to what one morally or rationally ought to do. As long as that is the case, it will be impossible to characterize a kind of action (without describing the kind in terms of its consequences) that will always be what one ought to do (or refrain from doing). But that poses a problem for a legal system that is trying to mirror morality. For laws to be useful, for laws to guide action, for laws to be enforceable, for juries to have a reasonable chance of reaching rational conclusions, laws need to be relatively straightforward. Those laws need to identify kinds of actions that are legally required, legally prohibited, and legally permissible. And they need to identify those kinds of actions in such a way that it would be practically possible for a legal system to accomplish its purposes.

If it is true that morality is as nuanced as law, as I have been arguing (we do need to talk more about this in next chapter), and if we want laws to mirror morality as much as possible, there are only two ways to proceed, neither of which will be at all practical. On the one hand, one can try to build into the statement of law as many morally relevant considerations as possible. Our laws would take the form: Do not steal from another unless it is the case that you could use the money to do A, B, C, D, E, . . . X, where the capital letters stand for all of the morally relevant considerations that would intuitively give you acceptable moral reasons for stealing. But the more complicated this list of conditions gets, the harder it would be to determine whether a law has been violated. This presents difficulties for police, prosecutors, judges, and juries. It wouldl also present difficulties for citizens contemplating whether or not to break the law. The more complicated that law is, the more difficult it is to determine what the law actually requires. *Nor will our hypothetical law ever succeed in anticipating all the factors that might pop up as perfectly good excuses for violating the law.*

An alternative suggestion might involve gesturing toward morally relevant factors by stating the law itself with reference to *whatever* morally relevant conditions obtain, but without making any effort to specify what those conditions are. Thus, one could imagine a legislature passing a law prohibiting people from trespassing unless, all things considered, they have good reason to do so. Our speed-limit laws would post maximum speeds, but in fine print below would allow people to exceed the stated speed limit if they have good reason to do so. If an attempt at fine-grained laws would create insuperable practical problems, laws that attempt to mirror metaethical principles that give no instruction as to what the relevant values are that need to be plugged in, give either no guidance or give guidance about which there is likely to be no consensus.

One might object at this point that the legal system, if not the law, has additional resources to make legal decisions fit fairly well with our intuitions about morality and rationality, resources that it should and sometimes does deploy. We all know that discretion is used by police, prosecutors, judges, and juries when deciding whether to enforce laws or their associated sanctions. The cop who finds you trespassing on my property while desperately looking for a telephone to call 911 probably isn't going to charge you with trespassing. Furthermore, even if the cop was so misguided as to follow the letter of the law, the prosecutor would doubtless refuse to prosecute.[10] Even with more serious violations of very important laws, laws defining and making murder illegal, for example, there is the possibility of jury nullification. Most of you are familiar with the plot behind *A Time to Kill*. The father, whose young daughter is brutally assaulted, raped, and left to die, illegally takes justice into his own hands. There is no doubt about his legal guilt,[11] but near the end of the movie the jury simply refuses to convict. They come to understand exactly why the enraged father would be justified (not legally, of course) in acting just as he did. So, measures do exist to align legal decisions more closely with morality. But the alignment doesn't always take place through the formulation of the law, and the measures in question are, in a sense, "extra-legal."

Reaching legal decisions concerning guilt and innocence is only one responsibility of a legal system. Together with juries, judges need to decide punishment (or, in the case of civil cases, restitution). And this is another opportunity to take into account all the subtle factors that go into our evaluations concerning the morality of an action. Where there is no mandatory sentencing, there is usually significant latitude in how one punishes someone found guilty of an offense. This is surely one of the ways that we recognize the thesis advanced in this section—that for all sorts of practical reasons, we won't be able to get a workable set of laws that mirrors exactly our conclusions about what was moral or rational to do.

Law and the Creation of Reason to Act

We will return to many of the controversies that have only briefly been introduced above. But before leaving the question of how to understand the relationship between morality and law, I want to put on the table one other significant reason why a rational person might not expect the laws of an ideal society to even *try* to mirror the moral positions of people in that society. It is entirely plausible to conclude, I will argue, that the purpose of many laws is not to formally recognize the reasons people have to act even in the absence of law, but, rather, to *create* reasons that people simply don't have to act or refrain from acting in certain ways in the absence of law. John Locke seemed to think that in an ideal world where everyone was able to know all moral truths and was equally disposed to act in a way consistent with such truths, there might be no need of law (1993, 124–125). In the real world, Locke recognized, there will be the sort of disagreement we discussed above, and in situations where we simply can't adopt a live-and-let-live attitude (because the desires of parties' conflict) someone (the state) is going to need to adjudicate the disputes. But the position I'm about to suggest here is quite different. It has nothing to do with the difficulty of finding consensus among people who are fallible and who will naturally disagree with each other, particularly about very complex moral controversies. It is, rather, that on reflection we may realize that perfectly rational people don't have any *reason* to act in certain ways absent of the existence of laws and their associated sanctions.

But how can that be? Don't we always want people to behave rationally? How could rational behavior—at least *ideally* rational behavior—present a problem for society? We can't fully answer this question until we talk more in the next chapter about what gives a person a reason to act and what makes an action, all things considered, rational. But many of the examples I have in mind concern situations in which perfectly rational people acting in perfectly rational ways will inevitably create for themselves a world much worse than a world they could have achieved but only through the creation of law and its related sanctions. Perhaps the best way to illustrate the basic idea is to talk a bit about Hobbes and his explanation of why rational people will give up freedom to ensure a better life. As we will see, Hobbes had a rather extreme view of human psychology, but the basic Hobbesian argument will apply even if we adopt a less cynical view of human nature.

Hobbesian Rationality and the Role of Law

I'm going to paint here with rather broad strokes. I don't want this discussion to turn into an extended exegetical discussion of the two historical figures to whom I will appeal. I believe, however, that the picture painted with these broad strokes is historically accurate. Hobbes held what I shall call a Humean conception of rationality. Briefly put, Hume thought that rational action was to be understood in terms of action that is an appropriate means to an end. In chapter 3, we will talk more about how one might refine this idea. But the basic idea is clear enough. You are acting rationally if you are taking effective means to achieve your ends. It is, of course, important to emphasize the fact that one may have many different ends, and the effectiveness of an action at achieving ends will most plausibly be understood comparatively. I have many different ends or goals, both positive and negative. There are states of the world I value and states of the world I disvalue. Actions can satisfy some interests and frustrate others. Earlier, we talked briefly about the consequentialist's intent to understand the right action to take in terms of the action that maximizes value, where the sum of the positive and negative values yields a net value, and the right thing to do is understood in terms of that action which yields the greatest net value.[12] Similarly, the Humean, now thinking in terms of ends or goals, will insist that we understand one's rational course of action in terms of the action which yields the greatest net satisfaction of one's goals (keeping in mind, that an action that does nothing but frustrate goals can be the most rational action should alternatives frustrate even more goals). As I understand Hume (and this is certainly controversial), one's ultimate goals are arational—neither rational nor irrational (1978, Book II, Part III, Sec. III). An agent's goals or ends are defined subjectively in terms of what that agent values intrinsically (values for its own sake). That is not to say that actions related to modifying one's goals might not be rational or irrational. So, for example, insofar as one values X for its own sake, and the fact of valuing X creates difficulties for one's satisfying other goals one has, one may have a reason for trying to change the fact that one values X. I would imagine, for example, that if one has sadistic tendencies but is otherwise concerned with one's own well-being, one should not only refrain from acting to achieve one's sadistic goals, but also, perhaps, try to get rid of the problematic desire for fear that one will give into disastrous temptation—disastrous in terms of one's ability to achieve one's other goals. This is all premised on the plausible thought that what goes around usually comes around. Given human nature, people who are hurt by you will usually make a concerted effort to hurt you in return.

In any event, one can quite consistently maintain that there is no rational evaluation of the having of a goal even if one also concludes that one can view someone as irrational for not *acting* so as to *alter* his or her goals. In the context of discussing morality, there are passages that complicate our picture of Hume. He sometimes seems to suggest that in making a *moral* judgment the only "passions" (as he calls them) that are relevant to moral evaluation are those that would arise were one considering the subject matter of one's evaluation from a disinterested perspective (1978, 472). But even if this distinction enters into the account of what one *morally* ought to do, other passages suggest that Hume rejects the idea that there is anything irrational about acting on "interested" passions (those passions one has because one is going to be negatively or positively impacted by the actions or events one is evaluating) (see again, Book II, Part III, Sec. III).

As I indicated above, I understand Hobbes as fully endorsing this means/ends conception of rational action (1994, 100). He further endorsed, I think, the idea that one can no more rationally criticize people for their psychological natures than one can rationally criticize them for the color of their eyes. And he thought that it was just a fact about human beings that we are all egoists—each person has as his or her sole goal or end his or her own "ease and sensual delight" (and presumably avoidance of discomfort and various forms of pain) (68). Putting this alleged fact about human nature together with the Humean conception of rationality yields the conclusion that the rational thing to do is to maximize one's own happiness (where again the net happiness must take into account not just the "positive" pleasures, but the "negative" pains). It doesn't follow from the fact that one is an egoist, of course, that one will *succeed* in acting rationally. Anyone who has lived for any length of time at all will realize that we make horrible mistakes even as we aim to achieve happiness. And some people are really kind of pathetic when it comes to making rational calculations about what it is rational to do.[13]

From the fact that someone is an egoist in the sense explained above, even an egoist with full knowledge of which actions are rational, nothing much follows about how that egoist will live his or her life. As Hobbes (1994, 100) points out, even if people are alike in terms of their *ultimate* goals or ends, they often differ dramatically in terms of what brings them ease and sensual delight. To take a trivial example, I get pleasure from listening to the Beach Boys (a fact that I realize full well ages me in a depressing way) while one of my colleagues despises that sort of music and gets pleasure from listening to Bach. Acting as an ideally rational agent, I'll end up listening to a different sort of music than will he. But for the Hobbesian this lesson will extend beyond tastes in music and food. Our aforementioned sadist, who gets enormous pleasure from seeing others suffer, *may* end up rationally acting in ways radically different from your favorite philanthropist, and that is so even if each, in his or her own way, is after ease and sensual delight.

What has anything of this to do with the subject matter of this section? We are, after all, trying to explain how the purpose of law might extend far beyond formally encoding what one ought to do even in the absence of law. Hobbes famously describes a hypothetical situation that he calls the state of nature (or the natural state of human beings). This is a condition in which we live without society, without law, without government. Egoists living in such a state, Hobbes suggests, will live a life that is "nasty, brutish, and short" (1994, 76). Their restless desire for the sort of power that will allow them to achieve their egoistic ends will inevitably lead to conflict. Ironically, conflict is precisely the sort of thing that will be anathema to one's *successfully* finding "ease and sensual delight" (68). The egoist in such a state needs to find a way out. Those of us who are already out of a state of nature, need to make sure we don't slip back into one. The solution, according to Hobbes, is not to change our nature—to become something other than egoists. That's not going to happen. Human nature, Hobbes believes, is immutable (99–100). We need to find a solution that, as Rousseau puts it, takes people as they are (1967, 49). And for Hobbes that solution is to form a commonwealth headed by a sovereign who will create and enforce laws, where the enforcement of such laws gives us reasons to act that we would lack without the threat of the sovereign's sword hanging over our heads.

The details of Hobbes's story, of course, are much more complicated. Furthermore, he brings to his argument many highly controversial assumptions. It is also an understatement to suggest that the Humean conception of rational action is controversial. We'll talk more about this in the next chapter. Additionally, all sorts of thought experiments suggest that most of us are not really egoists—that we value, even value for its own sake, the happiness or well-being of at least some other people. Most parents, I suspect, would sacrifice their lives for the lives of their children. One determined to construe all behavior as egoistic[14] might suppose that such parents are looking for rewards in another life, or are acting in the knowledge that their lives, not having made the sacrifice, would be filled with never-ending torment.[15] But we can easily change the thought experiment so that the parents making the sacrifice are convinced that there is no life after death and they live in a world in which pills are readily available that will induce effective amnesia or block feelings of guilt with its attendant suffering. It still seems likely to me that in such a world most parents would make the same sorts of sacrifices for their children.

To suggest that people are probably not egoists is not, however, to suggest that they exemplify the kind of impartiality that Mill seemed to think of as the moral ideal.[16] Mill argued that we should all be hedonistic utilitarians, people who regard happiness as intrinsically valuable, no matter whose happiness it is, and that the ideal person is such that, "As between his own happiness and that of others, utilitarianism requires him to be as strictly impartial as a disinterested and benevolent spectator" (1956, 16).

As we shall discuss in more detail later, people in the actual world clearly aren't impartial and disinterested in Mill's sense. Perhaps, they should be—that is a different question. But they simply aren't. I care about my wife, my children, my grandchildren, and my friends in ways, and to a degree that, I certainly don't care about strangers. I value the happiness of my "intimates" (as my colleague Diane Jeske describes them—see Jeske 2008) so much more than I value the happiness of people I don't know that I would trade almost unlimited amounts of the happiness of others to achieve the happiness of those I love. And I don't think I'm the slightest bit unusual in this respect. Again, these biases I have don't imply that I am an egoist. They don't even imply that I don't care *at all* about the happiness of total strangers. The claim is only that I care *much* more about some people than I care about others. And so do you.

If the above is true, and Hobbes had an unrealistically bleak view of human nature and what we value, it doesn't follow that his concerns about avoiding the "state of nature" were irrelevant. If one is a Humean about rationality and one acknowledges that we all have *different* values, values that will probably lead to conflict, we still might realize that we need to find a way to avoid the conflict. Just as conflict is often incompatible with achieving *egoistic* goals, so also conflict might be incompatible with securing the happiness of those others about whom I care very much. And it still might be true that it is only through establishing law and its sanctions that I can change the playing field so that others and I have reasons to refrain from acting in ways that would otherwise be quite rational.

There is another concern that is "internal" to the framework Hobbes adopts. One needs to worry that even if we grant Hobbes his conception of rational action and human nature, he didn't adequately consider alternative ways to escape the disastrous conflict that we would face were we living in a state of nature. One of Hobbes's dominant concerns is that we create a situation in which it is possible to secure cooperation among rational, self-interested people. The greatest power we have, Hobbes thought, is the power that comes from combining our individual powers in cooperative endeavors (1994, 50). But self-interest, or even interests that favor some over others, is a potential obstacle to cooperation. Cooperation involves agreements or "contracts" that often necessarily involve one party to act "first" and thus expose himself, herself, or themselves to the risk of the other party failing to live up to the terms of the contract. So, in a state of nature, a state without law or a sovereign's sharp sword to enforce that law, you and I might agree to help each other plant and harvest our crops. But after I help you, what is to prevent you from reneging on the agreement? You got what you wanted from me, you and I are both tired from our concerted effort, and, as a rational, self-interested person, you might well just turn your back on my need for your help. Creating a sovereign with a sword to enforce contracts is the solution, according to Hobbes. That sovereign will give both you and me a reason to do what might otherwise not be in our interest to do.

Very real questions arise concerning why one should expect a sovereign to expend time and energy enforcing the kinds of contracts we need enforced in order to ensure rational cooperation. As far as I can tell, Hobbes's only response to this concern is that an *enlightened* (i.e., clever and far-sighted) sovereign will realize that his, her, or their[17] own interest lies in having an economically prosperous state. A sovereign can only be as rich and powerful as the sovereign's state is rich and powerful. Moreover, if things get bad enough for the sovereign's subjects, they might well invoke what Hobbes calls their "right of nature," the one freedom that he believes that rational people should never give up for the benefit of creating a state. That right Hobbes describes as the freedom each person always has to do what is necessary to preserve his or her life (1994, 87). When it comes to agreements and contracts, all bets are off for a rational person facing death. According to Hobbes, a life-threating situation is the one sort of situation in which a rational person can consider reneging on the agreement to submit to a sovereign, and Hobbes makes clear that such situations arise not only from direct threat of physical force, but from deprivation of food, air, and medicine (142). And if you are a self-interested sovereign, you don't want people thinking about getting rid of you. Prosperity and freedom from conflict (including potentially life-threatening conflict) require the kind of cooperation that results from enforced contracts, so *rational* sovereigns will enforce contracts.

Note, however, that this response presupposes a rational and far-sighted sovereign. If one could count on people, *in general*, to have these attributes, it is not clear that one needs to take the drastic step of creating a sword hanging over one's head to give people reasons to keep those agreements, reasons that secure the possibility of cooperation. Even in a state of nature, you will usually have a strong reason to do what you said you would do. Consider again our example of the two individuals part-nering to harvest their crops. To be sure, you might think about leaving me in the lurch after you get from me the cooperation you wanted, but it wouldn't require a great deal of sophistication for you to realize that this might not be in your long-term interest. Harvesting is something that will need to be done again, and your work will be easier in the future if you can again secure help. Once you break your agreement with me, you are not likely to get *me* to fall for the same sort of agreement again. You might hope to pull the same routine on someone else, but, as they say, word gets around, and before very long people will realize that you are not the kind of person who is likely to keep an agreement, particularly when short-term advantage lies with breaking it. So, if you were rational and far-sighted, you would have a powerful reason to act in such a way as to secure the reputation of being someone who keeps agreements.

It is not hard to imagine what Hobbes's response would be to this suggestion. He does consider, at one point, the suggestion that he has an overly cynical view of what people are like and how they will behave. But he immediately reminds us that we lock our doors when we leave our houses (1994, 76–77). We don't trust our fellow human beings even when we live in a commonwealth, where laws are enforced "with the sword." Most people who break the law, particularly when there is a decent chance of getting caught and punished, are probably irrational by egoistic lights. The risk they are taking is usually too great for the reward. But at least some people are clearly not far-sighted enough to properly evaluate the risks. And while ideally rational, far-sighted people might not need the threat of punishment to give them egoistic reasons to coop-erate, Hobbes probably thinks that we often aren't dealing with people who are ideally rational and far-sighted. The more immediate threat of punishment might be a much more powerful motivating reason than the more subtle long-term gain of securing the kind of reputation that allows one to make agreements with others.

All this should leave Hobbes's critics worried about why he is so relatively sanguine about the sovereign being appropriately far-sighted. Of course, when one starts a commonwealth from scratch, one has the opportunity to try to select as one's sovereign a person or group of peo-ple who are particularly suited for the job, and those qualifications would surely include having the appropriate kind of perspective on long-term self-interest. In the case of a monarch, however, power (according to Hobbes 1994, chapter XIX) is usually inherited by children of the sove-reign, and the transfer of genetic traits is a slim reed on which to hang one's hopes. While Hobbes's didn't approve (generally) of democratic rule and found representative monarchy or aristocracy to be a kind of contradiction (since real power is always retained by the majority), we could hope in our system that we can select appropriately qualified people for government. But one needn't be the world's greatest cynic to wonder if our politicians are typically far-sighted in appropriate ways. More sympathetically, perhaps, one might appreciate the fact that given their need to get re-elected, they often can't simultaneously satisfy their desire for political power and be appropriately far-sighted. The electorate that they face every two, four, or six years doesn't seem to have much patience when it comes to waiting a long time for policies to bear their fruit.

SUMMARY AND CLARIFICATIONS

In this chapter, I have introduced the notion of *legal* rights, permissibility, and obligation. We have also examined the connection between law, morality, and rationality. I have warned against thinking that there is always, or usually, a close connection between what even ideal law dictates and what either morality or rationality, *independent* of the law, would require. There are laws whose purpose is to solve coordination problems and to clearly define terms that will be useful to employ in the formulation of other laws. For practical reasons, almost all laws need to be more course-grained than our moral conclusions. Rational moral conclusions about how people ought to behave take into account factors that we can't build into effective legislation. Lastly, and most controversially, I argued that the purpose of at least some important law might be to *give* people a reason to act in ways that would be otherwise irrational.

None of this suggests that our concepts of morality and rationality aren't conceptually and epistemically more fundamental than the concept of law. Trivially, the fundamental question concerning the law will always be what laws we *ought* to have. That italicized *ought* is not, of course, the *ought* of law. And the issues that dominate libertarian political thought concern what laws we ought to support or reject in order to insure appropriate freedom. To position ourselves to discuss that topic properly, we need to delve into complex and thorny meta-controversies concerning the nature of morality and rationality.

NOTES

1. Narveson has suggest to me that the first step should surely be to define the concept of a right simpliciter. But my intention is to explore the conceptual distinction between two quite different kinds of rights without presupposing that anything falls under the concept of a "moral right." As I will argue, the closest we can come to a coherent notion of a moral right is the notion of a reason to act or refrain from acting (a reason among others). That might allow us to capture something that looks a bit like a *very* weak concept of prima facie right. More about this later.

2. Of course, good legislators will keep an eye on morality when they do their business of making laws. So at least sometimes, moral truths will play a role in determining what the law is. The stronger and more interesting claim, that *necessarily* moral

truths play such a role, is what we find to be implausible: too many bad people throughout history have gotten work as legislators. See Aquinas (2001) and Finnis (1980) for an example of someone who wants a very tight connection between what the law can be and what morality requires.

3. I emphasize that *I* have these legal rights. The actual laws are complex and vary from state to state. In many states, if I have been convicted of a felony, then I don't have the legal right to own a gun. And one can certainly imagine a state that puts legal restrictions of various sorts on the kinds of cars one can buy and the kinds of people who can buy them.

4. See Dworkin (1986).

5. When I speak of an ideal society, I mean a society that is as good as you can make it given empirical facts about what people are like. I'm not talking about a world in which people have God-like powers.

6. One notable exception is Leo Katz (1996).

7. For those who don't know, the last two episodes of the series focused on the main characters of the sitcom having been arrested for failing to aid (and indeed finding amusing) the mugging of another person.

8. At least, by definition, if they are pro-choicers with respect to the moral issues. One can be pro-choice concerning the legality while simultaneously thinking that abortion is always, in all circumstances, morally wrong—the very point we are trying to emphasize here.

9. For a consequentialist, there is one way of describing a kind of action such that an action of that kind will always be the right action to take. One can always describe the action as being of the kind that maximizes value.

10. That's not to say that you would be completely in the clear. If you were to break into my house to make the call, you would almost certainly be made to pay for the damages. It is not that the court would find you morally reprehensible—quite the contrary. But somebody has to bear the cost of the damages, and there is no reason that the householder should do so. More complicated arrangements for this sort of case could be put in place—we could devise a system in which costs are shared via some public insurance policy, but we don't currently have such a system.

11. In the movie there is a token gesture at a defense of temporary insanity, but it quickly becomes clear that it won't fly.

12. Again, this will do for now. We will see shortly that this approach here and the similar approach to understanding rational action ignore important complications, some of which involve the assessment of risk and probability.

13. One can't let oneself be confused about all these uses of the adjective "rational." For the most part, we have been talking about what makes an action rational. We can also talk about whether or not a belief is epistemically rational. A belief is epistemically rational (in one view) if it enjoys a kind of justification that makes likely the truth of what one believes. See Fumerton (1996).

14. Perhaps it should be emphasized that an egoist need not be an egotist. The latter is that person (we all know one) who has a very high opinion of himself or herself—a person who thinks that they are the straw that stirs the drink. An egoist might have a very dim and depressing view of their own intelligence, wit, and charm.

15. Not unrelated to the old cliché that a coward dies a thousand deaths; a hero, but one.

16. There are no uncontroversial interpretations of Mill. It seems to me that in the most straightforward interpretation of *Utilitarianism*, Mill insists that one must be absolutely impartial as between one's own happiness and the happiness of others. Presumably, that impartiality also extends to the happiness of those one loves and the happiness of strangers. Narveson (1967) argues that Mill was really only suggesting that, from the moral point of view, rationality compels one to treat the desires of others as just as "reason giving" as one's own desires. In one interpretation of Narveson, the moral point of view is just the perspective one occupies once one is determined to engage in cooperative behavior. Put another way, the moral point of view is

just the perspective one occupies as a member of a group that decides what it is rational for "us" to do. As will become clear, I don't think that a rational person would ever approach decision-making from such a perspective. As will also become clear, I don't think that precludes a person taking the "egocentric" perspective from engaging in bargaining with others who have different interests.

17. For Hobbes, a sovereign can be an individual or a group. It can even (in a democracy) be constituted by the majority (either the majority on a given issue, or a majority agreeing to respect majority opinions on various matters).

THREE

Controversies in
Metaethics and Meta-Rationality

Chapter 2 introduced the idea of legal rights and explored a number of questions concerning the relationship between legal concepts and the concepts of morality and rationality. Some of those questions require a more careful look at controversies in both metaethics and meta-rationality. One of the primary concerns for this chapter is to determine whether or not we can make sense of rights outside of the context of law. The answer to this question might heavily influence views about how well ideal legal rights might be expected to mirror moral rights, particularly as such rights are invoked in arguments concerning freedom.

My approach will be to survey a number of views in metaethics and meta-rationality, comparing and contrasting their answers to the question raised above. In the context of this comparison, however, I will try to defend the view that I take to be most plausible.

VIRTUE THEORY

In what follows, I focus on views according to which the concepts of intrinsic positive and negative value, and the concept of what one ought to do are more fundamental that the concept of what makes a person virtuous. In general, one needs to distinguish carefully one's evaluation of what a person does from one's evaluation of the person. Good and virtuous people can unintentionally do very bad things. And bad people with the worst of motives can still end up doing the right thing. That's a claim on which almost everyone will agree. But there remains a controversy over which of our moral concepts are most plausibly viewed as the conceptual building blocks out of which we should construct the rest of our moral concepts. I mentioned briefly in chapter 1 that one version of virtue ethics takes the concept of a virtuous person to be more fundamental than the concepts of good and bad, or the concepts of what one should or shouldn't do. In a crude version of such a view, one acts the way one should when one acts as a virtuous person would act. For such an account to be informative, of course, one would need an account of what makes a person virtuous. And in the pain of vicious circularity, one couldn't go on to explain the virtues in terms of characteristics that lead one (typically) to do the right thing.

As I indicated earlier, I can't do justice to different versions of virtue ethics here. I'll just say here that I don't see how one could ever get a grip on what makes a character trait a virtue unless one first has independently an idea of what makes something good or bad, or what makes an action right or wrong.[1] That is not to reject the importance of understanding our talk about virtues. Nor is it to ignore the very real fact that in thinking about what we ought to do we should always consider, among other consequences, the effects our actions might have on *us*. If something we do, for example, might tend to make us more indifferent to the suffering of others, that might be a negative consequence of what we do that outweighs other good consequences that flow from the action. Procrastinating too often causes one to become a procrastinator and that's something one needs to worry about it—even on a day that cries out for golf instead of work. Both consequentialists and deontologists who recognize an important role for consequences to play should concede that what we do to ourselves often affects how we will act in the future. But that shouldn't lead us to lose sight of the fact that our evaluation of action is still more fundamental than our evaluation of character. In what follows I'll be examining what I take to be the most plausible competing views about the evaluation of action.

NATURAL LAW VS HUMAN LAW

There is a very old tradition in philosophy that sought to keep an almost exact parallel between at least some moral law and at least ideal law developed by humans embedded in cultures. Proponents of this theory thought that at least some legal rights and obligations should mirror moral rights and obligations that exist quite independently of law. It is this theory that Bentham characterized as "nonsense upon stilts."

The Natural Law as Divine Law or Commands

In one straightforward, though not very plausible, view, we might try to identify the moral law that *applies* to all humans, regardless of what actual human-made law requires, as the law of God. To hold the simplest version of this view, one needs to hold that there is a God, and that He has issued commands to us—commands that tell us what to do and refrain from doing in just the way that human laws tell us what to do and refrain from doing.[2] The view is sometimes called, appropriately enough, Divine Command Theory. Many philosophers take the problem of the *Euthyphro* to be a devastating problem for Divine Command Theory.[3] Let us suppose, for a moment, that there is a God and that He has commanded us to act in certain ways. Plato asked a question that (very liberally paraphrased) went like this: Would the kinds of actions that God commanded us to perform be morally right in virtue of the fact that God commanded us to act in those ways, or would God have commanded us to act in those ways because God (in His wisdom) realized that they were morally right? If the latter, then we are looking in the wrong place for what *makes* an action morally right or wrong when we look to God's commands. To understand rightness and wrongness, duty and obligation, we need to find in thought whatever it is that God found in order to issue His commands. If, on the other hand, the only thing that makes an action morally right or wrong is God's commands, then God's commands seem utterly capricious, and if we ought to obey those commands it will only be because God has the power to make us pay if we don't.

This is, of course, only one problem with any theory that makes what people ought to do dependent on God. While one does sometimes hear such dramatic claims, as *if God is "dead," there is no morality*, most think such concerns border on nonsense. Surely, if a former theist awakes one morning an atheist, that born-again atheist won't feel perfectly free to lie, steal, and torture puppies and small children. This at the very least suggests that even profound theists don't really *mean* by such terms as "right" and "wrong" anything that makes essential reference to a God and His commands.

Hypothetical Divine Command Theory

One might worry that the above argument is far too quick in dismissing the role that the concept of a God might play in understanding a moral law that resembles human-made law. Perhaps one can define the moral law not in terms of what some *actual* God commands, but rather in terms of what sorts of behavior a God-like being *would* command or prescribe (whether such a being exists or not).[4] To develop such a view, one would, of course, need to explain what the concept of a God or a God-like being is. On some standard philosophical views, a being is God only if the being is perfect. To be perfect is to be as good as it is possible to be. But if this is so, then one certainly can't use the above approach to understand *all* ethical concepts. One invokes the concept of good in the definition of God, and thus one could not, without vicious circularity, try to understand goodness in terms of anything one might say about an actual or possible God. But perhaps one might be willing to restrict the metaethical analysis proposed to one of rightness or wrongness, conceding that one will need an independent analysis of other ethical concepts such as goodness.

It is not clear, however, that turning to hypotheticals eliminates the problem of the *Euthyphro*. One still needs to know *why* a perfect being would command us to behave in this way or that. If one provides an answer—say that a certain sort of behavior will maximize value—then won't one have located the source of the moral law in something other than God's commands? Why wouldn't one be best construed as defending a version of consequentialism mentioned earlier and will be developing later? And if one refuses to answer the question of why a perfect being would command a certain sort of behavior, why shouldn't one think of the commands in question as capricious or whimsical?

Natural Law without God

The term "natural law theory" is used by some to cover far more than moral theories built on the concept of an actual or possible God and His commands. On one extreme, some will use the term to describe any philosophical view committed to universal moral principles or universal principles of rational action that are supposed to apply to all rational beings. So, Aristotle is sometimes called a natural law theorist because he thinks that human beings (like most other things) have a telos (a goal or end). The good life, the life one ought to lead, is the life that will achieve that goal or end, and there are universal principles that need to be followed in order to achieve that success. Even Thomas Hobbes in *Leviathan* adopts the terminology of "natural law" to describe various principles that he thinks rational people will follow, particularly in their dealings with their fellow human beings (1994, chapters XIV and XV). Hobbes may well have been an atheist,[5] and he certainly wouldn't have anything to do with Aristotle's conception of a *telos*. But he did think that there is such a thing as human nature. As we discussed earlier, he thought that, as a matter of fact, we are all egoists—we all have as our sole ultimate goal or end in acting, "ease and sensual delight" (68). Furthermore, he thought that there are unchanging facts about how people respond in various ways to how they are treated. As I suggested earlier, Hobbes also accepted (in my reading of Hobbes) that controversial Humean conception of rational action. Our *subjective* goals or ends are arational and rational action is all about achieving what we subjectively value. Hobbes's laws of nature are nothing more that pieces of advice that he thinks rational people will follow (given human nature and the circumstances in which they find themselves) in order to achieve their goals or ends.

Once we broaden the notion of natural law so much that it includes virtually any ethical theory that finds room for general principles, it seems to me best to discuss separately the quite disparate views that could fall under that label.

CONSEQUENTIALISM

In both chapters 1 and 2 we talked briefly about consequentialism. We also contrasted that view with a deontological approach to understanding morality. I will be arguing that the controversies concerning political freedom are best addressed from a consequentialist perspective. But we need to be clearer about precisely how to understand consequentialism and deontology. I'll first discuss consequentialism and then explore deontology primarily as a view that reacts to alleged difficulties with consequentialism. As we are about to see, there are both consequentialist accounts of rationality and consequentialist accounts of morality. Let's talk first about the former.

Consequentialist Accounts of Rationality

The most straightforward consequentialist account of rationality is the Humean/Hobbesean account sketched briefly in the previous chapter. The basic idea, again, is that a person's action is rational just insofar as that action is appropriately connected to that person's goals or ends. In the Humean/Hobbesian view, your ultimate goals or ends are defined in terms of what you value intrinsically.[6] It is worth emphasizing this idea of an *ultimate* goal or end. Certainly, as we normally talk, we often describe ourselves as having many goals, some of which are not *ultimate*. So, someone might describe herself as having the goal of becoming a partner in a law firm, of running in a marathon, of losing twenty pounds, and so on. But it is not at all clear that these are what I am calling ultimate goals. Among the things one values or cares about, some are valued only as a means to achieving something else that is valued. Others are valued just in virtue of what they are. And some might be valued both for what they are and as a means.[7] I suspect that most people want to lose weight only because they want to feel healthier or be more attractive. And it is *possible* that people want health or beauty only as means to some sort of pleasure (or freedom from pain) that they get from being healthy or attractive. But it doesn't seem to me coherent to suppose that *everything* you value, you value only as means to something else you value. There must be something you value just because of what it is. As we noted in the last chapter, Hobbes had the view that all people value intrinsically only their own "ease and sensual delight" (1994, 68). But as we also noted, it is not at all clear that Hobbes was right about what people do value intrinsically. Moreover, there is no reason to suppose that all people are the same in terms of what they value intrinsically. Furthermore, even if two people *are* alike with respect to what they value intrinsically, there may be differences among people with respect to the *strength* of the subjective valuing. You and I may both intrinsically value the happiness of Alexandra and Charlotte (my grandchildren), but I may value their happiness far more than you do.

I haven't said much about how precisely we should understand someone's valuing X intrinsically. This is ultimately a question for the philosophy of mind. But I will assume that Moore (1912) was wrong in thinking that we should understand someone's valuing X intrinsically in terms of someone's thinking that X is objectively good in itself. I'm certainly not denying *here* that there may be an intelligible concept of something's being good in itself that is distinct from the idea of someone's valuing X intrinsically. I'm only assuming that we can make sense of an attitude of valuing (and its opposite disvaluing) that we can understand independently of views about what is objectively intrinsically good (bad). But we'll discuss this issue more fully below.

As I suggested, it is a controversial issue in the philosophy of mind as to how precisely to understand what it is for someone to value X intrinsically.[8] My own view is that the concept is unanalyzable. We know what the mental state is, but we can't *define* it in terms of something more basic—something that is easier to understand.[9] In any event, let us proceed on the assumption that we know what it is to value X intrinsically, to value X for its own sake, and that we can understand someone's subjective ultimate goals or ends in terms of what that person values intrinsically.

Having defined the concept of something's being a goal or end for some person, we might define the concept of that person's having a reason to act in terms of the act satisfying one of that person's goals or ends. But this doesn't seem quite right. Suppose that you value X intrinsically and have a justified belief that some action, A, will bring about X. Surely that fact gives you a reason for doing A—even if your justified belief that A will bring about X turns out to be false. Perhaps, then, we should modify our account of having a reason to act as follows: Someone, S, has a reason to do A just insofar as S has a justified belief that A will bring about some X that one values. But even this seems to demand too much. A rational life involves rational gambles. If we have good reason to believe that some action A that we are contemplating *might* bring about some X that we value intrinsically, we again surely have *some* reason to do A. And if the goal, X,[10] that we might accomplish is important enough—is valued strongly enough—the reason to do A might be quite strong. So, in the approach we are considering, it would be more plausible to suggest that S has a reason to perform some act, A, just in so far as S has a justified belief that A *might* bring about some X that S values intrinsically. Put differently, S has a reason to do A just insofar as A might (relative to S's evidence) bring about X.

In the above view, as in any plausible view, reasons to act come in varying *strengths*. Indeed, if we allow that one has a reason to take some action, A, whenever one has a justified belief that A might satisfy some goal or end, one virtually always has *a* reason to take any action one contemplates. Assuming that I value intrinsically my life, I have *a* reason to stay in my house tomorrow in virtue of the fact that if I leave the house there is a tiny probability that I will get hit by debris falling from outer space. But I also have *a* reason to leave the house in that there is also a tiny probability that the same sort of debris will fall on my house. I have *a* reason to kill you in that there is a non-zero probability (relative to my evidence) that you plan to kill me. I also have *a* reason not to kill you in that there is a non-zero probability that you will stop a plot to kill me. While this consequence of the view might seem initially absurd, it is relatively harmless once one realizes that incredibly weak reasons for and against acting in some way will almost always cancel each other out. For every very weak reason for doing A there will be a very weak reason against doing A, and we will be left contemplating more significant reasons in trying to decide what to do. (We'll say more about how one might understand differences in strength of reasons in what follows.)

If it isn't already obvious, then, a Humean account of rational action will need to capture the idea of what we have the *most* reason to do. In life, we are faced with choices. There will be reasons for and against taking each of the alternatives open to us. The rational alternative for us to take is that action which we have the most reason to take, or at least is that action which we have as much reason to take as any other alternative (again, ties will obviously be possible). We need to introduce the idea of weighing reasons for and against alternatives in order to generate the concept of what is rational to do, *all things being considered*. On the Humean view, we have as one of our conceptual building blocks the concept of a goal or end (defined in terms of what we value and disvalue intrinsically). But once we allow that even the *possibility* of realizing a goal or end can give us a reason to act, and we reflect on the fact that there is a continuum of probability (relative to the evidence one possesses), it seems obvious that when we weigh our reasons we are going to need to take into account the *probability* of a given goal or end being satisfied by the various alternatives we are considering. And the classic way to do this gives us the view that is sometimes called a "maximizing expected utility" account of rational action. Although my label is uglier, I prefer to call the account of rational action explained below, the *value adjusted possible consequence* (VAPC) view of rational action:

Of the available alternatives open to S, A is the rational action for S to take when the sum of the adjusted value (adjusted for probability) of the possible consequences of A is greater than the sum of the adjusted value of the possible consequences of any alternative open to A.

That is a bit of a mouthful, but the basic idea is clear enough. Each alternative open to us has possible consequences. We either value or disvalue intrinsically each of those possible consequences. We ignore those that we don't care about and assign a kind of weight (positive or negative) to the possible consequences we do care about, a weight that reflects how *much* we care about the relevant consequences. But we need to adjust downward whatever weight we assign to a possible consequence in virtue of its probability. So, if it is 99 percent likely that some goal, Y, we have will be satisfied by doing A, then in "summing" the adjusted values of the possible consequences, we get to take into account 99 percent of the value we have assigned to Y (based on how much we value intrinsically Y). If Y, by contrast, had only a 1-percent chance of occurring, we would take only that fraction of the value we assigned to Y.

It might be helpful to think of the assignment of values (positive and negative) to the possible consequences of an act as if we were assigning positive and negative integers along a scale representing the strength of positive and negative attitudes. We assign 0 to everything toward which we are indifferent. Positive numbers represent the degree to which we value something intrinsically, and negative numbers represent the degree to which we disvalue something intrinsically. After we adjust the "numbers" for the probabilities, there is a sum for each alternative that would represent the addition of the adjusted numbers. It is probably best to emphasize that this is just a useful picture or model. We don't have a measurement scale for strength of subjective value. And although there may *be* specific facts about how likely our evidence makes some occurrence, we are hardly in a position to *assess*, with a high degree of specificity, that likelihood. None of that makes the view incoherent, however. We can obviously rank values. We can make the judgement that we intrinsically value X more than Y and Y more than Z. And we can also usually do a decent enough job estimating relative probabilities. So, I don't see why we can't *understand* the concept of net adjusted value required by the view.

Clarifications

Let me make a few quick points of clarification. The reader unfamiliar with the idea of expected value might wonder why we restricted the relevant values to what we value intrinsically. The idea is simply that if A has as a consequence something we value instrumentally, that instrumental value will be "picked" up by the further consequence that is valued intrinsically and is the *source* of the instrumental value. It would be a kind of needless "double counting" to sum both the instrumental value of one possible consequence and the intrinsic value of another that is the ultimate source of the instrumental value (though doing so would be essentially harmless as long as one did the assignment of valuing and summing *consistently* for all of the alternatives open to one).

It is also important to realize that, as I use the term, the consequences of an action are not restricted to the *causal* effects of that action. I might value intrinsically being an Olympic champion in some sport without caring what sport it is.[11] Given that my being a member of an Olympic-champion bobsled team will *logically* imply being an Olympic champion, taking an action to achieve the former would still have as its consequence achieving the goal of being a world champion. With this caveat, we can also allow for the possibility that I value intrinsically some action just in virtue of the kind of action it is. So, it is at least conceivable that I value intrinsically being honest, and if I do, an act of telling the truth will have intrinsic value for me (though it might also have many consequences I disvalue).

I haven't said much about the idea of alternatives open to one. As we ordinarily think about choices, we virtually always restrict ourselves to thinking about a relatively small number of alternatives from which we will be choosing. As I sit at my desk typing, I am starting to think about whether I will continue for another hour or two or whether I will head for the golf course—it's a pretty nice day. But, strictly speaking, there are indefinitely many other actions open to me in the next few minutes. I could stop typing and kill one of my colleagues. I could stop typing and do some volunteer work for a local charity. I could stop typing and sit in a kind of semi-comatose state just staring blankly at the screen in front of me.

It is important, even if a bit disturbing, to realize that there is no opting out of choice in life. In foreign policy decisions, one often hears politicians argue that when we are really unsure as to the consequences of taking action of one sort another, we should just do nothing. But doing nothing is an alternative among other alternatives. It is a choice that has all sorts of consequences (in the broad sense of "consequence" I am using) just as do all of the alternatives to doing nothing. And doing nothing, whether it is seeing the doctor about some strange sensation one feels in one's chest or failing to confront, as early as possible, a threat from a foreign country, can have absolutely disastrous consequences—far worse than many actions one could have taken.

As we noted earlier, it should also be obvious that an ideally rational course of action could have primarily horrible consequences. The rationality of an action is always a function of how it compares to alternatives. The world is often an unfortunate place in which, either through no fault of our own, but also, sometimes through fault of our own, we are confronted with nothing but disaster whichever way we turn. There may still be a course of action that will minimize net disvalue, and that will be the rational course of action to take.

Lastly, it is important to distinguish VAPC consequentialism as an account of what makes an action rational from the quite different view that rational people should attempt to make decisions by making calculations about consequences and probabilities. It is perfectly consistent with VAPC consequentialism that it would be unwise for many people to attempt to do their own calculations. There is a truth-maker for a true claim about the sum of a large number of figures. If you are not very good at adding, however, you are probably better off using a calculator, or asking someone else to do the addition, rather than trying to figure out the truth "directly." It should be obvious that in the view described above, truths about what it is rational to do are exceedingly complex. Many people would be far better off just asking for advice when it comes to trying to reach a conclusion about what they rationally ought to do (though they would still face the often-daunting task of deciding whom to ask).

A similar point holds for what one rationally ought to *tell* people with respect to what makes an action rational. Philosophers have the comfort of knowing that most people don't read what they write, and those that do usually don't accept the relevant conclusions. If we couldn't rely on that, we would need to be much more careful with respect to what we argue for. When we give advice to children about how they ought to behave, we often couch that advice in terms of such relatively simple and often universal prescriptions as: Always tell the truth; always do what your parents tell you to do; never hit your sister. But as most thoughtful people will conclude, we don't really think a child would always be acting rationally if they strictly followed the advice. Just as we saw in the last chapter that claims about morality are nuanced, so also are claims about rationality. There are, surely, circumstances in which it would be rational for a child to lie. On the other hand, we might not think it is a good idea for a child to *know* that there are circumstances in which it would be rational to lie. We might anticipate, probably correctly, that a child who thinks about such matters will end up lying far too often. We don't trust children to make the relevant calculations. But it is surely, in principle, possible that many people are just like children in this respect. They might generally fare better in life falsely thinking that there are universal rules laying down what it is rational and moral to do—rules that they ought to follow no matter what. [12]

The Relativization of Rationality

The above account of rational action relativizes the rationality of an action to a person or group. An action is rational only relative to a person's or group's goals or ends, and a person's or group's available *evidence* relative to which we can make sense of the probability of various consequences. If you and I have quite different goals or ends, what it is rational for you to do in a given situation might be quite different from what it is rational for me to do in that same situation. And if you and I have at our disposal quite different evidence, then even if we share the same goals or ends, it may still be rational for me to act in a way that is quite different from what rationality dictates that you do. As you will see, this is a source of profound uneasiness about the view. The problem, some will argue, is that the view leaves open no way of assessing the intrinsic rationality of one's goals or ends. But before we address such criticism, we should probably admit that there is ambiguity that even the relativist should admit is inherent in our talk about reasons for acting. It is easiest to illustrate the ambiguity with an example.

Suppose that, unbeknownst to me, you have put arsenic in the bottle of Diet Coke from which Jones is about to drink. You are aware of the situation and start screaming at Jones not to drink the Coke. I ask you, "Why?" Is there any reason he shouldn't have his drink? What is the correct answer to the question? Certainly, there is a very clear, and very natural, answer that you might give. There *is* a reason for Jones not to drink the Coke—doing so will kill him. It's just not a reason of which Jones is aware. Of course, there is another equally clear and natural sense in which, absent of the warning, Jones would have no reason not to drink his Coke. A thirsty Jones would be paradigmatically rational to drink from a bottle that he justifiably believes will quench his thirst. The first sort of reason—the reason that there is for Jones not to drink, whether he knows it or not—might be understood in terms of what it would be rational for Jones to do *were* he aware of certain truths. The second sort of reason—the reason that Jones lacks to refrain from drinking—is the kind of reason that would be relevant in assessing how rational *Jones* was in choosing to drink.

The above distinction gets blurred constantly, particularly in political discussion. Let us suppose, for the sake of argument (I realize that the hypothesis is disputed), that when the United States and its allies launched the second Iraq war, they had relatively strong evidence for thinking that Iraq was developing a nuclear program. In one sense (again let us suppose) that evidence gave them at least some reason to start the war. We then discovered that the intelligence was misleading—the justified belief was false. We then heard a lot of people claiming that there was no reason (of the sort often put forth) for going to war. The potential ambiguity here is precisely the same illustrated with unfortunate Jones. And we simply aren't going to be clear about what rationality demands of someone unless we keep in mind the distinction between what *would have been* a reason to act or refrain from acting were the agent to acquire certain evidence, and what *was* rational for the agent to do relative to the knowledge the agent actually possessed.

One might try to understand the contrast between the two sorts of reasons as paralleling two concepts of probability. People sometimes talk about objective probability versus subjective probability. But the latter is itself ambiguous. As philosophers sometimes discuss these matters, the subjective probability *for you* of something, X, happening is understood in terms of the degree to which you believe (rationally or irrationally) that X will occur. And one can develop a corresponding sense of "reason" defined in terms of *that* concept of probability. So the paranoid schizophrenic who strongly believes that I am about to murder him has a strong reason to kill me in an act of self-defense. But the "subjective" probability and the corresponding concept of reason, that I think is more interesting in defining genuinely rational action, is probability relativized to evidence. In this sense, I have a genuine reason to do X just insofar as I have *evidence* that X will (or might) lead to the satisfaction of some goal or end. The paranoid is paradigmatically irrational (in the sense relevant to evaluating the overall rationality of a person's action) precisely because he or she doesn't have evidence supporting those paranoid beliefs. And there is a sense in which, in my view, there is nothing "subjective" about what evidence a person possesses and what is likely relative to that evidence. But the topic of epistemic probability relative to evidence is a subject for another book.[13]

The Rationality of Group Action

We noted that the consequentialist view of rational action described above relativizes what it is rational to do to a person or a group—the rationality of an action is relativized both to the person's or group's values and the person's or group's evidence. There are special problems, though, in assessing the rationality of group action. These derive primarily from difficulties about how to understand a group's values and a group's evidence base. In an infamous passage from *Utilitarianism* (1979, 34–45), Mill was trying to get to the conclusion that, as a matter of fact, the general happiness is desired as an end. He wanted that conclusion because he appeared to think that there was some sort of connection between being able to show that the general happiness is desired as an end and convincing us that the general happiness is desir*able* as an end (good in itself).[14] Mill seemed to endorse the following reasoning—at least he seemed to *need* the following reasoning: Each person desires as an end his or her own happiness. Therefore, the general happiness (the happiness of all) is desired by the aggregate (the group made up of all of these individuals). As it stands, of course, the argument seems to be terrible. I might desire my happiness, and you, yours, but nothing follows from this about whether I care one whit about your happiness or you, mine. Mill's reasoning seems so bad because we think that one can correctly describe a group as desiring something, X, only if each member, or at the very least most members, of the group desire it. Americans love professional football, for example, only if most individual Americans do.

Americans like little puppies only if most Americans do. And Americans care about the general happiness only if most individual Americans do. The problem, of course, for Mill is that most individual Americans *don't* care about the happiness of others, at least they don't care about it *as much as* they care about their own happiness and the happiness of those with whom they are intimate.

The above presupposes that if we can make sense of talk about a group's values, we will need to translate that talk into talk about individuals and what they value. To be sure, this view is not uncontroversial. There are those who think that a social group is something over and above its "parts" related in various ways, and that one can correctly ascribe to groups the same kind of characteristics that are also exemplified by individual people.[15] I'm not going to discuss such views in any sort of detail other than to warn against being seduced by superficial arguments that are ultimately unsound. It is certainly true that we often talk about a "group" or "mob" mentality. It is notoriously the case that when in a group people will sometimes act and respond emotionally in ways that they wouldn't were they alone. Laughter, sadness, hatred, joy, fear, and many other states are "contagious." Many of us will find ourselves laughing at a show just because others are even when we don't really think that the show is very funny. And even as we might think that there is something very odd about the way in which people respond to college sports, we might easily get caught up in the emotional reaction of the fans with whom we are watching a game. But none of this suggests in the least that we need to think of the group and its "characteristics" as something over and above the individuals who make up the group. We need only understand that there are complex causal connections that hold between being a person related in complex ways to other people and the attitudes and emotions that person has. One can still effectively define the attitudes and actions of the group in terms of the attitudes and actions of the individuals who comprise the group.

But we haven't answered the critical question. Within the framework of what I've called the Humean conception of rational action, how are we to understand the concept of what it is rational for a group to do? The question is particularly acute in the context of political philosophy. While we certainly can ask what legislation would be rational for you or me to support, we also need to make decisions about what legislation it is rational for *us* to support. If we are to employ the concept of subjective value to define the goals or ends that in turn (partially) define rational action, we need to find a way of understanding what *our* goals or ends are. We could try to define the collective's goals in terms of what everyone in the collective values intrinsically. The problem, of course, is that there might be nothing that *everyone* values intrinsically. And even if there are some things we all value intrinsically, it is doubtful that we value those things with the same intensity. I have already noted that it seems almost painfully obvious that I value intrinsically my happiness and the happiness of my family and friends far more than you value my happiness and the happiness of my family and friends. And the reverse, of course, holds true as well.

It won't really help to understand the relevant group's goals in terms of what *most* people in the group value intrinsically, for the point made above still applies. If we are defining goals both in terms of what people value and how much they value it, it is doubtful that we can even find a majority who share the same goals or ends. Our best hope, then, for understanding group rationality is probably to understand it in terms of actions that are instrumentally rational for the majority of people who make up the group. Let me explain.

Let's suppose that you and I own an investment property together. To make things simple, let's suppose that my sole goal in buying the property was to make a profit for myself, and your sole goal in that same investment was to make a profit for yourself. We have different goals or ends, but the act of selling the property at the height of a real-estate bubble might be precisely the (joint) action that is maximally rational for each of us (relative to our respective goals or ends). Can a model that simple help us understand the idea of rational action for a society to take?

There does seem to be something plausible about the idea, the ancient idea,[16] that people live together in society partly as a way of efficiently achieving their goals or ends. As philosophers from Plato to modern times have pointed out, there are things that people can accomplish acting in concert that they could never accomplish acting alone. Just as you and I might purchase a summer home together in the realization that neither could afford the house by ourselves, so you and I and a whole lot of other people can "purchase," through a pooling of resources (such as we achieve with a system of taxation), efficient ways of producing energy, defense (from external and internal threats), transportation, education, recreation, and the innumerable other structures, entities, and resources in our society that we "jointly own." I take it that most of these joint endeavors are instrumentally rational for most of us to support. Most of us succeed in satisfying our basic goals in such ways.[17]

As I said, there seems to be something generally right about the above approach to understanding what it is rational for members of a group to do. Matters become much more complicated as we look at more detailed decisions. Most of will probably decide that a system of parks and recreation will be instrumentally rational to support. But we'll start separating ourselves into subgroups fairly quickly when it comes to what precisely we'll do with that jointly owned property. I like golf, tennis, and hockey. You might think that golf is one of the more inane activities invented by conscious beings—that public golf courses are an inexcusable waste of money of which you want no part. So, the process of bargaining begins.

As long as we are committed to joint action, we need to find a way of making these sorts of decisions.[18]

Another simple analogy might be helpful. Anyone who belongs to a large family is familiar with the situation in which the family decides it would be fun to go out for dinner. Then the tortuous process begins — finding a place that the group will agree upon. I like Chinese food and always give that suggestion a try. My wife virtually always does her best to veto that proposal. My grandkids like McDonalds, and while we love our grandchildren dearly, my wife and I are both going to veto that idea for our family culinary excursion. My daughter likes seafood restaurants; my son likes steak houses. What to do?

In the context of his discussion of an ideal society, Rousseau seemed to suggest that such a state must have policies and laws that are in accord with "the general will." Unfortunately, he was unclear about what precisely he meant by saying of some policy that it is in accord with the general will. There are passages that suggest rather strongly that he meant by the general will neither the "will of all" nor even "the will of the majority."[19] Cryptically, he suggests that the general will is something that emerges from a *clash* of wills:

> There is often a great difference between the will of all [what all individuals want] and the general will; the general will studies only the common interest while the will of all studies private interest, and is indeed no more than the sum of individual desires. But if we take away from these same wills the pluses and minuses which cancel each other out, the sum of the difference is the general will. (1967, 72)

And in a footnote to the passage, he quotes the Marquis d'Argenson, as saying that "Harmony of two interests is created by opposition to that of a third," and goes on to suggest that d'Argenson could have gone on to hold that

> the harmony of all interests is created by opposition to those of each. If there were no different interests, we should hardly be conscious of a common interest, as there would be no resistance to it. (1967, 73)

Rousseau wasn't thinking about dinner reservations, but I think his idea is relevant. Our family, *determined to find a place to eat together*, will usually find their restaurant through a clash of interests. My "plus" (my favorite Chinese restaurant) is cancelled by my wife's "minus" (she hates Chinese food). My daughter's "plus" (the seafood restaurant) is cancelled by my son's "minus" (his strong preference for steak over seafood). We keep going until we find something with which we can all be relatively happy, *or* we don't achieve our goal of eating together. The latter is, of course, a possibility. We can give up on our joint project, or we can lose members of the group. But we keep trying to find compromise as long as we have as one of our strongest goals eating together. We can also be imaginative when it comes to the nature of the compromise. If the family seeking compromise over where to eat plans to eat together relatively often in the future, we might agree to take turns on deciding where to eat. This time, we'll go with my favorite restaurant; the next time, my wife's; the time after that, my daughter's; and so on. And "deals" can become even more complicated. If we are planning weekend family excursions occasionally, the rest of the family might agree to give me my first choice of a restaurant, if they get their first choice of where to vacation a couple of weeks from now.

So how does all of this help with golf courses, tennis courts, and hockey rinks? Well, as we'll see later, there are different ways of achieving consensus. We could try to find something most of us enjoy doing at least a bit and use the publicly owned space for that purpose. But it is not clear that we'll have all that much luck, and, in any event, we almost all enjoy engaging in different activities at different times. But we can use the same sort of imagination we illustrated above. Fortunately, we own a lot of public space, and our compromise can often take the form of using one public space for my sub-group's preferences, a different public space for yours. Or we can use a given public space for one activity or one group on certain days of the week, while we use it for a different purpose or a different group on other days of the week. Again, we'll return to this very basic idea in much more detail when we explore various arguments for freedom that are still consistent with a commitment to "public" ownership of land and the projects we associate with that land.

The other obvious source of contention when it comes to joint endeavors is the question of who is going to pay for what. It is one thing to suggest that most of us can agree that we want to jointly own space that we couldn't afford to purchase on our own. It is quite another to figure out how to "pay" for the public space and the projects we develop for use of that public space. For all intents and purposes, in the United States we pay for what we jointly own through our taxes. Wealthy people obviously pay a great deal more for the construction and maintenance of publicly owned land, infrastructure, and recreation than do poorer people. Generally, they probably use more of what they pay more for, but that is a matter that needs further discussion (chapter 7). As we will see, the issues about how to pay for what we (collectively) want lie at the heart of many of the controversies concerning economic freedom.

A Fundamental Objection to the Humean Conception of Rational Action

There is a fundamental, perhaps obvious, objection to a consequentialist account of rational action built partly on the concept of a person's subjective goals or ends. Specifically, one might object that the view provides no framework for a rational assessment of one's goals or ends. Surely, the argument goes, a person might value as an end something that it would be *irrational* to value as an end. And one might fail to value as an end something that *rational* people should value. If that is possible, why would we think we could successfully define rational action in terms of the satisfaction of goals or ends (however *irrational* those goals or ends might be)? On the Humean view, a person who values intrinsically the suffering of other people, and who values intrinsically his own suffering, might act rationally in causing all sorts of mayhem. Such a person might not even be deterred by the prospects of punishment, given the extreme nature of the masochism.

The Humean might make certain concessions to those who find absurd the suggestion that one cannot critically assess one's goals or ends. Earlier (chapter 3) we noted that the Humeans can certainly allow that, in their view, it might be irrational not to act in an attempt to *rid* oneself of some of one's goals or ends. It also might be rational to act so as to *acquire* certain goals or ends. If, for example, my having certain values tempts me to act in ways that frustrate my maximally satisfying my other goals or ends (tempts me to act irrationally in the sense defined above), then it *might* be rational to get rid of this potentially troublesome value/goal. Alternatively, it *might* be rational to live with a frustrated goal. After all, the attempt to rid oneself of a fundamental desire will almost certainly have all sorts of consequences that matter to one. It is equally *possible* that the chances of my achieving certain goals or ends will increase were I to acquire some new goal or end. In any event, even if one thinks that there is nothing intrinsically irrational (or rational) about having certain goals or ends, one can critically assess actions that might have an impact on whether or not one continues to have or acquires those goals or ends. All this is perfectly compatible with the Humean consequentialism defined above and involves no modification of the view.

Still operating with the basic assumptions of Humean consequentialism, one might allow that one can plausibly restrict the kind of goals or ends that enter into the account of rational action. So, for example, one might argue that only when one subjectively values X as an end, after vividly imagining X, does the value count as one that will partially define what it is rational for one to do. Richard Brandt once argued (1979) that only values that would survive "cognitive therapy" are rational and thus relevant to what it would be rational to do. So, for example, he suggested that if one values (Brandt more often talks about desiring) something, X, intrinsically but only because one has certain false or irrational beliefs, one's valuing X as an end would be irrelevant to what one rationally ought to do. At least, such a value would be irrational if it could be "extinguished" through the right sort of therapy. [20]

Frankfurt (1988) suggests that first-level desires (where a first-level desire is a desire for something that is not partly constituted by desires) can be irrational and irrelevant to rational action if the person with those desires would not "endorse" those desires with a second-level desire (where a second-level desire is just a desire that takes as its object a first-level desire). According to this view, I might desire as an end the pleasure I would get from having an affair with one of my students, but I might also despise myself for having that desire—I might have a strong desire not to have that desire. And if that is true, that first-order desire will be irrelevant to the rationality of actions designed to satisfy it. It is not clear what would license one to stop at the second level, but let's not worry about that here.

Brandt's and Frankfurt's views are still in the spirit of what some would take to be the "cruder" Humeanism with which I began. And it won't matter much to the overall argument of this book if you find such qualifications to Humeanism plausible. There is, however, a much more radical diagnosis of what it is wrong with an account of rational action that relativizes what it is rational for a person to do to that person's subjective goals. This critic argues that we are missing the most obvious explanation of what would make certain fundamental values irrational. That explanation is that it is possible for someone to value something, X, as an end when X is intrinsically worthless or even intrinsically bad. Any such view owes us an account of what makes something intrinsically good or bad. The most straightforward view about intrinsic objective value was famously advanced by G. E. Moore (1903). After making the distinction between instrumental and intrinsic goodness, Moore gave a list of states that he took to be intrinsically good. When asked to define being intrinsically good, Moore unapologetically asserted that the concept is indefinable. In Moore's view, illuminating philosophical definitions involves breaking complex ideas or properties[21] down into their simpler constituents (1903, 59–60). But some ideas are simple—they are the conceptual "atoms," so to speak, out of which other ideas are built. And the conceptual atoms of ethics, Moore thought, are the ideas of being intrinsically good and being intrinsically bad.

There is obviously much one could say by way of critically evaluating Moore's view and his arguments for that view. To put it bluntly, some philosophers, like Hume and Hobbes, for example, reject the idea of objective goodness essentially because they find the idea to be unintelligible. Moore is confident that if you "look" in the right way for intrinsic goodness/badness and aren't distracted by other different properties that may always be exemplified along with objective value, you'll just find "before your mind" the property he is talking about. Hume is equally confident that you can search for objective value until you are blue in face and you won't find anything that is a plausible candidate for what you are talking about when you use value expressions. You won't find value "out there" in the world, Hume argued. You'll only find it when you turn your attention inward and find, in yourself, certain subjective reactions to actions, character traits, and states of the world that you contemplate (1978, 468–469). Phenomenological appeals are essentially appeals to what is before your mind when you pay close attention to the character of your experience. Moore and his followers and Hume and his followers are in a phenomenological stand-off.

Hume suggested another reason, however, for rejecting the idea that there is such a thing as objective value. He seemed to suggest that it is just obvious that moral judgments go beyond "the calm and indolent judgments of the understanding" (457). And by that he seemed to mean that it is in the very nature of one's moral judgments that they move one to act. But he thought that it was equally obvious that the only thing that can ultimately move one to act is desire (or what he called passion), and from that he thought it followed that the "subject matter" of moral judgments involved the passions. The view is sometimes called "motive internalism." The basic idea is clear enough. Even if there were such a thing as objective value, it seems possible that someone might be completely and utterly indifferent to it (or worse, loathe things in virtue of their having the property). A person who was indifferent to objective goodness wouldn't have the slightest tendency to act so as to bring about good things. But we would have trouble even understanding people who simultaneously concede that X is intrinsically good while they announce that they have no inclination whatsoever to pursue X.

Motive internalism should be sharply distinguished from what we might call reason internalism. Hume probably implicitly endorsed both views. Reason internalism, as a view about ethical judgments, comes in various forms. The weakest is basically the idea that one cannot, without contradiction, assert that one morally ought to do X while one also concedes that one has no reason at all to do X. The strongest form of reason internalism is the view that it involves contradiction to suppose that one morally ought to do X while one concedes that X isn't what one has the *most* reason to do.

One can write entire books on internalism/externalism controversies in ethics. And regardless of which side of these controversies one endorses, it is still not clear that it will settle the dispute between subjectivists and objectivists about value. Some objectivists argue that it is impossible to recognize that something is intrinsically good without caring about that thing and, thus, that even if moral judgments necessarily motivate, and even if only affective states like desire can motivate, they can accommodate these facts.[22] And, as we have already seen above, some reason internalists will insist that there is a connection between what one morally ought to do and what one has reason to do, but only because it is ultimately the fact that something has objective value that one has a reason to care about that thing and to act so as to bring it about.

Consequentialist Accounts of Morality

If one is an objectivist about intrinsic value, one can turn a consequentialist view about rational action into a consequentialist view about what one morally ought to do by understanding the value one attaches to consequences, not in terms of how much the agent values intrinsically those consequences but by how intrinsically valuable they are. We'll still understand the best course of action to take in terms of the alternative that yields the greatest net value (which might be positive or negative), but the "summing" of values will be understood in terms of the "summing" of the intrinsic goodness and badness of consequences. Everything else we said about consequentialist accounts of rational action will apply *mutatis mutandis* to consequentialist accounts of what one morally ought to do. We can still introduce the notion of having *a* moral reason to act in a certain way, and we will still need to decide whether it is actual or possible consequences that should define what we morally ought to do. If it is the latter, we will still need to take into account probability, decide how to understand that probability, and adjust assignments of value to a consequence for the probability of that consequence occurring.

I briefly sketched Moore's view about objective intrinsic value, but, of course, there are many others, and one can employ in one's consequentialist account whatever conception of value one takes to be most plausible. However, one understands being objectively, intrinsically good/bad, one also needs an account of what actually has objective value (positive or negative) if one is to reach conclusions about what one ought to do. There might be a happy correlation between what people subjectively value and how much they subjectively value it, and one's view about what is objectively valuable and how valuable it is, but it is difficult to argue for the conclusion that these two cannot come apart.

A radical subjectivist about value—someone who thinks that the only value in the world is brought to the world by conscious beings and what they subjectively value—has some fundamental decisions to make concerning the connection between morality and rationality. Reductionists, as the name implies, are inclined to think that one can "translate" talk about what is intrinsically good and bad into talk about what is valued and disvalued intrinsically. But there are many different ways of attempting such a reduction. We could try to define being intrinsically good in terms of what all people value intrinsically, what most people value intrinsically, or we could insist that being intrinsically good is itself a *relative* notion. In such a view, we can only talk about what is intrinsically good *for* some person or group, S, and define that relativized intrinsic goodness in terms of what S values intrinsically.[23] And as we briefly noted above, we could qualify the kind of subjective valuing that we think we should employ in our analysis of goodness. We could insist that it is only subjective values that would be "endorsed" by the person with those values, only subjective values that will survive full exposure to vivid imagination, the truth, cognitive therapy, or what have you. One could even insist that in analyzing moral judgments one must recognize important differences between kinds of affective states, and further insist that only *some* kinds of those states should enter into an analysis of what we mean when we talk about intrinsic goodness and badness. There is a reading of Hume, for example, in which he was trying to call our attention to a specific kind of sentiment (he called it a moral sentiment) that is different from other sorts of "passions." You are more likely to find that sentiment if you think about certain sorts of feelings that arise in you when you consider matters from a "disinterested" perspective (a perspective you occupy when you are not materially affected by the object of your evaluation).[24]

Reduction isn't the only alternative for a philosopher who rejects the existence of objective value. Such a philosopher could, instead, turn to error theory. J. L. Mackie (1977, chapter 1), for example, rejected the idea that there is objective value, but found equally implausible attempts to reduce talk about goodness and badness to talk about what people subjectively value. He concluded, in effect, that we are simply confused. We think we are making true claims about the goodness or badness of this and that, but whenever we make such claims, we fail to pick out any property and thus fail to say anything true. Our value judgments have the same status as the judgments some people used to make about people being possessed by demons. On the assumption that there are no demons, claims about demon possession were always false.[25]

One might, of course, embrace the existence of objective value, endorse a consequentialist account of what one morally ought to do, but retain a subjectivist and relativist account of what one rationally ought to do. There is an ancient question in ethics: Why ought I be moral? It was one of the most important question raised in Plato's *Republic* (first by Thrasymachus and later by Glaucon and Adeimentus—Books I and II). But it is a question to which philosophers have returned over the millennia, and it is a question that has probably occurred to a number of ordinary people who would sometimes really rather not act as they think morality requires them to act. The question can be interpreted in such a way that it is utterly trivial. If to be *moral* is to act as one *ought*, then the question, "Why *ought* I be moral?" reduces to the question, "Why *ought* I act the way I *ought* to act?" And the answer would be that it is *trivially* true (in technical philosophical language, a tautology) that people ought to do what they ought to do. Red things are red, round things are round, and what people ought to do, they ought to do. The trouble is that the question doesn't strike us as trivial. Intelligent people have thought that it is a difficult question that requires a great deal of thought to answer. But why is this so?

One possible answer is that there is more than one "ought." And indeed, we have already had occasion to note in the last chapter that this is almost obviously true. There we argued that, at the very least, we need to distinguish what one legally ought to do, from what one morally ought to do. Arguably, there is yet another quite different "ought" that epistemologists use in characterizing beliefs that are supported by evidence. We often talk in that context about what a person ought to believe, given his or her evidence. Perhaps there is yet another "ought" of etiquette, the kind of "ought" employed by people like Emily Post when she wrote books about when you ought to send a handwritten thank-you note and how long you are allowed to wait before you do it. But, importantly, for our present discussion, we might wonder whether there is an "ought" of rationality that is distinct from an "ought" of morality. That question raised in *Republic* (and in the nineteenth century famously by Sidgwick 1981) of whether one ought to act morally might be understood as the question of whether it is (always, or usually, or ever) rational to act morally.

There is a huge price one pays if one lets the "oughts" of rationality and morality come apart. If they do, then we need to figure out whether we *ought* to do what we rationally ought to, or what we morally ought to do. But if we ask the question this way, we obviously need to figure out which "ought" we are employing in trying to resolve our dilemma. If it is the "ought" of rationality, the question answers itself, and if it is the "ought" of morality, the answer is equally obvious. If one introduces yet a third "ought" to ask the question, we only increase our difficulties, for we will still need to figure out which of the now three different "oughts" will inform our ultimate decisions about what to do.

I have argued elsewhere (1990a) that there is considerable rhetorical force behind the suggestion that we all want to be ideally rational, and that if rational action can diverge from moral action, a rational person must side with rationality. If morality tells you to sacrifice your child for the greater objective good, but rationality tells you to ignore that moral advice, then as a *rational* person you will listen to *reason*.

In *Reason and Morality*, I tried to sort out all these complex positions and, given the topic of this book, I can't try to turn this chapter into a summary of all of the arguments and positions taken in that book. My own view is that there is no such thing as objective value and, thus, in understanding the content of value claims, one's real decision is between reduction, Mackie-style error theory, or something in between. By the last I mean to suggest that people might be confused about the subject matter of their value judgments, but also be inclined to accept eventually certain reductions as the "best they can do" to make sense of how they use value terms. In much of what we will argue later in the book, it might not matter how one assigns those values that are a crucial part of the consequentialist conception of what makes it rational to pursue one alternative or another. As we shall see, however, there is a significant advantage for the consequentialist who thinks of the relevant values as reflecting subjective values that vary from person to person.

ACT CONSEQUENTIALISM AND THE LAW

The versions of consequentialism sketched above are all versions of what is sometimes called act consequentialism. The act consequentialist takes the relevant alternatives to be specific actions, each of which has consequences whose values are relevant to which alternative we ought to choose. Below, we shall have occasion to contrast act consequentialism with another view that still often goes under the label "consequentialism."

Whether we are act consequentialists about rational action who relativize what it is rational for a person or group to do to that person or group's subjective values (and probability relativized to their evidence), or we are consequentialists about morality who define what one ought to do in terms of the objective value of consequences adjusted for the probability of those consequences occurring, the view will have difficulty finding moral *rules* that parallel the legal rules of even an ideal society. The difficulty, put simply, is that the consequences of a certain kind of act (for example, stealing, lying, torturing, breaking the law of one's land) can vary significantly from situation to situation. Lying usually has consequences that we disvalue (or that the objectivist might characterize as objectively bad). But telling the truth can also have disastrous consequences (on just about any way of evaluating consequences). There will be no general rule about telling the truth that *always* gives you the correct answer concerning what you ought to do on any given occasion. As we noted in the previous chapter, the law, by its nature, needs to be general so that it can be predictable and so that it is manageable to apply. On act consequentialist grounds, we may decide we need a law governing torture. Taking into account all of the relevant consequences, we might decide that we'll do best with a general legal rule prohibiting torture. And again, as we noted in the previous chapter, we may simultaneously realize that there will be circumstances in which we nevertheless ought to torture someone—we ought, that is, to break the law. Our consequentialism will be compatible with all of the following being simultaneously true:

We ought to have a law prohibiting torture.
We ought to pretend that we follow that law scrupulously.
We ought to violate that law from time to time.
Sometimes, we ought to punish those who violate that law even when
they behaved precisely as they should.

Sometimes investigators, prosecutors, or juries ought to find some way of ignoring the law so as to let violators "walk" in those situations in which they behaved precisely as they should.

For the consequentialist, we only confuse the debate if we don't recognize that all of these are *separate* judgments. (And, of course, if we are recognizing a distinction between an "ought" of morality and an "ought" of rationality, the distinctions we need to make automatically double.)

CRITICISMS OF ACT CONSEQUENTIALISM

Many will cringe at the idea that the claims made above are compatible. Some endorse a principle stating that the law must be, in some sense, *transparent*. One cannot, the argument goes, *sincerely* endorse a law while simultaneously thinking that one ought to violate said law on occasion. One cannot legitimately endorse a policy that one plans to ignore on occasion. One cannot endorse a policy without being willing to endorse *publicly* the policy. There are all sorts of problems with a principle of transparency, particularly as it relates to law or policy. A relatively trivial example might illustrate some of these problems. It was alleged that a bookstore I know of (I won't name the store) had a policy of reporting shoplifters to the police, but only the *second* time they were caught. I'm not at all sure of the wisdom of having such a policy, but I am sure that it would be a serious mistake to adopt the policy *and* to be transparent about the fact that it is in place. One surely doesn't want potential shoplifters to know that they get one free book before they get themselves in trouble.

But set aside concerns about transparency. More generally, act consequentialism, particularly consequentialism about morality, has been thought to face devastating counterexamples. Its critics are convinced that we can easily imagine situations in which consequentialists will be forced to utterly absurd conclusions about how people ought to behave. Let's briefly consider a sample.

At one time, some philosophers thought that it was effective to ask us to think about the implications of consequentialism for what they took to be the obvious moral implications of making a promise. When we promise someone to act in a certain way, they sometimes argued, we place ourselves under a moral obligation to perform the act.[26] On the strongest version of the objection, the alleged obligation is claimed to be such that it cannot be overridden by other considerations. But on more modest versions of the view, the obligation is only prima facie, and other reasons might ultimately determine that one not act as one prima facie ought to act. Either way, the idea is that one cannot justify one's failure to keep a promise on the grounds that one calculated the value and probability of consequences and concluded that the greatest net value sided with breaking the promise. A Kantian might even argue that a world in which everyone behaved that way would be a world in which one couldn't even engage in the practice of promise making. Once you realize that after I promise to do X, I will do X only if it has the best consequences, why would you pay any attention to the fact that I made the promise? If you know I am a consequentialist, then you know that I'll do X only if it has the best consequences.

It is not clear that the objection succeeds, even on its own terms. We might have a kind of informal agreement with each other that once we utter the words "I promise," we have just ratcheted up the stakes when it comes to not doing what we promised to do. Promising is a way of giving assurance and I know in advance that a good many people are going to get upset with me (and perhaps try to get even with me) if I don't do what I've assured them I will do. If I break too many promises, I will also lose my ability to give people assurance in the future and getting people to believe me is often valuable to me. To avoid some of these practical considerations, the hypothetical situations to which the critic appeals often become "death bed" promises, where the failure to follow through will never be known to anyone. I promise my dying Aunt Mary to deliver her secret stash of money to her favorite charity. She's heard that I'm a consequentialist, so she goes out of her way to make me promise not to engage in any sort of consequentialist reasoning in deciding whether or not to fulfill the promise. Being a kind person who doesn't want Aunt Mary's last moments to be unpleasant, I solemnly promise to do as she asks. And then she dies.

While initially planning to deliver the money as promised, however, I happen to read, shortly after making the promise, that Aunt Mary's selected charity is one of the worst. The executives at the charity take most of the donations to pay their salaries and only a small fraction trickles down to those in need. I conclude that I ought to give the money to a different charity—after all, lives are at stake. Some would argue that I cannot legitimately break the promise. But I've found that the vast majority of students these days don't even feel the pull of the claim that it would be wrong to break one's word. They really react precisely as one would expect a consequentialist to act. Aunt Mary is dead. You did the right thing to promise—it made her last moments more peaceful. And you did the right thing by breaking the promise. You helped all sorts of other people.[27]

The act consequentialist's critics, however, are hardly out of ammunition. There are all sorts of other vivid counterexamples to which they appeal. Remember that act consequentialism implies that any kind of act might be the right act to choose, given relevant circumstances.[28] There are possible circumstances under which one ought to lie, steal, cheat, commit adultery, kill innocent people, torture innocent people, frame innocent people for crimes they didn't commit, and so on. Take, for example, the case of torturing the innocent. Many can bring themselves to conclude that if the lives of millions are at stake, one ought to torture a known terrorist if one has reason to believe that such torture will prevent the slaughter of innocents. But suppose one knows (never mind how) that while the terrorist would probably remain silent in the case of his own torture, he would fold if he had to watch the torture of his eight-year-old child. On any likely assignment of intrinsic value to consequences, it would be difficult to resist the conclusion that one ought to begin the torture of his child.[29] As Smart (1956) pointed out years ago, there is a natural revulsion to the idea of acting in ways that are almost always wrong. We have probably labored long and hard to influence the behavior of those we raised by inculcating in them the kind of character that would result in these affective responses. I'm not even sure that normal human beings could ever bring themselves to engage in the torture envisioned above, no matter how convinced they became that it was the right thing to do. But all that might be quite compatible with the conclusion that the act in question is demanded by reason.

With this example, one can, with effort, weaken the initial response many people have. Certainly, when we reflect on just wars, we also realize that one probably can't fight and win a just war against a powerful enemy without being willing to act in ways that one knows will cause pain and suffering to people who by any plausible standards are completely innocent. Indeed, the more psychologically depraved one's enemy is, the harder it will be to avoid hurting the innocent. We have heard reports of various groups that deliberately position rockets and communication centers in the heart of civilian neighborhoods, or even elementary schools or hospitals, with the hope that their enemy will be unwilling to sacrifice the few for the perceived greater good of the many. Some will argue that there is a crucial difference between intentionally killing and acting in a way that one knows will result in death, but the distinction is a difficult one for a consequentialist to view as significant. Death and suffering is the same where it was a foreseen means to an end or an intentional means to an end.[30]

In terms of swaying intuitions, Harman's (1977, chapter 1) now familiar example of organ transplants is one of the most successful. In Harman's sort of example, you are to imagine that you are a surgeon in desperate need of organs to save the lives of four people—you need a heart for one, a liver for another, and a couple of kidneys for two more. The circumstances are unusual (you can fill in the imaginary situation with as many details as you like) and you simply can't find suitable organs. Joe, a nice-enough guy but a bit of a klutz, comes wandering into the surgery unit looking for dermatology. And Joe is wearing an organ donor bracelet. You know how to kill a person and make it look like an accident and there is almost no chance you will be caught (we don't want to worry about subtle and long-term consequences of *that* happening).

Should you kill Joe to save the four? Almost everyone says "No," but it is difficult to reconcile that conclusion with a commitment to act consequentialism. Wouldn't a trade of one life for four be a good trade by the act consequentialist's lights?

Consider one more kind of example, one illustrated by what is sometimes called the voter's paradox. There are all sorts of situations in which it seems plausible to suppose that an individual acting in a certain way has a negligible impact on anything we value. The individual polluter doesn't, all by himself or herself, do much of anything to the environment. In times of drought, my watering my lawn will hardly make a crucial difference to whether the water supply survives. And as the term "voter's paradox" suggests, one person's vote in a large election has almost no chance of affecting the outcome of the election. You probably have a better chance of accidentally killing a child on your way to the polls than you do of being the deciding vote in a national election (or the perception of the outcome of the election, or the perception that it was a healthy turnout, and so on). But surely, the critic of consequentialism suggests, it is obvious that we ought to vote if we are citizens in a democracy.

The psychological power of the last two examples is undeniable. One can try to "outsmart"[31] one's critic by playing again on the distinction between what it is rational to tell people about how they should act and how it is actually rational for them to act. In the case of voting, one can appeal to the fact that there is a kind of vicarious pleasure that people get from participating in elections (a consequence that must be factored in with all other possible consequences), or one might even appeal to the fact that people are just irrational (and consequently we can't trust their intuitions about these matters). It does seem to be an empirical fact that when news networks project early the outcome of a national election it does depress the vote in states whose polls haven't closed. And why would that be unless individuals were acting with the almost absurd supposition that their individual vote might make the difference in the outcome of the election?

I actually think the above kinds of response are on the right track. But we should at least quickly look at alternative views of morality and rationality inspired by worries about these sorts of cases. And both of the views I will consider are more friendly to the idea that in morality and rationality we might find a more robust role for *rules* to play—rules that might look a bit more like the laws of an ideal state.

RULE CONSEQUENTIALISM

In a classic paper, "Two Concepts of Rules," John Rawls distinguishes two kinds of rules. We can best illustrate the two kinds of rules first with an example of each (1995). Games (at least some games) seem literally to be defined by a set of rules describing what players may and must do. So, the rules governing chess, for example, permit one to move the bishop diagonally but not through other pieces, the rooks move vertically and horizontally but not through other pieces, and so on. There are rules that determine when a piece is captured and when the game is won. Again, these rules *define* the game and following them partially constitutes what it is to play chess. They are sometimes described for that reason as *constitutive* rules.

Constitutive rules are contrasted with what are sometimes called rules of thumb,[32] or summary rules. As a rule, we might say, children who are given too much too early become very spoiled. As a rule, people get angry if they are deliberately insulted. As a rule, successful politicians at the national level are independently wealthy. These rules seem to be nothing more than statistical generalizations supported by past experience. The "rules" in questions are not purported to be exceptionless and they certainly don't *define* what it is to be spoiled, or angry, or a successful politician.

Painting with a broad stroke, the rule consequentialist thinks that morality, like games, and arguably like law, is *defined* by a set of rules. What determines what one morally ought to do is a rule that governs the act in question. So, consider the voting paradox we discussed above. According to the rule consequentialist, one ought to vote if the correct rule governing voting dictates that one vote. What makes a rule the correct rule? This is where consequences again enter the picture. Earlier we talked about alternative actions open to one, and the act consequentialist's conviction that what makes an alternative correct is some fact about the sum of value (adjusted perhaps for probability) of that alternative compared to sums calculated similarly for alternatives. The correct rule, the rule consequentialist argues, is a function of the consequences of people following that rule compared to the consequences of people following alternative rules. Just as with act consequentialism, we can think of the consequences as actual or possible, and if we go with the latter, we will want to adjust the value that attaches to various consequences for the probability of their occurring.

Back to voting. If we are comparing only two possible rules governing voting (*Vote* or *Don't Vote*), it seems plausible to suppose that in any natural way of calculating the value of consequences, the *Vote* rule will win out over the *Don't Vote* rule. If everyone were to vote, we would have a nice healthy election, people would respect the results, our democracy would be hailed as strong, and so on. If everyone were to follow the *Don't Vote* rule, the country would probably collapse. Every state across the nation would be reporting 0-0 ties. The result would probably be complete anarchy. What you ought to do is a function of the correct rule for voting, so you ought to vote.

So far, so good. But it doesn't take much imagination to see dark clouds on the horizon. There are more than two possible rules governing voting. I've always thought that it is a complete waste of time for people to vote if they don't know anything about the issues or the positions of the candidates, for example. So, we ought to throw into the mix the rule: *Vote if, but only if, you have kept yourself moderately informed.* Let Aunt Mary enter the picture one more time. She is on her deathbed again, and just as you were heading to the polls, you receive a call telling you that she desperately wants to see her favorite relative before she dies. Do you ignore your dying aunt to follow a *Vote* rule? Of course not. Or suppose that on your way to the polls you see the victim of a hit-and-run accident. If you stop to help, you will miss your chance to vote. Should you follow the *Vote* rule? Of course not. Or suppose that. . . . Philosophers have good imaginations and there will be no end to the list of possible situations in which the value of doing something other than voting trumps the value of voting. And if you are a rule consequentialist, you had better not impatiently suggest the rule *Vote unless you can produce more value by not voting*, for the act consequentialism will, at this point, simply welcome you back into the fold!

There are possible responses to this well-known argument that rule consequentialism "collapses" back into act consequentialism. One might argue that the test for a correct rule concerns, not the consequences of people actually following the rule, but of people *trying* to follow the rule. Furthermore, given this criterion, the "consequentialist" rule described above will not necessarily "win" the contest of rules, precisely because the consequences of everyone "trying" to follow the rule *Vote unless you can produce more value by not voting* will probably be the same disastrous consequences described earlier. In "bridge" the card game begins with an "auction" through which partners try to communicate with each other the character and strength of their respective hands. The legal rules of communication allow for very complex conventions, some of which would be extremely effective *if* partners were to succeed in following them. But many bridge players learn fairly quickly that the consequences of people trying to follow these very complex rules are often disastrous, particularly for those who are not experts. Instead, some would argue, one should only try to follow "KISS" (keep it simple, stupid) rules. The same might be true of rules designed to guide normal human contact. The rules that would be effective were people to act on them might be relatively simple rules.

If moral rules are simple, however, the rule consequentialist faces another problem. Simple rules will inevitably conflict in certain situations. Let's say that two rules, R1 and R2, "conflict" in a given situation, S, when the rules tell one to act in impossible ways. So, for example, a simple "Always vote" rule will conflict with a simple "Always save innocent lives" rule in the situation described above where one can only save the hit-and-run victim by foregoing the opportunity to vote. So, our rule consequentialist with simple rules will obviously need a further view about how to choose between conflicting rules. And there will need to be indefinitely many such rules, for, of course, the conflicts can exist between many different rules. To keep a promise, I might need to hurt an innocent person and fail to act on a rule requiring me to care for my children.

There are all sorts of proposals for dealing with these conflicts. One is to suggest that one employs the same sort of consequentialist test for alternative "meta" rules—rules governing what to do when first-level rules conflict. And if the meta-rules conflict, one can turn again to a consequentialist test for the relevant meta-meta-rules. The criteria for deciding what one ought to do might get enormously complex, but the rule consequentialist might shrug and insist that the question of what one ought to do is often exceedingly complex. It is no mark against a view that it acknowledges that fact.

But note how far our rule consequentialist has strayed from the "constitutive" rules of a game that were supposed to be the model for moral rules. The rules of a game define the game. As such they admit of no exceptions. The first-level rules of morality will be nothing like the first-level rules of chess or baseball. They won't define what we may or may not do in life.

Rule Consequentialist Accounts of Rationality

Just as one can advance a rule consequentialist account of morality, one might also try a rule consequentialist account of rational action—assuming, of course, that one thinks morality and rationality can come apart. We might illustrate the idea with the famous hypothetical situation called "Prisoner's Dilemma." In the example, two people, A and B, are captured by a philosophically interesting enemy who asks them to confess to their spying. They are informed that if they both confess, they will get five years in prison. If one confesses and the other remains silent, the one who confesses will go free; the one who remains silent will be executed. If they both remain silent, they will spend only a year in prison. In the version I'm imagining, they can discuss their choice for a few days before they make it. In a classic version of the dilemma, it is supposed that A and B are "non-empathetic" egoists. Each value intrinsically only his own well-being (broadly) construed, and neither is empathetic—neither is affectively moved by the plight of the other. But we can construct the same sort of dilemma as long as we suppose that the two prisoners value intrinsically different outcomes—for example, that each values intrinsically the well-being of his family and cares not a whit about the well-being of the other's family. In that case, we imagine the outcomes (jail, execution) applying to the family members. To simplify matters, we are also asked to suppose (unrealistically, of course) that the prisoners' decisions will never be discovered by anyone else—we stipulate this so that we don't need to consider consequences, such as the determination of others to seek revenge.[33]

The interesting feature of the dilemma is that on a Humean conception of rational action, each should conclude that the choice of confessing "dominates" (using a technical term from decision theory). A can correctly conclude that no matter what B does, A's confessing will leave A better off in that situation than he would be were he to remain silent. If B confesses, A is better off confessing; if B remains silent, A is better off confessing. B, of course, can reach the same correct conclusion concerning B's choice, so as ideally rational agents, each will confess. Ironically, they end up in a far worse position than they would have been in had rationality allowed them both to remain silent.

If rational behavior were determined by the *rule* each should follow for a choice of this sort, rational behavior would have allowed the prisoners to find the benefits of cooperation. At least that is so if the correctness of the rule is determined by the consequences of everyone involved following the rule. Following the "Remain Silent" rule leaves each better off than following the "Confess" rule. Of course, if you reason on the basis of such rules, you had better hope that your fellow prisoner is not an *act* consequentialist about rationality. Your last thought before execution might well be that you should have paid more attention to that possibility.

A FUNDAMENTAL OBJECTION TO RULE CONSEQUENTIALISM

The following is not much of an argument, though I find it ultimately persuasive. Some critics of rule consequentialism think that the view reflects a bizarre form of "rule worship." In the final analysis, we are surely interested in making the world the best place we can (either from the perspective of an objectivist about value or from the perspective of one evaluating that world in terms of what is valued intrinsically). When following a rule doesn't have that effect, why on earth would one follow the rule? There may be good reasons for having rules of thumb. As Mill pointed out (1979, 23–24), one hasn't *time* prior to action to consider all of the potential effects of each action open to one, so one had better go out on the "sea of life" with navigation charts in the form of rules learned from past experience. But there is simply no point in thinking of these rules as exceptionless. When we do have the time to think through the consequences of the alternatives open to one, and particularly when we are in unusual situations that call for careful thought, why wouldn't we engage in thought about will yield the best outcome?

DEONTOLOGICAL ACCOUNTS OF MORALITY

The rule consequentialist still takes consequences to be relevant just inso-far as the view defines the correctness of rules in terms of the value and disvalue of the consequences of people following those rules (compared to others). There is another "rule-based" account of morality that is superficially similar to rule consequentialism, but that differs in its ulti-mate metaethical underpinnings. Unlike the consequentialist (act or rule), the *deontologist* doesn't think one can *define* rightness and wrongness, what one should or shouldn't do, in terms of intrinsic value. Like the rule consequentialist, the deontologist thinks that what one ought to do is a function of kinds of action that are either right or wrong simpliciter (on a very strong version of the view) or prima facie right or wrong (on a less extreme version of the view). As we saw earlier, it is more than a little difficult to make plausible the claim that there are kinds of action that are always morally required no matter what the circumstances. It is precisely this fact that might make one lean toward act consequentialism. As we also saw, however, it is probably true that one usually ought to tell the truth. But wouldn't one need to be a fanatic to conclude that one ought to tell the truth when thousands of innocent lives would be lost as a result? It is entirely plausible to suppose that there are very few situations in which one ought to engage in torture, but almost anyone can *imagine* an extremely unusual situation in which the relevant consequences mandate that one ought to do what is almost always wrong.

The deontologist who builds a view on the idea of an action kind being prima facie right or prima facie wrong has other resources to ac-commodate our consequentialist inclinations. Ross, we saw earlier, will include among the relevant prima facie obligations a prima facie obliga-tion to produce good consequences and avoid harmful consequences. He was quick to point out that prima facie duties might be outweighed by others. According to this sort of deontologist, promising, occupying a position of trust, contracting, being in an intimate relation with some-one—all these and many more—carry with them various prima facie obligations to act that must be weighed against the good and bad conse-quences that the act of keeping a promise, say, would have.

Ross didn't try to define the concept of being prima facie right. Just as Moore thought that the idea of something's being intrinsically valuable was a simple concept that we just grasp but cannot define in terms of anything simpler, so also Ross thought that the idea of something's being prima facie obligatory was a simple concept that we grasp but cannot define.[34] Of course, one might try to provide an analysis of the critical concept and if one succeeded one could employ the analyzed concept within the very same framework for which Ross argued.

The line between certain versions of act consequentialism and Ross-style deontology can become very fine. We have had occasion to note that a general acceptance of act consequentialism leaves open the question of what actually has intrinsic value. Hedonistic consequentialists think that only pleasure has intrinsic value, but "generic" (or, as it is sometimes called, "ideal") consequentialism allows one to adopt a pluralistic view about what is intrinsically good or bad. So, there is nothing to stop an act consequentialist from insisting that acting in certain kinds of ways is intrinsically valuable. An act consequentialist might conclude that telling the truth, keeping a promise or a more formal contract, participating in an electoral process, are all examples of kinds of actions that are intrinsically good. And the value that attaches to acting in these ways must be factored in along with all the other positive and negative value that attaches to various consequences in analyzing what one ought to do.

But what is the difference between the deontologist who talks about a *prima facie* reason to tell the truth, a reason that could be outweighed by other considerations, and an act consequentialist who allows that telling the truth is intrinsically valuable, but where the value of telling the truth might be outweighed by other considerations? The answer is subtle. If one tries to co-opt the deontologist by assigning *objective* intrinsic value to certain action kinds, one will still need to allow that you're acting in the way that has objective value has no *more* objective value than anyone else acting in that way. But that, the deontologist claims, will lead to implausible consequences. Consider just one example. Most of us probably think that we have special obligations to our children that we don't have to strangers. If I had to choose between saving my child and saving two or three other children that I don't even know, I ought to save my child. At the very least, it would be permissible. Both Ross and the act consequentialist who assigns objective value to a parent's saving his or her child can reach this conclusion. But suppose that the only way I can save my child is to prevent other parents from saving their children. When we "add" up the value, the sum would seem to favor allowing the other parents to save their children at the expense of my saving my child (other things being equal). And that's not the result we want. But note that this would be a problem only for the act consequentialist who tries to solve the problem with the assignment of objective values. As we noted earlier, one can embrace act consequentialism with a subjectivist, relativist concept of value. The Humean might insist that my child's happiness has a degree of intrinsic value *for me* that your child's happiness doesn't have. And that will be correctly reflected in my assignment of intrinsic value to the consequences of actions open to me.[35] The act consequentialist who is a *relativist* about value and the Rossian objectivist who offers a deontological account of prima facie obligation can reach the same conclusion about the hypothetical just described. But there is still a world of difference between the conceptual framework each brings to their understanding of what one ought to do.

As we pointed out in the last chapter, the kind of deontology Ross defended still won't allow one to find much of a parallel between the kind of generality *law* requires and the kind of generality the deontologist might allow in morality. The Rossian deontologist insists that there are general principles describing what kinds of actions are prima facie right. But the view insists that we distinguish carefully between what is prima facie right and what is right, *all things being considered*. It will be no easier for the deontologist to find general truths about kinds of action that are always right, all things considered, than it is for the act consequentialist or even the rule consequentialist who admits that the relevant rules can conflict in indefinitely many ways.

MORALITY AS AGREEMENT

There is another historically influential "rule-based" conception of morality that rejects the idea of objective prima facie obligation developed by deontologists like Ross, but still might find a structural similarity between morality and law. In this view, morality is construed as a system of rules, but those rules are thought of as agreements to which people who are committed to living together have explicitly or implicitly accepted. Later in the book, we'll talk again about the idea that the source of *political* obligation is our explicit or implicit acceptance of some sort of contract or agreement with our fellow citizens—the so-called social contract theory of political obligation. The view we are considering here is a kind of contract theory of *morality*. As I indicated earlier in the book, this *kind* of view can be traced back as far as Glaucon (playing devil's advocate) in Plato's *Republic*. A version of it is defended by Harman (1975). But throughout his career, Gauthier has developed what I take to be the most sophisticated and subtle view that morality is a matter of agreement.[36]

The idea that morality is best construed as a system of agreements faces the task of explaining just how, and by whom, these agreements are supposed to have been made. Since it seems highly implausible to suppose that any of us have literally hammered out with other people some set of constraints on our interpersonal behavior, the proponent of this sort of view will usually appeal either to *implicit* agreements,[37] or to agreements ideally rational people *would* accept. We have discussed the possibility of distinguishing theories of rational action from theories of morality. There is a sense in which a contract theory of morality is typically *parasitic* upon some understanding of individual rational action. The relevant agreements that constitute some system of morality just are agreements that are rational to accept. We have also warned, however, about the potential danger of divorcing the concepts of rational and moral action. Any attempt to identify morality with a set of agreements into which rational agents would enter faces a version of the "fool's" objection to Hobbes's idea that the state comes into existence as an attempt by rational people to escape the "nasty, brutish, short" existence they face without the protection of laws enforced by a sovereign. The fool, as Hobbes describes him, doesn't deny that it might be rational to *enter into* various agreements, but insists that we distinguish the question of whether it is rational to enter into an agreement from the question of whether it is rational to *keep* that agreement. And the fool doesn't understand why the very considerations that make it rational to make an agreement might not also sometimes make it rational to break the agreement. If, for example, it is self-interest that leads one to agree to cooperate with others in various ways, then, surely, self-interest might lead one to stop cooperating (for example, when one can profit enormously by violating an agreement with little or no chance of facing repercussions associated with getting caught).[38] One needn't presuppose that the parties to the agreement are rational egoists, however, to generate the concern. As long as the rationality of one's action is a function of fundamental values that can vary from individual to individual, a cost/benefit analysis might at one time lead one to enter into an agreement, while at a later time that same sort of analysis leads one to violate that agreement.

Throughout his work, Gauthier has been worried about how to reconcile his attempt to construe morality in terms of rational agreements with the obvious force of the worry that one can't preclude the possibility that the very rationality that leads to agreement can, in principle, require one to turn one's back on the agreement. I can't do justice to the various attempts Gauthier has made to prevent rationality from leading one to violate a morality understood in terms of agreement. He does correctly remind us that consequentialist calculations need to be subtle. As I see it, he ultimately rests his case on the concern that a willingness to violate contracts will likely develop character traits that in the long run will frustrate one achieving one's ultimate goals or ends. Such considerations certainly are relevant.[39] Lying gets easier the more one lies. Procrastination gets easier the more one procrastinates. Breaking promises gets easier the more one breaks promises. And if it gets too easy to lie, procrastinate, or break a promise, it is, perhaps, likely that one will act in these ways far too often—act in these ways when rationality doesn't recommend the action. So before one lies, procrastinates, or breaks a promise, one should factor into one's calculations the disvalue of *this* sort of possible consequence. All this is true, but it won't faze the fool. Factor in what you want, the fool argues, but the most subtle and sophisticated reasoning will still *sometimes* lead one to break the agreements that might have been once rational to make. A morality understood in terms of agreement will drive a wedge between the concept of rationality and the concept of morality. And, again, it seems to me close to a tautology to suggest that rational people will act rationally. Of course, a contractarian about morality might just shrug off the worry that sometimes it might be rational to ignore morality. After all, I have argued, and will continue to argue, that sometimes it might be rational to ignore what the law requires. And that shouldn't stop us from thinking that important questions concerning what the law should be are reached through agreement, consensus, and compromise. But once we have the concept of rational action and the concept of law, why introduce yet another system of rules that raise all of the same questions as law?[40]

None of what I just said should be taken to disparage the importance of agreements forged through compromise. We do need to make collective decisions about what laws to have and enforce. Those sympathetic to libertarian conclusions will want those laws to protect a great deal of freedom. As I will argue in later chapters, the consequentialist road to freedom often runs through compromise.

SUMMARY

We have surveyed some of the main competing accounts of morality and rationality. We have done so primarily with a view to understanding the implications of these views for the idea that we can view ideal law as paralleling in some straightforward sense moral truths. Later in this book, it will become apparent that I am most sympathetic to act consequentialist accounts of rational action. If morality is distinct from rationality, so much the worse for morality.

It is also important to emphasize that just because law doesn't parallel rationality or morality, it doesn't follow that our account of what we ought to do has no implications for what the law ought to be. Law is just one of many instruments that serve our goals or ends. But it is a particularly important instrument, and we need to figure out what laws we ought to have. Given the primary subject of this book, it is particularly important that we reach correct conclusions about how much we ought to respect freedom in constructing our laws.

We have discussed the importance of theory and the potential difficulties that face a philosopher trying to apply theory to first-level ethical controversies, in particular, controversies concerning the extent to which we ought to embrace law that protects freedom. In Part II, with our eyes wide open to those difficulties, we'll look at some of the most important controversies that arise in a defense of freedom.

NOTES

1. The objection I am raising here is very similar to the objection to form of Divine Command Theory that is discussed below.

2. That there be obligations to which humans are bound requires the existence of God. There is another, subtly related, but importantly different theory, one according to which when people make moral judgments, they *are asserting* that there is a God

who has issued commands or who has preferences. But their assertions might be false. On such an "error" theory, people never succeed in making true claims about what they are obligated to do (though I suppose they can make true claims about what they are not obligated to do—without God they would not be obligated to do anything).

3. Raised by Plato in his famous dialogue *Euthyprho.*

4. See Firth (1952) for one of the most clear and sophisticated versions of such a theory.

5. There is an entire third book of *Leviathan* (not read nearly as often as the other two) devoted to the interpretation of the bible. Still, Hobbes admitted he was timid, and it is not wildly implausible to suppose that this was an elaborate effort to save him from the dangers of an openly defended atheism.

6. This terminology is the one I favor. Hume is more likely to talk about attitudes of approbation (a species of what he calls passions) and Hobbes is more likely to talk simply about what people desire. The verb "value" is more flexible in that it allows one easily to talk about valuing something that is past or present. Verbs like "desire" are most at home when what is desired is something in the future.

7. The distinction is at least as old as Plato's *Republic* (1974).

8. I discuss various possibilities of interpretation in Fumerton (1990a, chapter 5).

9. One might suggest that one values X intrinsically when one values X and would value it even if one were to have no beliefs about its consequences. But this sort of definition is tricky. If one didn't have beliefs about certain consequences of X, one might not be the same sort of person one is. That fact might change other facts about oneself, including facts about one's affective states. Other more extreme views might try to define talk about value in terms of dispositions to behave in certain ways. But behaviorism is a wildly implausible view.

10. There is a very real complication I am ignoring. In presenting the view, I took for granted that the values of an agent, relevant to what the agent has reason to do, are the values the agent has at the time the choice is made. We all know that people change over time. There are plenty of people who were young liberals and who are now old conservatives. Suppose that I know or suspect that my future self will have quite different values from the values I have now. How would those future values factor into an account of what I rationally ought to do? My own view is that one still sticks to the present. Of course, I might now care very much about my future happiness, and I might realize that if I don't get my future desires satisfied, I will be unhappy. This will give me a way of factoring in the values that my future self will have. See L. A. Paul (2014) for an extensive discussion of various problems associated with knowing and taking into account possible changes in one's future self—particularly changes that Paul describes as transformative.

11. See MacDonald (1991).

12. See Smart's (1956) discussion of this issue, and (in one reading) Gauthier (1986).

13. See Fumerton (1996).

14. So, there is a really interesting question as to whether Mill implicitly adopted something like a consequentialism defined in terms of desire satisfaction, where it is analytic that what is desired as an end by S is good as an end for S. It would then be a contingent fact (if a fact at all) that people desire, as an end, happiness (their own or the general happiness). For a defense of the view that Mill is a "desire satisfaction" consequentialist, see Fumerton in Donner and Fumerton (2009, 189–194). The interpretation of Mill on the goal of morality is, however, decidedly complicated. Brink (2013) argues that while no interpretation is perfectly consistent with all of the passages in Mill's text, Mill is best understood as endorsing a "perfectionist" account of happiness. The details of Brink's view are subtle and complex, but as I understand him, Brink places considerable emphasis on Mill's well-known suggestion that the desires relevant to determining value are those of "competent judges." Minimally, competent judges have experience with a wide range of pleasures—both physical and mental. Perhaps, however, they also need to be ideally rational agents who are appropriately "progressive" in their intellectual development. If Mill held such a view, then he needs

an account of what makes a given subject both ideally rational and appropriately progressive. That account would require an analysis of these concepts that involves no normatively laden terms lest the view become problematically circular.

15. See Fumerton (1990b) for a detailed discussion and criticism of this approach.

16. See Glaucon's suggestion early in Book II of *The Republic* (Plato, 1974).

17. So, one might infer that I am talking here about what Samuelson (1954) called public goods. In one way of understanding public goods, these are just goods that belong to all and to which all have equal access. A great deal depends on what it means to describe something as a good to which all have access. Anyone can use public tennis courts, but their "availability" isn't of much use to those who are paralyzed, or, for that matter, those who don't know how to play tennis. We'll talk later about how best to understand rational decisions about how to "create" jointly owned property, goods, and services.

18. There is an important distinction between endorsing the obvious truth that it is often rational to engage in bargaining that involves compromise, and the more radical thesis that morality is best understood in terms of a commitment to the results of such compromise.

19. He says (1967, 72) "that there is often a great difference between the will of all . . . and the general will." He goes on to make clear that everyone might want something even if it is not in accord with the general will. If all people can want something when it is not the general will that it be done, then *a fortiori* most people can want something even if it is not the general will that it be done.

20. For a critique of Brandt's view on this matter, see Fumerton (1990, 143–150).

21. For Moore, an idea was just a property "in mind" and thus he felt comfortable switching back and forth between talk of ideas and talk of properties.

22. See Butchvarov (1989, chapter 3).

23. Narveson (1967, chapter 9) seems to think that it is most natural to understand the claim that X has value for S as a claim about what S *believes* has value. He interprets Mill as using the "for/to" language in this way. But while one *can* understand relativized value claims that way, there is another equally plausible understanding of relativized value. In that view, X has value for me just insofar as I subjectively value X. As we'll see, it is important to distinguish general claims about relativized value from claims about what has *intrinsic* value for some person.

24. There is another, equally plausible, interpretation of Hume in which the distinction he is trying to make is defined not in terms of the character of the sentiment but in terms of the fact that it is a sentiment that would arise in you from a disinterred perspective. The distinction is subtle but crucial. In the one view, one is emphasizing a kind of feeling and one is "pointing" to that feeling by talking about situations (disinterested perspectives) in which it arises. In the other view, one is defining the reaction that is relevant to the subject matter of moral judgments in terms of the fact that it is a sentiment that would arise from that disinterred perspective. Either view presents problems for Hume's "internalism." In Hume's own view, all sorts of passions are potentially motivating, and if we carve out a subset of passions that are the subject matter of moral judgments, we have lost any tight connection between our moral conclusions and what we are likely to do.

25. It gets complicated. If Mackie's view were correct, there is a sense in which if one asserts that something is not intrinsically good, one is saying something true, just as if there are no demons and one says that someone is not possessed by a demon, one is also saying something true.

26. See Ross (1988, 17–18), as an example.

27. It's true that the intuitions might change a bit if the expected gain from breaking the promise is only marginal. And yet the marginal gain, in the consequentialist's view, would still seem to justify breaking the promise.

28. With the trivial exception of the act kind that is defined by the act consequentialist as the right thing to do (i.e., the act that maximizes value).

29. In any *likely* assignment of values. We have already noted that a generic commitment to consequentialism leaves open how one assigns intrinsic value. One could assign enormous negative intrinsic value to the act of torture—a negative value so high it would be difficult to compensate for it with the positive value of saving the lives of countless other innocent people (including innocent eight-year-olds) who might suffer painful death were we unwilling to engage in the torture of one innocent eight-year-old.

30. The issue is, of course, very complicated. The doctrine of "double effect"—the doctrine that there is a significant distinction between doing what one knows will cause X and acting with the intent of causing X—has been debated for thousands of years.

31. The expression is a tongue-in-cheek reference to the way which J. J. C. Smart is perceived as sometimes responding to objections by "biting the bullet" and simply accepting counter-intuitive consequences of positions.

32. There is a highly dubious view that the expression "rule of thumb" has its origin in common law that allowed a husband to beat a wife with a stick with a diameter no greater than the man's thumb. It's much more likely that it has to do with the way in which one sometimes uses one's thumb (or portions of it) for purposes of measurement.

33. And again, it is important to emphasize that we are stipulating that the prisoners have no other relevant desires or interests. It seems to me that it is *possible* for a person to value intrinsically just about anything. It is possible to value intrinsically a decision-making process that counts the desires of others as being just as important as one's own desires. *I'm* not like that and I don't think that you are like that. See Gaus (2008), though, for a "solution" to the prisoners' dilemma that suggests that the right sort of rational person with the right sort of values can find their way clear to cooperating.

34. In correspondence, Narveson has suggested to me that Ross did define what it is for an act to be prima facie right. He defined that concept in terms of being right, all things considered. Specifically, the idea is that X is prima facie right in virtue of being of kind F when X would be right in virtue of being F if there were no other features of X that are morally relevant. That claim might be true, but it isn't plausibly regarded as an *analysis* of prima facie rightness. There is implicit reliance on our understanding of prima facie duties in the reference to no other relevant features. The features in question are features that make an act prima facie right or wrong. Ross didn't think that there is an algorithm for calculating what is right, all things considered, but it is not clear that the problem he envisioned was practical or theoretical.

35. See Jeske and Fumerton (1997) for further discussion of this point.

36. He has written a great deal on the topics but Gauthier (1986) is still one of the best and most influential presentations and defenses of the view.

37. An implicit agreement is something like the arrangement my wife and I have concerning distribution of labor around the house. We never sat down and agreed that I would do this and she would do that, but an "understanding" developed over the years and all hell would break loose if either of us suddenly refused to perform our respective "tasks."

38. Even facing sanctions, it might be rational to break an agreement. Corporate lawyers make a great deal of money litigating suits brought against companies who quite openly violate an agreement into which they entered. A company will sometimes conclude that complying with the agreement will have such dire consequences that it would be better to face the relevant sanctions.

39. As I emphasized in our brief discussion of virtue theory.

40. I suppose an answer might just be that we save *law* for regulations of matters that are *very* important to us. We have another slew of rules that we want people to follow, many of which aren't important enough to encode in law. The rules of etiquette are, presumably, like that.

Part II

Defending Freedom

FOUR

Mill's Defense of Freedom

No discussion of the importance of freedom would be complete without taking into account John Stuart Mill's classic *On Liberty*. The book was rhetorically powerful and influential. To many, it captures the fundamental principles underlying libertarian political thought. But as is true of many philosophical classics, superficial clarity and power sometimes disguises underlying complexity. The discussion of metaethical and metarational controversies in chapter 3 will help us uncover internal tension within Mill's own thought, tension that should lead us to wonder about the underlying structure of Mill's arguments.

MILL'S SEARCH FOR A PRINCIPLED DEFENSE OF FREEDOM

I've already described Mill as one of the most famous defenders of freedom. But even that claim is misleading given Mill's own words. In *On Liberty*, after deploring the lack of a *principled* approach to issues concerning freedom he complains that

> [p]eople decide according to their personal preferences. Some, whenever, they see any good to be done, or evil to be remedied, would willingly instigate the government to undertake the business, while others prefer to bear almost any amount of social evil rather than add one more to the departments of human interests amenable to governmental control. And men range themselves on one or the other side in any particular case, according to this general direction of their sentiments, or according to the degree of interest which they feel in the particular thing which it is proposed that the government should do, or according to the belief they entertain that the government would, or would not, do it in the manner they prefer; but very rarely on account of any opinion to which they consistently adhere, as to what things are fit to

79

be done by a government. And it seems to me that in consequence of this absence of rule or principle, one side is at present as often wrong as the other; the interference of government is, with about equal frequency, improperly invoked and improperly condemned. (1956, 12)

In this passage one can almost hear both current right- and left-wing caricatures of their respective political opponents. And in his concluding sentence Mill seems to suggest a "pox" upon both their houses. That said, the rest of the book has a decided emphasis on the importance of various sorts of freedom, and Mill unequivocally aligns himself with de Tocqueville's concern that even with the rise of democracies we still need to be on guard against the "tyranny of the majority:"

[I]n political speculations "the tyranny of the majority" is now generally included among the evils against which society requires to be on its guard. (6)

Our problem, Mill argues, is that we need a *principled* way of deciding issues of freedom, and he clearly thinks that *On Liberty* is supposed to solve that problem. After some rhetorical flourishes, he suggests a principle that will do the trick:

That the sole end for which mankind are warranted, individually or collectively, in interfering with the liberty of action of any of their number is self-protection. (13)

The principle is immediately restated in the form that gave it its name— the harm principle:

That the only purpose for which power can be rightfully exercised over any member of a civilized community, against his will, is to prevent harm to others. His own good, either physical or moral, is not a sufficient warrant. He cannot rightfully be compelled to do or forbear because it will be better for him to do so, because it will make him happier, because, in the opinions of others, to do so would be wise or even right. (13)

The basic idea behind the principle is intuitive and compelling. If we really want to live in a society that respects freedom, we should leave people alone to do as they please as long as they are not hurting another person against that person's will. But in philosophy the devil is in the details. To evaluate the principle we need a careful interpretation of what constitutes harm, and an equally careful interpretation of what constitutes *producing* harm—an account of the circumstances under which a given individual can be said to have *relevantly* caused harm to another.[1]

Before addressing these two critical questions, however, it is crucial to note that the harm principle, even if plausible, will not live up to its billing. Mill was looking for a principle that we could use to *decide* controversies over whether someone should be free to act as he or she chooses. But the harm principle clearly states only a *necessary* condition for legitimate interference with the freedom of another; it does not state a *sufficient* condition for correctly engaging in such interference. The principle tells us that we must not interfere with someone's freedom if that person is not harming another (against the other's will), but it doesn't tell us that we always, or even usually, should act so as to prevent such harm when it occurs. If there is any doubt as to whether Mill himself understands his principle that way, it is removed unequivocally in chapter V where Mill says:

> In the first place, it must by no means be supposed, because damage, or probability of damage, to the interests of others can alone justify the interference of society, that therefore it always does justify such interference. In many cases an individual, in pursuing a legitimate object, necessarily and therefore legitimately causes pain or loss to others, or intercepts a good which they had a reasonable hope of obtaining. Such oppositions of interest between individuals often arise from bad social institutions, but are unavoidable while those institutions last; and some would be unavoidable under any institutions. Whoever succeeds in an overcrowded profession or in a competitive examination, whoever is preferred to another in any contest for an object which both desire, reaps benefit from the loss of others, from their wasted exertion and their disappointment. But it is, by common admission, better for the general interest of mankind that persons should pursue their objects undeterred by this sort of consequences. (1956, 114)

So, we are clearly going to need other principles before we act so as to restrict freedom, and in particular before we pass and enforce laws that restrict freedom. As we'll see later, Mill does have another principle, but the availability of that principle makes the role of the harm principle in *On Liberty* difficult to understand. We'll return do that issue shortly.

After presenting the harm principle, Mill adds an obvious qualification. The principle is not intended to apply to children. And in a comment revealing that even the most "enlightened" of thinkers can display deplorable world views, Mill also makes clear that he thinks of many races and ethnic groups as analogous to children:

> It is, perhaps, hardly necessary to say that this doctrine is meant to apply only to human beings in the maturity of their faculties. We are not speaking of children or young persons below the age which the law may fix as that of manhood or womanhood. Those who are still in a state to require being taken care of by others must be protected against their own actions as well as against external injury. For the same reason we may leave out of consideration those backward states of society in which the race itself may be considered as in its nonage. (13)

Setting aside the disturbing racism,[2] one might worry about a slippery slope inherent in Mill's exceptions to the harm principle. It is obviously difficult to decide just when someone reaches the "age of reason." In the United States, we deem eighteen-year-olds rational enough to vote or to decide to serve in the armed services, but we apparently don't think that they are equipped to decide whether or not to consume alcohol. And it obviously isn't one's *physical* age that determines whether one has reached the age of reason.[3] There is a continuum from those who suffer severe and debilitating mental problems to those who just aren't very bright, and it won't be easy to decide where along this continuum we should treat people more like children than competent adults.

It would be a mistake, however, to worry too much about this very real practical problem. We make perfectly useful distinctions that involve these sorts of continua all the time. There is a real "sorites" puzzle (the puzzle of the "heap"). The puzzle arises when we try to specify how many grains of sand make a heap, what percentage of lost hairs renders someone bald, at what height a man moves from being short to not short, and so on. And one had better be careful dealing with the puzzle. Obviously, a person who is, say, 3′ tall is short for an American adult man. And it is tempting to think that if a person is short, adding a billionth of an inch to that person's height is never going to change that fact. But acceptance of the *general* principal forces one to the conclusion that a man 9′ tall is short. Just keeping adding a billionth of an inch to that 3′ tall man 72 billion billion times! So, it seems that a billionth of an inch must make a difference somewhere along the line, even if we feel foolish trying to specify where *precisely* that crucial billionth of an inch matters. But, however puzzling this is, it would be a mistake to infer that we should not describe people using adjectives like "short" and "tall." The existence of borderline cases doesn't render the distinctions that have vague borders useless. And that's probably the moral we should draw about what sort of intellectual capacities are relevant to whether one falls under the protection of something like a harm principle.

There are other comments Mill makes that provide clues as to how he wanted his harm principle to be understood. Shortly after introducing the principle he makes clear that there are circumstances under which we might not only legitimately force a person to refrain from acting so as to produce harm, but also legitimately force a person to benefit another (*act* so as to prevent harm). He immediately emphasizes, albeit cryptically, that the latter should be the exception rather than the rule:

> A person may cause evil to others not only by his actions but by his inaction, and in either case he is justly accountable to them for the injury. The latter case it is true, requires a much more cautious exercise of compulsion than the former. To make someone answerable for doing evil is the rule; to make him answerable for not preventing evil is, comparatively speaking, the exception. (1956, 15)

This admission that both action and inaction can be subject to legitimate regulation will pose no end of difficulty for Mill trying to make use of his harm principle.

Another term that makes its appearance in one of the quotes above is usually missing from Mill's discussion but is crucial for any charitable interpretation. In that quote, Mill refers not just to an action causing harm to another, but also to an action involving the *probability* of harm to another, potentially justifying regulation of the action in question. But for reasons similar to those we discussed, when arguing about how to understand a plausible consequentialism, Mill would surely be quickly forced to admit that one can legitimately regulate actions that *might* produce harm even when the probability is rather low.

Consider, for example, those cultures that routinely celebrate such events as soccer victories by firing automatic weapons in the air. We wouldn't allow such behavior here in the United States, and for good reason. Bullets that go up come down, and it is a sad fact that this sort of celebration takes its toll on both life and property. Why would we want to risk needlessly this sort of harm for the sake of the pleasure our hypothetical revelers get from their display of fire power? Or take a more familiar sort of example. Most of us are OK with laws prohibiting people from driving a car under the influence of alcohol or behavior-altering drugs. Though it is probably not a good idea to advertise this fact, it is almost certainly true that the probability of someone just over the legal limit hurting another is relatively small. But the reasonable consensus is surely that we don't want to put up with this *needless* increase in the probably of damage to life and property. A key term in the discussion of these examples is the word "needless." We put up with increases in the probability of harm to others all of the time. Allowing people to drive cars increases the probability of harm to pedestrians. Allowing planes to fly overhead obviously increases, however slightly, the probability of a plane's crashing down on our heads. But we think that, all things considered, we ought to put up with those increases in the probability of harm. And Mill is, or should be, fine with all of this, for as we emphasized above, the harm principle doesn't tell you that you should stop *all* behavior that involves harm, probability of harm, or (now we are including) possibility of harm to others. The only point is that any plausible interpretation of the harm principle would state the necessary condition for legitimate regulation of behavior in terms of the action (or failure to act) that increases the probability (by however slight an amount) of harm to others (against their will).

The above comments all focus on how a *plausible* harm principle should understand the relevant connection between actions[4] and harm in order for the act in question to lose the protection of the harm principle. But there are also a host of questions concerning the relevant concept of harm. Physical injury is obviously going to make the list. When you stick a knife in my chest, we surely want to count that as your harming me. Or do we? Whether I am harmed by your action (at least as we normally think about these things) makes critical reference to a base line. The surgeon who operates on me to save my life plunges a knife (a scalpel) into my chest, but isn't appropriately described as harming me. Indeed, she is more often described as benefiting me. And that's presumably because her action doesn't make me worse off (all things considered) than I otherwise would have been.[5] But this can get tricky. Imagine that a taxi driver negligently drives his taxi into a tree, injuring his passenger, a passenger who then proceeds to claim damages. As it happens, the passenger was on his way to a flight that crashed killing all on board. Was the passenger harmed by the taxi driver's negligent behavior? The passenger was certainly better off than he would have been had the cab driver been driving properly. But I'll bet the passenger would still expect to win the suit.

Complications aside, we should probably conclude that even with physical injury (including, of course, death) we are going to need a way to take into account base lines. But having done so, we still obviously want to conclude that under certain conditions one way of making someone worse off is to physically injure them. We can also obviously injure people by injuring their property interests. So, if for no good reason I burn down your house, vandalize your car, break your computer, and so on, we are going to want to include such behavior as harmful in the sense relevant to deciding whether that behavior forfeits the protection of the harm principle. Property damage can be subtle, however, and often results indirectly from the psychological effects actions have on others. So, let's turn to that vexing issue. Shall we include as harm (relative to a baseline) such factors as psychological stress, fear, aesthetic revulsion, and so on?

In discussing this question, let's distinguish the question of how *Mill* wanted us to understand the notion of harm from the question of how one might most plausibly construe a harm principle. Did Mill want to allow the fact that someone finds certain behavior distasteful or repugnant, or the effects of such behavior distasteful or repugnant, to count as an instance of that person being *harmed* by the relevant behavior? Mill himself sent somewhat mixed signals. The Muslims who are disgusted by the idea of eating pork, Mill seems to suggest, are not harmed by those who eat pork, at least in the sense of harm relevant to issues concerning the application of the harm principle (1956, 103–104). Similarly, he indicates no sympathy for Catholics who claim to be "harmed" due to the emotional distress they feel at people practicing religions other than Catholicism (105). On the other hand, almost as an afterthought, Mill endorses laws prohibiting acts of public indecency (119). With respect to the latter, perhaps the critical emphasis should be on acts that are *public*. We'll talk more about the private/public distinction below. But before we do, let's explore in more detail the question of whether one can be harmed by someone's behavior in virtue of the *psychological* effects that behavior has.

Think about the following:

1. You threaten me with violence creating a reasonable fear that you might actually do what you threaten to do.
2. You are my neighbor. You paint your house purple with diagonal orange stripes across the exterior;
3. The next day you add to your lawn realistic replicas of severed animal heads stuck on stakes and spurting water dyed to look like blood;
4. Finally, you add to the ambience non-stop golden hits from old Pat Boone albums blaring all day long.
5. You and your partner are an openly gay couple in a neighborhood that is socially very conservative.
6. You and your friends are members of a neo-Nazi party that marches in a heavily Jewish neighborhood of Chicago where some of the last survivors of the Holocaust still live.[6]
7. You are an avid golfer but enjoy playing in the nude. Your body is not exactly a paradigm of fitness.
8. You are an author (film maker, television personality) who publishes or produces hate-filled diatribes against one societal subgroup after another.
9. You don't bathe and when you pass people on the street (or sit on a bus or train) you make others feel like gagging.
10. You make pornographic movies and try to advertise the content of one movie with a billboard outside the movie theater showing its most graphic scene.
11. You breast feed your twelve-year-old son at restaurants.
12. You pack your own lunch that you proceed to eat in your workplace's common room. It consists of live cockroaches and worms.

The list, of course, can go on and on. Some of the items on the list fall into the category of what Feinberg (1984) describes not as harmful behavior but as *offensive* behavior (behavior that is offensive to normal aesthetic sensibility). Of course, what is normal is often relative to a given culture. In an old film, *Mondo Cane*, one that I still remember vividly, the film portrays people eating live slugs gathered from a rotting log, a cuisine that was considered quite the delicacy by members of their culture. Smells that are offensive to some are quite pleasurable to others. Eighteen-year-old boys might be positively thrilled to gawk at the billboard's display of graphic sexual acts. Threats and the fear they produce, and behavior specifically designed to torment those who have already suffered (that Nazi march through Skokie), fall into a different category still.

How are we going to sort all of this out? Before we try, we would be wise to note that one cannot so easily disentangle questions of significantly offensive behavior from property damage. Even if my neighbors stop with the garish purple and orange painting of their house, they will probably have damaged the resale value of my house. Indeed, I suspect it might cut the value by more than 70 percent. Whether we like it or not, there are probably still parts of the United States where an openly gay couple moving into the neighborhood will significantly decrease property values. And the non-stop medley of Pat Boone's greatest hits will make houses in the neighborhood virtually impossible to sell. So, one can damage someone's property more or less directly, but also indirectly by doing something with one's own property that others living nearby find repugnant or distasteful.

Set that problem aside for the moment. If we allow that people can be harmed by behavior of which the mere *knowledge* of upsets others, then even if we accept the harm principle we might find it utterly useless as a principle designed to adjudicate *controversial* cases that arise concerning freedom. A case is controversial, after all, precisely because at least some people care whether or not the behavior is regulated. And if some people want society to use its resources to stop me from behaving in a certain way, it is a safe bet that most of those people will be upset if they don't get their way. And if my upsetting someone is a form of harming them, then even if we accept the harm principle, I won't be able to use it to defend my liberty in the relevant case. Repeating what is, and will continue to be, a common refrain, it doesn't follow that I won't be able to argue plausibly that I should be left alone—the harm principle states only a necessary condition, not a sufficient condition, for the state to legitimately interfere with my freedom. But I won't be able to use *the harm principle* to defend the cause of freedom if we get too promiscuous with the concept of what counts as producing harm.

If we want the harm principle to be an effective weapon in the arsenal of those defending the cause of freedom, then we had better think long and hard before we allow that offensive behavior counts as harmful behavior. But even after we think long and hard, how are we going to avoid the conclusion that there are circumstances in which we can prevent others from behaving in certain ways, but where the sole reason we have for regulating the behavior is its psychological effects? Neither you nor I want to be subjected to music next door that we find distasteful. I don't want to see realistic models of severed animal heads spurting realistic fake blood as I drive home from a long day at work. And I certainly don't want to be subjected to the disgusting odors of those who refuse to engage in minimal hygiene.

One might try to get around the problem by subsuming at least some of these cases under acts that produce or increase the probability of producing harmful *physical* effects. Given my current state, I have no doubt that were I subjected to five or six hours of Pat Boone's greatest hits, my blood pressure would begin to soar to life-threatening levels. And the same might be said for any other action that produces in me significant fear, disgust, or aggravation. But the beauty of philosophical thought experiments is that they are not held hostage to empirical facts. We can simply stipulate that we have evolved in such a way that there are no relevant physical harms associated with the unpalatable psychological effects produced by various obnoxious and offensive behaviors. And I don't think that would give us much less reason to want society to protect us from those who would produce the relevant fear and disgust.

As we noted earlier, Mill himself did make a point of distinguishing offensive behavior done *publicly* from that same behavior done in the privacy of one's home. And whatever *Mill* was trying to do with the distinction, it is surely a distinction worth exploring for anyone trying to find a *plausible* interpretation of harm relevant to developing an effective harm principle. We could suggest that we won't count as harm the disgust or distaste people feel from the mere knowledge (or belief) that others are acting in a certain way. But we will count as harmful that same offensive behavior if it is done in *publicly* owned space, or if it "creeps" into my own privately owned space. So, take the relatively easy case of the neighbor playing non-stop the music that I don't want to hear. We can surely accuse that neighbor of "invading" my property. It is not a case of trespass as it is usually understood, but the neighbor has unleashed sound waves from which I cannot protect myself without considerable expense or difficulty. And, of course, that is precisely why there are ordinances almost everywhere that will allow the police to force people to respect our "privacy" from unusually loud or boisterous parties. Logically, it isn't that hard to move from sound waves to light waves. The hideous way in which you decorate your property directly affects what I am virtually forced to see as I drive to my house. I can hardly be expected to close my eyes as I aim for my garage and hope for the best. I could build a fence high enough to block the sight of everything you have done to your house, but fences that high are very expensive, and they destroy views that one might reasonably want to keep unobscured.

The above examples concern intrusion by others into my own privately owned property. But, given the way our society is currently structured, we also have jointly owned "public" space. Perhaps we shouldn't have such space—we can argue about that later. But as of now we do. And we have already conceded that we will need to find procedures for us to make decisions concerning what can and cannot be done on the property we own collectively.[7] Given the shape I am in now, I guess I can sympathize with those who don't want to see me without a shirt on at the local golf course, or a public park. And I'm sure the "collective" decision to prohibit such behavior would become even more intense should I decide to relieve myself of even more clothing. All of this would be completely contingent on the "collective" attitudes and dispositions that causally affect states like fear, disgust, contempt, revulsion, and the like. But we might be on the way to finding a compromise that still has a healthy respect for the freedom we want people to have to do as they please in the privacy of their own homes, and the restrictions we might want to place on those who "inflict" their behavior on others, either by "intrud-ing" on our private property, or by acting in ways that we collectively decide to prohibit in jointly owned space.

How would such a proposal fare with respect to the examples Mill considers? You will recall that he didn't want a predominantly Muslim society to be able to prohibit the eating of pork, or a predominantly Catholic society to prohibit the practice of religions other than Catholi-cism. But if we make the private/public distinction all bets are off con-cerning whether the Muslims could legitimately prohibit the eating of pork at a sidewalk café, or even whether the Catholics might legitimately prohibit *public* displays of non-Catholic religions. If a society were homo-phobic, that society might still be entitled by our revised harm principle to consider banning *public* displays of affection by gay people. Puritanical societies might legitimately ban public displays of affection by anyone. And all of this must sound a bit horrifying to anyone trying to defend the cause of freedom.

But recall one more time that a defender of the harm principle is committed to the view that our argument for freedom isn't lost just be-cause we give up on the harm principle as the most effective *way* to defend that freedom. We noted earlier that one probably can't even de-fend our freedom to drive a car using the harm principle. We will later be exploring other ways in which to argue for liberty, but for now we need only emphasize that even if we accept the harm principle as *one* weapon in the arsenal of those defending freedom, we aren't committed to the view that it is the only weapon one can deploy.

That said, there is a concern that has already started to emerge rather clearly. Even if we can find a version of the harm principle that is accept-able, the principle might turn out to be relatively useless as a principle that will help us decide genuinely controversial cases. In the actual world, the harm principle could probably be successfully deployed to defend my freedom to wear a blue shirt, at least on my day off. But then nobody wants to stop me from wearing that color in the first place. The question is whether we can find a realistic example of a genuine contro-versy, where the harm principle would win the day for those committed to the cause of freedom.

One certainly might suggest examples of so-called victimless crimes — behavior that has been criminalized even though it poses no risks to anyone not consenting to the behavior. The criminalization of prostitu-tion is an example often given. On the face of it, prostitution, at least prostitution involving consenting adults (who satisfy the other condi-tions discussed earlier), involves one person paying another to have sex with him or her. The prostitute may or may not be harmed in various ways, but almost all versions of the harm principle protect behavior among *consenting* adults even if there are clear risks for one or the other of the consenting parties.[8] So, for example, professional boxing would seem to be protected by the harm principle even though there is an obvious risk of rather severe physical harm to each of the parties engaged in a boxing match. To be sure, there is a question as to how "libertarian" we will be when it comes to consenting adults agreeing to participate in dangerous activities. As we noted earlier, in these days of reality TV it wouldn't be that hard to imagine a show involving gladiatorial combat, a show in which the gladiators, let us suppose paid many millions of dollars, literally fight to the death. If the consent were genuine (as it might be, given the right sort of person and the right sort of financial incentive), then why would a proponent of the harm principal support *legislation* designed to make such combat illegal? Or to take that less fanciful example discussed earlier, we might reflect on the fact that at one time dueling was perfectly legal in most states. It is now illegal throughout the United States. But what interpretation of the harm principle would allow us to prevent consenting adults from engaging in a duel—even a duel to the death?

Although the case isn't nearly as *prima facie* plausible, critics of U.S. criminalization of recreational drugs have long argued that this legal incursion into the habits of adult citizens violates the freedom everyone should have to do to their own bodies whatever they please. When we endorse the harm principle, after all, we view as unacceptable forced interference with another's behavior on paternalistic grounds. The use of recreational drugs might be harmful to the user. It might be stupid to use such drugs. But Mill would argue that we can't interfere until that harm spreads to others who want no part of the risk. And similar arguments have been used to argue for a hands-off approach to those who choose (however foolishly) to ride a motorcycle without wearing a helmet or drive a car without wearing a seatbelt.

At this point, a defender of the harm principle who nevertheless wants to make illegal many of the behaviors described above might seek to cast a wider net in an attempt to find *non-consenting* adults who are at least indirectly harmed by the behaviors in question. The most radical version of this move essentially involves the cliché that "no person is an island." When one harms, or increases the probability of harm to oneself, that harm will inevitably reach others. Interestingly, Mill himself rather eloquently presents a version of this argument that he expects he will get from his critics:

> The distinction here pointed out between the part of a person's life which concerns only himself and that which concerns others, many persons will refuse to admit. How (it may be asked) can any part of the conduct of a member of society be a matter of indifference to the other members? No person is an entirely isolated being; it is impossible for a person to do anything seriously or permanently hurtful to himself without mischief reaching at least to his near connections, and often far beyond them. If he injures his property, he does harm to those who

directly or indirectly derived support from it, and usually diminishes, by a greater or less amount, the general resources of the community. If he deteriorates his bodily or mental faculties, he not only brings evil upon all who depended upon him for a portion of their happiness, but disqualifies himself for rendering the services which he owes to his fellow creatures generally, perhaps becomes a burden on their affection or benevolence; and if such conduct were very frequent hardly any offense that is committed would detract more from the general sum of good. Finally, if by his vices and follies a person does no direct harm to others, he is nevertheless (it may be said) injurious by his example, and ought to be compelled to control himself for the sake of those whom the sight or knowledge of his conduct might corrupt or mislead. (1956, 78)

In the next paragraph, he imagines those who wonder why it isn't permissible to engage in paternalistic behavior when those who have fallen into moral disrepair are so corrupt that they can't see the wisdom of various truths concerning proper conduct, truths that we have learned through the accumulated wisdom of generations.

But first let us look more carefully at the rather eloquent statement of the objection that is intended to strike at the very heart of the idea that we will find controversies in which something like the harm principle will prove effective in defending freedom. A great deal will depend on whether we are going to allow that we should at least sometimes count as harm certain psychological effects. Given our current culture, many women or men would be deeply hurt, psychologically crushed, to find out that their husband or wife was regularly seeing a prostitute. Perhaps they shouldn't be. Perhaps that's just a vestige of a religious upbringing that one should shed. But evaluating the effects of one's actions on others is a function of how things are, not how they could be. And that intimates have been psychologically hurt by this behavior, on the part of those they trusted, is surely undeniable.

A number of other behaviors described above might initially seem only self-regarding, but obviously also pose risks of the sort Mill imagines his critic emphasizing. When you do something that poses a risk to yourself, you also risk harming those near and dear to you. They may have been depending on you for financial support, but even if that were not the case, your genuine friends depend on you for emotional support, for friendship, and all the benefits that come with friendship. And if you have good enough friends, they will be emotionally crushed when the risk you take results in your serious injury or even death.

Mill worries about becoming a burden on one's affection. When the motorcyclist without a helmet crashes into a tree and becomes a vegetable, what precisely is society to do? We could require such people to pay much more in insurance, but suppose our hypothetical motorcyclist doesn't do what he was supposed to do, or that his insurance has run out.

We could just deny that person medical care. We could designate a hold-ing area of the hospital to keep those who are bleeding to death, dying from lack of oxygen to the brain, or what have you, with a sign on the outside: "For those who didn't carry appropriate insurance." But that's not what we do. We are compassionate people (most of the time) and we can't stand the thought of someone dying a slow painful death without at least trying to help. So, we provide care and pay for it out of our collec-tive pocket. To be sure, this was a voluntary act on our part—we weren't forced by anyone to contribute in this way.[9] But we didn't *want* to be put in the position where we *had* to make this decision. The moral dilemma was *forced* on us by the person whose behavior resulted in that person becoming (in Mill's words) a "burden on our affection."

If we decide that people who don't wear helmets on motorcycles or don't wear seat belts while driving cars forfeit the protection of the harm principle, then it will be difficult to avoid the conclusion that anyone who takes unnecessary risks forfeits the protection of the harm principle. I have a friend whose hobby is climbing—serious climbing. As it turns out, climbing is among the most dangerous of athletic hobbies. He certainly risks more in the way of harming himself and others indirectly than the person who doesn't wear a seatbelt. People who climb Mount Everest are essentially playing Russian roulette with the weather. The climb itself isn't that difficult, but the lack of oxygen has a significant negative effect on most people. But the weather patterns are notoriously difficult to pre-dict, and if you get caught in a sudden storm, you are dead. Now again, thrill seekers don't need to panic that if we accept the harm principle then they will lose their freedom to take risks. In that familiar refrain, the harm principle was never intended to state anything other than a necessary condition for legitimately interfering with another's freedom. Once that necessary condition is met, we might still be able to find all sorts of excellent reasons for allowing people to take risks, to put themselves in the path of danger. The clearly emerging worry, however, is it that the harm principle, even if true, will be useless.

Earlier, we mentioned briefly that Mill opened a hornets' nest of prob-lems for one hoping that the harm principle could do some serious work in the defense of freedom when he allowed that one can harm others by failing to provide benefits to society. If we look at the quote above, Mill imagines his critic taking advantage of this admission by complaining that he who harms himself "disqualifies" himself "for rendering the ser-vices he owes to his fellow creatures generally." Mill had better have a response to this complaint, for if he doesn't, we are all harming people all of the time through our indefinitely many failures to act. I'm lying in a hammock in my backyard enjoying the afternoon sun—having not a care in the world and bothering no one. If a harm principle protects any free-dom, one might suppose, then it should surely cover this situation. But, of course, there are all sorts of things I am *not* doing by virtue of lying in the hammock. I'm not volunteering at the local senior center, at the local hospital, or the local animal shelter. I'm not participating in the neighborhood watch group that afternoon or working for some political cause. There are all sorts of ways in which I could be helping others. So why can't I be accused of harming those whom I fail to benefit—harming them through my failure to act?[10]

So, Mill *must* have a response. He wouldn't have considered the objection unless he thought he knew how to reply. Respond he does, but it is not clear that he addresses the point. Here is some of what he says:

> I fully admit that the mischief which a person does to himself may seriously affect, both through their sympathies and their interests, those nearly connected with him and, in a minor degree, society at large. When, by conduct of this sort, a person is led to violate an assignable obligation to any other person or persons, the case is taken out of the self-regarding class and becomes amenable to moral disapprobation in the proper sense of the term. If, for example, a man, through intemperance or extravagance, becomes unable to pay his debts, or, having undertaken the moral responsibility of a family, becomes from the same cause incapable of supporting or education them, he is deservedly reprobated and might be justly punished; but it is for the breach of duty to his family or creditors, not for the extravagance. . . .
>
> But with regard to the merely contingent or, as it may be called, constructive injury which a person causes to society by conduct which neither violates any specific duty to the public, nor occasions perceptible hurt to any assignable individual except himself, the inconvenience is one which society can afford to bear, for the sake of the greater good of human freedom. (1956, 80)

And later he adds some cautionary advice to those thinking of trying to force others to better themselves:

> If there be among those whom it is attempted to coerce into prudence or temperance any of the material of which vigorous and independent characters are made, they will infallibly rebel against the yoke. No such person will ever feel that others have a right to control him in his concerns, such as they have to prevent him from injuring them in theirs; and it easily comes to be considered a mark of spirit and courage to fly in the face of such usurped authority and do with ostentation the exact opposition of what it enjoins. (102)

Anyone who has raised children can sympathize with Mill's point here—the struggles to get them to do what you want are often titantic indeed, in part for the reason that Mill discusses.

Finally, Mill adds this slightly odd comment:

> But the strongest of all the arguments against the interference of the public with purely personal conduct is that when it does interfere, the odds are that it interferes wrongly and in the wrong place. (102)

Here, I take it that Mill is underscoring his oft-stated view that by and large people are the best judge of where their own happiness lies.[11]

So, let's take stock of Mill's replies to the criticism he anticipates. *First,* he does explicitly admit that one can harm others by harming oneself in such a way that one fails to benefit those others and that if there is some sort of formal or informal *contractual* duty to the others who are thereby harmed, one can not only morally condemn the person who caused the harm but potentially impose legal sanctions on that person. So, if I'm a lifeguard at the pool, fall asleep, and fail to save a drowning child, I might be not only civilly but criminally liable. And in Mill's illustration, if I am a parent who has undertaken the responsibility of raising a child and become a hopeless drug addict unable to fulfill that responsibility, society, through its laws, can come after me.

Second, however, Mill wants to distinguish these cases from others, where, as he puts it, there is no *specific* duty to another or to the public at large. Of course, this language already begs the question against his critic who is wondering why we might not think of people as having a general obligation to contribute to the well-being of society. It is, after all, Mill who warned us, in introducing the harm principle, that one can harm others not only through action but, also by failing to act—failing to bene-fit or prevent harm. So, what is an objection *based on the harm principle* to conscripting people to engage in what would otherwise have been volun-tary charitable work? Again, such conscription might be a really bad idea—it might even be a foolish idea. But the question we are asking here is the narrow question of whether such coercion would violate a harm principle that allows for the *possibility* of legitimate interference once oth-ers are being harmed (either by actions or failure to receive benefits). If anything, Mill seems to admit in the end that his critic is perfectly cor-rect—that when one harms oneself one *does* hurt the interests of others. And that conclusion is reinforced when he goes on to suggest that, all things considered, we should put up with this sort of harm for "the greater good of human freedom." It may well be true that if we do the cost/benefit analysis (an analysis that one always must do once one de-cides that an individual's freedom isn't protected by the harm principle), we will often, perhaps almost always, stay away from "paternalistic" efforts to stop people from destroying their lives. But that doesn't even speak to the question of whether *the harm principle* can be used to reach this conclusion.

When we look at the additional reasons Mill gives against paternalis-tic intervention (even with the longer-term interests of society in mind), they seem primarily *epistemic* in nature. And that's perfectly appropriate once one engages in cost/benefit analysis. As I admitted above, there is something to the idea that people will rebel against the yoke. Young people, particularly, will sometimes "do ostentatiously" what their "eld-ers" try to get them to stop doing. And if one's goal is to stop people from behaving in ways that are directly detrimental to their well-being and indirectly detrimental to the well-being of society, one certainly would be well-advised to consider how difficult it is to predict what will make another person's life go well. To take some relatively trivial examples, most of us have had friends who dated people we thought were horribly wrong for them. And many of us have had children who were making "disastrous" decisions when it comes to matters of the heart. But as we get older, we probably get a bit more modest about whether or not we really know what works for another person. As they say, people "fit" with each other in all sorts of strange ways. And even when a couple doesn't look particularly happy together, there is no telling how much more unhappy they would be without each other.

People also have all sorts of coping mechanisms. Some of them probably do fall somewhere along a continuum of self-destructive behavior, but we would always do well to realize that it might be the case that the realistic alternative to at least some mildly self-destructive behavior is behavior is even more self-destructive. So, all of Mill's cautionary warnings are important to take into account before one engages in attempts to help society by preventing self-destructive behavior. But, again, none of this even *speaks* to the question of whether the harm principle can be used effectively to argue for freedom. It seems to me that *all* of the heavy lifting in *all* of the controversial cases we consider is done by the cost/benefit analysis that *follows* the conclusion that there is harm that we may legitimately seek to prevent. Furthermore, for all of the fanfare with which Mill introduces the harm principle, he tacitly admits as much himself.

MILL'S UTILITARIANISM AND THE HARM PRINCIPLE

As soon as we realized that Mill's harm principle states only a necessary (not a sufficient) condition for correctly concluding that we ought to interfere with someone's freedom, we knew that Mill would need at least one other principle to decide controversial cases. There are, Mill admits, countless examples of situations in which we will rationally conclude that it is better to allow the relevant harm to occur than to try to do something about it. Above, we started talking about cost/benefit analyses, but that is really just shorthand for talking about consequentialist considerations of a sort that we distinguished in the previous chapter. And interestingly enough, Mill is just as famous for his support of utilitarianism, a paradigmatic *consequentialist* approach to understanding what one ought to do, as he is for his defense of the harm principle.

We talked earlier about the terminological distinction between utilitarianism and consequentialism. As I understand utilitarianism, it just is consequentialism with added details concerning what sorts of things can be intrinsically good and bad. Typically, a utilitarian has an objectivist conception of value, and, more controversially, one according to which that objective value attaches only to states of conscious beings. Mill, following both his father James and the influential political philosopher Jeremy Bentham, defended a form of utilitarianism that is called *hedonistic* utilitarianism. In its most straightforward form, the hedonistic utilitarian is a consequentialist who thinks only pleasure is intrinsically good, only pain is intrinsically bad. But like Plato (1974, Book IX), Mill was quick to insist that some pleasures are much better than others. Specifically, Mill argued, mental pleasures are far superior, both in terms of quantity, but more importantly, also in terms of quality (1979, 7–8). The quantitative superiority of the mental (intellectual) is probably better put in terms of the quantity of pleasure one gets from the activity that leads to the pleasure. So, for example, Mill (like Plato before him) thought that many of the physical pleasures are relatively short-lived, and the activities that produce them are "costly." Mill didn't do much by way of defining the two sorts of pleasures, nor did he elaborate much on what the relevant costs were of pursuing them. A few passages suggest that he might be willing to operationally define the bodily or physical pleasures as those that even lower animals like pigs or cats are capable of experiencing. The mental pleasures are those that involve aesthetic appreciation—appreciation of art, music, a good philosophical argument, and so on. The problem, of course, is that in human beings, the bodily and mental pleasures are often thoroughly mingled. So pigs no doubt experience sexual pleasure, but most humans are capable of turning the sex act into almost a work of art that can be appreciated on many different levels. Pigs and humans can both experience the pleasure of eating, but humans can view a fabulous meal as a work of art. So any discussion of mental and bodily pleasures is going to get very complicated if it is to be appropriately sophisticated. Plato did a much better job than Mill of warning us about the risks of pursuing the pleasures associated with what he called appetite. The desire for such pleasures, Plato argued, are a kind of pain or suffering, and it is easy to confuse the resulting diminution of pain and suffering that comes from satisfying the appetite with a genuine pleasure. Worse, many of the appetites grow stronger the more they are "fed," and the result is that the kind of pain and suffering that is the appetite can take over one's life (think of the wretched existence of a heroin addict). And perhaps worse still, as these appetites take over one's life they crowd out of that life the ability to nurture the skills that allow one to experience the lasting and rewarding pleasures of the intellect.

With respect to the intrinsic superiority of intellectual pleasures over physical pleasures, Mill suggests (1979, 8) that all that he means is that people who have experienced both give a decided preference to the intellectual pleasures over the bodily. In his more extreme comments, he seems to suggest the obviously false idea, that we would *never* trade any intellectual pleasure for a physical pleasure. In other passages, a charitable reading might suggest that he only meant to say that no one would trade for a life filled to the brim with physical pleasures if it meant living without *any* of the intellectual pleasures. In any event Mill's "competent" judge test for what makes one thing intrinsically more valuable than another, has always suggested to me that *at heart* he wasn't an objectivist about value at all—indeed that he was probably a meta-ethical subjectivist (and perhaps even a relativist). It is for that reason that I've always worried about defining utilitarianism in terms of the utilitarian's meta-ethical views about value. It would be more than a bit awkward if history's most famous utilitarian turned out not to be a utilitarian, given the way in which some philosophers use the term.

The close connection that Mill thinks exists between what we value for its own sake and what is intrinsically good also casts doubt on the conclusion that Mill was really a *hedonistic* utilitarian. To be sure, he *says* he is one, and it takes a bit of nerve to ignore that fact in interpreting Mill. But in response to suggestions that people desire, for its own sake, things besides pleasure, it is clear that Mill's conception of pleasure and happiness just gets more and more expansive. For example, when he imagines his critic claiming that a miser can come to desire having money for its own sake, Mill responds by arguing that if the miser really does desire having money for its own sake, then money is just a part of the miser's happiness—not a means to happiness, but something that is literally constitutive of happiness (1979, 36).

We can't close this very brief discussion of Mill's utilitarianism without commenting on his (in)famous "proof" for the principle of utility. Mill makes clear that to be a utilitarian, in his sense, you have to hold that pleasure is intrinsically good, no matter whose pleasure it is. He says of the utilitarian: "As between his own happiness and that of others, utilitarianism requires him to be as strictly impartial as a disinterested and benevolent spectator" (16). It is perhaps an understatement that it would be difficult to be a hedonistic utilitarian in Mill's sense. Worse, perhaps, Mill tries to convince us that we all *do* have as our sole goal or end the "general" happiness understood this way. Suggesting again that you can only convince people that something is intrinsically desirable if they do in fact desire it as an end, Mill points out that each of us desires, as an end, our own happiness and therefore my happiness is desirable (good) as end for me (note the relativization); your happiness is desirable (good) as an end for you.[12] And these claims are followed by the startling conclusion that the general happiness is desirable as an end for the aggregate. The suppressed premise is presumably that the aggregate (the collection of all people) desires, as an end, the general happiness. But aggregates desire only what all (most, many) of the people who make up the aggregate desire. And even if it were true that all or most people care a bit about the happiness of others, it is surely absurd to suppose that each of us *equally* desires, as an end, the happiness of each and every other human being. You would probably be horrified at how many strangers' happiness I would sacrifice to ensure the happiness of my two grandchildren. And while some of you might be less extreme than I am, you also care about the happiness of all sorts of people much, much more than you care about the happiness of strangers.[13]

In the final analysis, it is hard to figure out how Mill is trying to defend his utilitarianism, or even precisely what his utilitarian principle is. He did warn us (1979, 34) that you can't really argue for "first principles" (shortly before giving his argument), and some might argue that he was just trying something out given that the only alternative was asking you to just "see" the objective value of pleasure. I don't believe that is a correct understanding of Mill, partly because if that were his view, he could have said it fairly easily, but also partly because in every other area of his philosophy Mill was a radical reductionist determined to translate everything that he could (including all talk about the physical world) into talk about affective states and sensations that people do or would have under certain conditions. He's just not the kind of philosopher to recognize the existence of *objective*, intrinsic goodness.

Set aside, though, the details of Mill's utilitarianism. The main puzzle, in the context of our discussion of the harm principle and the need to supplement it with some other principle, is how precisely utilitarianism of any form fits with Mill's ideas. A utilitarian, after all, has a perfectly *general* principle that defines what one ought to do. The principle places no restrictions on the subject matter of the choice. After carefully defining the concept of maximizing value (and we saw that there are different ways to do that), the utilitarian advances the view that one ought to act so as to maximize value. The principle applies to choices of schools, decisions about where to go for dinner, decisions about whether to go to war, and decisions about when to restrict someone's freedom to do as that person chooses. Again, the principle is perfectly *general*. So why wasn't the first chapter of *On Liberty* really short?

> Hi. I'm Mill. I'm a utilitarian you know. There are a lot of controversies concerning freedom. I bet you'd like a nice, simple principle that will make it easy for you to decide when to support freedom. Well, you are not going to get one. It's a messy business. But when you are trying to decide what laws to pass, make sure the decisions you make maximize utility. And work hard in making the decision because it will be really complicated. Thanks for your attention.

Lest there be any question that Mill abandoned his utilitarianism when writing *On Liberty*, he removes that doubt unequivocally:

> It is proper to state that I forego any advantage which could be derived to my argument from the idea of abstract right as a thing independent of utility. I regard utility as the ultimate appeal on all ethical questions;

> but it must be utility in the largest sense, grounded on the permanent
> interests of man as a progressive being. (1956, 14)

Notice how emphatic Mill is. He regards utility as the ultimate appeal on
all ethical issues. Not most, not some, not those that don't involve the
law, but *all* ethical issues. It is the utilitarian principle that is the supreme
principle governing what one should do. So why do we need another
principle?

As we saw earlier, the harm principle might be a useful *rule of thumb*
that experience reveals will get us a correct answer, more often than not.
But it will still require interpretation, and to be useful, even as a rule of
thumb, it would need to be interpreted in such a way that it will give us
rough and ready conclusions about when we shouldn't interfere with
freedom. The problem, as we have seen, is that once we add highly plausible qualifications to the principle, it isn't even useful as a rule of thumb.
The rule just doesn't apply to real-life controversies where there will
virtually always be the possibility of harm that results from the controversial action (or failure to act). For it to be a useful rule of thumb, we are
going to need to put the emphasis on Mill's own distinction between
direct and indirect harm. The principle will need to be interpreted in
something like the following way:

> When people are acting (or failing to act) in ways that only very indi-
> rectly and tenuously increase the probability of harm to others one
> should be exceedingly cautious in interfering with their freedom—the
> more tenuous the connection is the more reluctant one ought to be to
> get involved. (HP revised)

And even this exceedingly vague principle will need at least some clarification. One can get some sense of various notions of directness through
examples, but even the examples will send quite different messages. That
aesthetic issue Mill concedes is relevant when it comes to laws concerning public decency sends (to me at least) exactly the opposite message
from the one he sent when he talked about the distaste Muslims might
have for people eating pork (supposing, at least, that he would reach the
same conclusion even if the pork eating were done in public). Directness
clearly can't have much to do with the proximity in time between cause
and effect. I might devise an elaborate scheme to kill you—one that involves a series of actions that take place over a number of years. To
minimize getting caught, I put in place a plan that involves hiring someone who will later hire someone to hire someone to hire someone to hire
someone who eventually kills you. However temporally remote the effect
is from the cause, once the police trace the causal chain back to me,
virtually everyone would be OK with my being punished.

Directness can't have much to do with obviousness either. My plot to
commit murder might have been so sophisticated that it would be very
difficult to get any jury to convict me. As we noted earlier, however, we

can distinguish between the distaste, concern, revulsion, and so on, that people feel from the mere knowledge that people are behaving in certain ways, from similar reactions that people have when the behavior in question is inflicted on them through intrusion into private space or performance in public space. We might insist that a good rule of thumb will always ignore the former when it comes to deciding whether or not to try to force another person to alter his or her lifestyle.

SUMMARY

We have seen that the initially plausible harm principle can easily become almost useless as a way of defending robust freedom. Once we qualify the principle (as reason will compel us to do) it will be exceedingly difficult to find controversies that will be decided in favor of freedom. The most we can hope for is a watered-down rule of thumb that suggests that we should almost always ignore "harm" that consists of disapprobation, disapproval, disgust, distaste, revulsion, and so on, where these are reactions that come from the mere knowledge or belief that consenting adults are behaving in certain ways. But that will still leave enormous areas of our life open to the possibility of legitimate interference by others. As we stressed so often, even a defender of the harm principle will, or at least should, insist that a battle for freedom is not over just because it can't be won using the harm principle. Since the harm principle stated only a necessary, and not a sufficient condition for legitimate interference with someone's freedom, we need at least one other principle to reach our ultimate conclusion about whether or not we should make someone refrain from doing, or do, something that person doesn't want to do. Mill and consequentialists generally have that other principle ready at hand. It is the very consequentialist principle that we discussed in some detail in chapter 3. Furthermore, one of the great ironies of Mill's *On Liberty* is that the harm principle that was introduced with such fanfare virtually disappears when Mill gets around to arguing for various freedoms — particularly freedom of thought and expression and freedom of individuality (freedom of lifestyle). The arguments Mill gives are essentially consequentialist in nature. And that is a good thing, because, as we will see, he would have failed had he tried to use his harm principle to reach his conclusions. His consequentialist arguments, by contrast, while still controversial, make subtle and important points that anyone interested in matters concerning freedom needs to consider carefully. In the following chapters, we'll see how far we can get by explicitly focusing on consequentialist considerations in defending freedom of thought and expression, tolerance of radically different life choices, and a modest, laissez-faire capitalism.

NOTES

1. We will also need an account of when someone has genuinely agreed to the actions that causes him or her harm. So, for example, almost everyone agrees that a free society can legitimately outlaw dueling or gladiatorial combat (chosen for a huge salary). On the face of it, such restrictions violate the harm principle. To be sure, someone will be harmed, but the activity in question seems to be among consenting adults. One might try to argue that no rational human being can genuinely consent to engage in behavior that is likely to cause harm. It is not clear to me, however, that one can make much of a case for that. In the alternative, however extreme it might seem, perhaps the committed libertarian should have no objection to dueling or gladiatorial combat provided that the participants are genuinely consenting adults.

2. Mill is writing at the height of the glorious British Empire.

3. See Smith (2015) for a discussion of what makes someone "accountable" for his or her own action.

4. Unless otherwise indicated, I mean to include failures to act or omissions among actions.

5. Again, this oversimplifies matters. A plausible view would make references to probabilities. Surgery that actually kills me might have been such that it would probably have made my life better. Or even if that isn't true, my life might have been so bad that the non-negligible change of improvement might made the surgery rational.

6. A reference to the famous, actual case of Nazis marching in Skokie, IL.

7. Again, one can think of this publicly owned property as what Samuelson (1954) called a public good; but see note 49 for an important reservation about the application of this concept to what is owned publicly.

8. That the prostituted person is harmed whether or not prostitution is legal seems to me overwhelming likely; see Farley (2004). Moen (2014) seems to argue that these harms might be mitigated by changing the existing law. But again, our concern here is interaction among *consenting* adults, whether or not the consent is wise.

9. This is an oversimplification. In a democracy, we decide through majority vote who will represent us and, indirectly, what policies we will support. Those policies include laws determining how much tax I will pay on a given income and how the money collected from tax revenue will be spent. Whether I voted for my representative or not, supported the relevant policies or not, I will be forced by the majority to abide by their decisions.

10. Singer (1972) forcefully argues for this very point.

11. A claim that is certainly controversial. It seems to me that many people are very bad about figuring out how to make themselves happy and they would profit enormously from input from others. And some would probably benefit from paternalist action by others.

12. Again, Narveson (1967) interprets the relativization as most naturally interpreted as a way of talking about what someone believes. In this view, to say that something has intrinsic value *for me* is just a way of saying that I *believe* that that thing has value. The more plausible alternative, I think, is that the relativization is just what it seems to be—a relativization. X has intrinsic value for me just insofar as I value X intrinsically.

13. As I discussed earlier, Narveson (1967) offers the interesting suggestion that Mill was really just trying to argue that *in the context of morality,* one cannot consistently think that one's own subjective interests provide one with reasons to act without also thinking that the interests of others are equally reason giving. Korsgaard (1996) tries to offer a similar way of requiring that rational agents take into account the desires/interests of others. Nagel (1986) also suggests that there is a kind of reason that emerges from what he calls a "view from nowhere." As should have been obvious from my earlier discussion of accounts of rational action, I don't see how one can pull this rabbit out of a hat. Your interests may provide you with reasons to act, but how would they give me any sort of reasons to act absent the fact that I care about what

you want, or rationally believe that you're getting what you want will further my interests? And even if one defines something like "the moral point of view" as a perspective from which one treats the interests of all as having equal weight, one will inevitably face the problem that reasons one has from the egocentric perspective may conflict with reasons one has from the "Moral" perspective. One will then be in danger of divorcing rationality (understood in terms of what one has reason to do all things considered) from morality (understood in terms of what one has reason to do from a restricted perspective.

FIVE

Consequentialist Arguments for Freedom of Thought and Expression

We noted in chapter 4 that while Mill introduces his harm principle as if it were going to play a central role in arguments over freedom, the principle is made conspicuous by its absence from the more specific arguments he gives in support of various sorts of freedom.[1] Nowhere is that more evident than in his discussion of freedom of thought and expression. Mill's often passionate defense of freedom of thought and expression essentially proceeds by emphasizing the benefits, short-term, but also long-term, to society of allowing people to freely express their views. He seldom, however, acknowledges the harms that freedom of thought and expression can produce and, as a result, runs the risk of presenting a discussion that his critics will find one-sided. In what follows, we'll discuss both the good and bad consequences that might result from various forms of freedom concerning thought and expression, and try to reach a conclusion similar to Mill's but through a broader and more explicit consideration of all of the relevant consequences.

MAKING RELEVANT DISTINCTIONS

Anyone seriously thinking about freedom of expression soon comes to grips with the realization that no rational person wants to allow people the freedom to express their views (or engage in various forms of artistic and nonverbal political expression) *wherever* and *whenever* they please. You may have strong views about who should be elected the next president of the United States, but even the most ardent lovers of freedom don't want to live in a society in which you can force your way into my living room and begin a two-hour speech extolling the virtues of your favorite candidate. Unless I specifically invite you, I don't want you on any other part of my property either. You can call me on the phone, but I can block the number. You can e-mail me, but I can arrange to have your e-mails sent straight to junk mail. Students are not, and should not be, permitted to disrupt a professor's classes with boisterous political protesting, and, personally, I don't appreciate it when protestors block major thoroughfares (without seeking permission in advance) to call attention to their causes. Freedom is a two-way street. Obviously, many people want the freedom to be heard; others want the freedom to be left alone, the freedom to enjoy some peace and quiet on their day off. So, when we defend a person's right[2] to express various attitudes, opinions, and forms of art, we shouldn't be taken to imply that we are going to defend that person's right to say what they want whenever and wherever they want to say it.[3]

There is a closely related question concerning the manner in which we support or fail to support the mode in which one tries to convey one's messages. I take it that most of us who support some form of free speech (more generally free expression) are not inclined to think that the legal right we are interested in preserving comes with a corresponding duty to financially support all particular platforms someone would like to use in order to convey their ideas or art to others. In some sense, for example, we are surely going to defend my right to defend some rather outrageous philosophical positions. But your defense of that right doesn't include an obligation on your part to publish, or arrange for the publication of, my views. You aren't in any straightforward way obligated to arrange and pay for media time, stage performances, billboards I might want to use, or any number of other, often expensive, means of my getting the attention of others for my views or my art. As we'll see, it may be that the public (the collective) has fairly strong reason to ensure *some* opportunities to get exposure for people who lack resources that are easily available to others. But as we noted earlier, we'll almost certainly want those opportunities to respect the freedom of others to refuse to listen, should they so choose.

The title of this chapter refers to freedom of thought and expression. The "thought" part is a bit puzzling, perhaps, as one might suppose that no one is in a position to control the thoughts of another. All of the emphasis, one might suppose, should be on expression. But as we all know, there are a number of countries, including the United States, that have made the motivations underlying various legally prohibited acts part of what defines the act that is legally prohibited. In one sense, that seems relatively unproblematic. We probably are going to want to distinguish premeditated murder from murder in the heat of passion. We'll want to treat differently reckless endangerment (something that doesn't require intent) from second-degree murder (that does). The more controversial cases, however, involve so-called hate crimes, where our legal system wants to make a distinction between the intentional killing of another where certain sorts of racist or sexist attitudes played a causal role in causing the intention, and intentional killing not related to these "problematic" psychological causes. So even if one tries to keep one's thoughts to oneself and thus immune from outside interference, the state will sometimes think that it has a legitimate interest in trying to figure out what you were thinking in deciding whether or not to charge you with some crime.[4] And I suppose we could even imagine some futuristic scenario where it is far easier to determine what people are actually thinking than it is now. In such a (depressingly scary) society, we might be able to detect "problematic" thought and try to pass laws designed to control it.[5]

MILL'S ARGUMENTS FOR FREEDOM OF THOUGHT AND EXPRESSION

In *On Liberty*, Mill offered several eloquent and powerful arguments for supporting freedom of thought and expression. As I indicated, they consisted almost exclusively of pointing out *benefits* that we will receive from allowing freedom and unnecessary *risks* we take from stifling freedom. As I also suggested above, the story is much more complicated. In particular, Mill didn't give much balance to his discussion, nor did he spend a great deal of time on the "how and where" questions that need to be addressed, even if we agree with him that we want people to have opportunities to freely express their views. But let's begin with the benefits and risks that Mill did discuss.

Fallibilism

On most matters, Mill endorsed a rather extreme form of epistemic fallibilism (1956, 21–23). A fallibilist with respect to the kind of justification we have for holding some set of beliefs argues that no matter how much justification we have in support of those beliefs, that justification will never *guarantee* the truth of what we believe—the justification will never eliminate the possibility of error. Mill is sometimes thought to have held that fallibilism applies unequivocally and universally. But like his modern predecessors, even those famous for their skepticism (like Hume), Mill clearly thought that it made no sense to suppose that certain propositions were false (like, for example, propositions describing the intrinsic character of one's own sense experience; see Donner and Fumerton 2009, chapter 10). But for the vast majority of beliefs we entertain, the evidence that supports what we believe, at best, makes probable those beliefs.

Mill's fallibilism drives the first of his arguments against censorship. When we censor a given view, we unnecessarily risk driving into the dark a belief or a theory that turns out to be true. And when we suppress the truth, we risk forfeiting untold advances from which we might have benefited, advances that could have been built upon that truth.

Note a couple of points here. First, the freedom of expression that Mill seems to emphasize in this discussion and in his discussion of most other examples focuses squarely on claims and theories that have a truth value. There is very little discussion in Mill of what we now call artistic freedom. And his emphasis on censorship of views that have a truth value might be understandable, given that he lived not long after people could lose their lives for holding "heretical" views and lived during a period when people could lose their livelihood for holding unpopular views.[6] As we shall see, in contemporary universities, we seem to be moving backward toward a time when the wrong speech at the wrong time in the wrong place can cost teachers their employment or cost students their enrollment.

The second very important point I want to stress is that Mill's argument based on fallibilism seems to require something like the value adjusted possible consequence consequentialism (again, Mill calls his view hedonistic utilitarianism) that we discussed in chapter 3. Mill clearly opposes censorship, not only of very unpopular views but also of views that are, given the available evidence, very likely to be false. His idea isn't that by engaging in censorship of some particular view one will *probably* be suppressing the truth. With respect to many views that people hold, such a conclusion would be absurd. All one needs to do is google conspiracy theories to discover how many truly crazy theories people put forward, theories that cover everything along a continuum that includes the U.S. government bringing down the twin towers in New York, the current whereabouts of Elvis, how Bigfoot evades capture, and who was really behind the assassination of JFK. If Mill were around today, he would want people to be legally free to put forward such views, but he wouldn't think any of those theories has but the tiniest chance of being true. The possible consequence consequentialist, however, insists that even very unlikely consequences of actions are relevant to whether or not an action ought to be taken. The more unlikely the consequence is, the less of an impact that possible consequence will make on the net value of possible consequences. On the other hand, if there is a very unlikely possible positive outcome of an action and no countervailing possible negative consequences, the possible consequence might still carry the day when it comes to deciding what to do.

Mill's second argument is closely related to his first but is more subtle. He reminds us that even if a theory consists mostly of false claims, there might be embedded the odd grain of truth in that theory. By censoring the theory as a whole, one runs the risk of losing those potentially valuable seeds of truth. The plausibility of Mill's claim here hardly needs any argument. I'm a philosopher, so I can probably speak most knowledgably about my own field. Over the years I have read many philosophy articles that are truly bad. They contain confusions, equivocations, implausible interpretations of the views of others, depressingly poor reasoning, and the like. And some really have had no redeeming features that I can find. But the Millian point is correct. At least some of those bad publications had valuable thoughts buried in them—a distinction here or there that is useful to think about going forward, or an alternative to a received inter-pretation of an important figure's view that really is kind of plausible and would allow one to read that philosopher's work in a different way. And what is true of philosophy is surely true of just about any other field of inquiry. A theory, as a whole, might be almost comically implausible while it still contains ideas that can be culled that are important to take into account as one moves forward. When we censor, we kill everything contained in the material we censor. Using censorship is like using very powerful chemicals that will indeed kill the weeds, but will also kill everything else in the yard, some of which we want to grow.

The first considerations Mill raises concerning censorship involve risks society runs by depriving itself of truth. But Mill and many others are equally concerned with the potential cost of censorship when it comes to the intellectual health of society. It is only by allowing our ideas to be challenged that we are forced to defend those ideas. When we attempt to defend our ideas, we will need to get as clear as we can about just what we believe and why we believe it. In mounting such a defense, we will either succeed or fail. If we succeed, our beliefs will be that much strong-er, and we will be less vulnerable to the many sophists we encounter who will try to persuade us with rhetoric and fallacious reasoning. If we fail, we will have learned that there is a good chance that we need to look elsewhere for the truth. Either way, we will benefit in the long run.

There is, of course, a presupposition here that it is usually better to have true beliefs than to have false beliefs, and, by and large, having true beliefs—indeed having knowledge (true belief supported in the right way by evidence)—is something that will be good, at least in the long run. The presupposition is not obviously true, at least if it is unrestricted with respect to its subject matter. We are better off not knowing, and not even believing, all sorts of truths. Some true beliefs are just clutter—worthless beliefs that needlessly take up "storage" in our memory. If I were bored enough, I might count the number of tiles covering the floor of my office. But even if my depressing boredom led me to a truth about this matter, neither I nor the rest of the world is better off for the discov-ery. And having made the discovery, I would probably be better off forgetting it than using even a tiny amount of energy to remember it.

But it is not just trivial truths that have no value. There are all sorts of contexts in which people are probably better off going through life not knowing various sorts of truths. As I discovered in the recesses of my closet the suit I wore for my job interview forty-six years ago, it occurred to me that those to whom I gave the interview might have thought I looked ridiculous—the suit certainly looks ridiculous to me now. But should that be the truth, I am certain that I was better off at the time not knowing it. Even now, I'm not particularly thrilled with the fact that the belief in question has seeped into my consciousness. Examples go on and on. The now happily married couple, neither of whom know about the past infidelities of the other, might be better off having false beliefs about such matters. The truth might be that I don't have much more than a snowball's chance in hell of beating my next tennis opponent, but it certainly isn't going to do me any good to have a realistic assessment of my chances. If I am depressed enough about the thought of death, maybe I would be better off if I convince myself that there is an afterlife, even if that conviction is false.

I suspect, however, that Mill wasn't thinking of examples like this. He was, rather, thinking primarily of science, history, mathematics, and philosophy—fields of enquiry where almost everyone will concede that, on the whole, we are better off when the truth is known.[7] And in these fields Mill's arguments resonate. I write at a time when, in academic circles, those who reject the idea that there is significant human-caused climate change are ridiculed. But there are outliers—indeed, outliers who seem to be perfectly respectable scholars in their fields—who have alternative views.[8] And Mill is surely right that it would be absurd to try to shut down their research (at least shut down their research through *law*) just because most scholars currently think that the views of the outliers are probably wrong. Even the staunchest defender of the received view will surely concede that given the recent history of climatology as a science, there is an outside chance that the current, most commonly held view is false.

The risks Mill was concerned with can also be illustrated through common mistakes people make in approaching research in other fields of inquiry. I have a good friend, a former PhD student in philosophy, who changed fields and received a doctorate in chemistry. He worked for one of the world's leading chemical companies. According to my friend, the company isn't nearly as successful as it could be precisely because it failed to learn Mill's lesson. The company's financial model rewards success in research and, essentially, punishes failure. Researchers learn the lesson quickly and become very conservative in what projects they pursue. They conduct research that isn't that exciting but is relatively likely to enjoy some modest level of success. But you don't want *everyone* to be pursuing conservative strategies. The huge potential profits for the company may well lie along a research path that is unlikely to have a payoff. It is precisely because there is the possible great payoff that you want at least some of your employees to be working in areas less well-trodden.

Often, if you don't take great risks, you won't have a chance at great rewards.

Intellectual Health and the Exercise of the Mind

The arguments discussed above focus directly or indirectly on truth. Censorship is to be avoided because we don't want to risk suppressing truth, or partial truth, and because we want people either to believe more firmly what is true or abandon belief in what cannot be defended. But Mill also appropriately stresses the intellectual "exercise" that is involved in confronting views with which we don't agree, an exercise that involves finding reasons to reject those views and finding reasons that support one's own views. The muscles of the body atrophy if they aren't used, and it is tempting to think that the powers of the mind become weaker if they aren't used.[9]

There are, of course, many ways in which one can "exercise" one's mind and participating in a clash of ideas is only one. A recluse can work on philosophical problems, take practice LSAT tests, solve puzzles of various sort, paint, learn an instrument, or keep mentally active in any number of other familiar ways. So, one doesn't want to oversell Mill's idea that a society in which there is little debate will *necessarily* become a society of people with weaker intellect. But one can usefully relativize intellectual skills to various subject matters. The skills you learn working on crossword puzzles, or figuring out how to create the illusion of depth in a painting, might not automatically transfer to decision-making, philosophy, or political thought, for example. And one might argue that a well-rounded person should develop, through exercise, mental skills that apply to a wide range of intellectually stimulating topics. There is surely something to Mill's idea that if we don't expose ourselves to alternative viewpoints—even radically different viewpoints—we will lose the opportunity to exercise skills necessary to evaluate critically those views.[10] There is in today's world a depressingly large percentage of political liberals who get their news and political discussion primarily from MSNBC, an overtly left-leaning network. And there is an equally large percentage of political conservatives who seek knowledge and enlightenment only from FOX news, an overtly right-leaning network. One can't help but think that both groups would be better off if they exposed themselves to the world views of their political opponents. At the very least they would better understand the perspectives of their political opponents and be able to think more clearly about how to convince those opponents to abandon or modify their views.

ADDITIONAL ARGUMENTS

It is not a very original thought, but one of the benefits of letting people freely express their views is that we are more likely to find out what people actually believe. This can, of course, accrue to our benefit. If we discover that a great many people believe something controversial, we might start taking the view more seriously and eventually discover, to our surprise, that there is something to what those people believe. But this is already covered by Mill's concerns about inadvertently suppressing truth or partial truth. It is also, however, useful to know what people believe even when we judge that there is almost no probability of their beliefs even coming close to the truth. We might decide that it would be prudent to spend time and energy trying to convince people to abandon certain positions. The importance of this point only increases when the beliefs about which we learn are potentially dangerous—the kinds of beliefs that if spread could truly undermine society. One needs to know where danger lies so one can guard against it, and one of the dangers that sometimes exists in society are widespread views that have been driven so far underground that we aren't even aware that we should be engaging in relevant debate in an effort to change minds.[11] In the United States this isn't really much of a problem. The American public seems not the slightest bit shy about posting on various web sites even the most bizarre and obnoxious views. And they aren't shy about participating in polls. The results are sometimes a bit scary. We have already noted that there are weirdly high percentages of people who believe in far-fetched conspiracy theories of one sort or another, for example. But it is also good that we know that there are so many people with outlandish beliefs. Perhaps there is more we need to do through open discussion by way of persuading at least some of these people that there aren't dark forces out to undermine their very existence.

As I said, because we have such a free society, I don't worry that much about the United States encountering the dangers of driving people's views underground through fear of *formal* sanctions. Mill, however, stressed in *On Liberty* that he was also worried about the more informal sanctions people can impose on those with whom they disagree. Such sanctions can include everything from ridicule and shunning to economic sanctions, such as not hiring, or firing, or failing to promote, for examples, those with whom we disagree. This is more of a problem. I have the good fortune to be an academic—the best job anyone could possibly have. We do what we love to do, we have enormous flexibility, and we are paid rather generously. But I do worry more and more about an intellectual climate that is becoming all too common at universities—a climate of political, or even scientific, correctness that discourages many from saying what they think about various controversial issues.[12] It's not that I really think that those with controversial views will get fired or won't receive tenure. I do think it is entirely possible, however, that they won't get hired in the first place. And I do think it is entirely possible to hurt one's department financially if one gets a reputation for having the "wrong" sorts of views about controversial social and political issues, including, of course, the controversial internal politics of a university. I know for a fact that there are academics who are afraid to openly say what they think about certain matters for fear of more subtle sorts of retribution. If ever there is a place where one wants to encourage free exchange of even very controversial ideas, a university is surely such a place. We'll talk a bit more about this issue toward the end of this chapter.

ARTISTIC FREEDOM

We have been talking mainly about benefits that accrue to us from allowing the free expression of views that have a truth value. But the potential targets of censorship go far beyond scientific and political worldviews. For millennia, people have wanted to regulate poets, authors, artists, and musicians. And while we sometimes talk about truth revealed through art, it is not always clear to me what those who talk that way have in mind. But at least some of the arguments we have been discussing transfer to the benefits of allowing freedom in this dimension. Earlier, for example, we talked about Mill's idea that through censorship one runs the risk of not exposing society to truth or grains of truth. Aesthetic appreciation of art, poetry, writing, music, and the like are often very much an acquired taste. Consider the analogy of food. As I recall, when I was a child I liked hot dogs, grilled cheese sandwiches, french fries, and that was about it. Over the years, I was coaxed, cajoled, or sometimes forced to try other sorts of food, and over those same years I acquired the ability to get enormous pleasure from some of the foods that seemed initially inedible (and drinks that seemed undrinkable). The process was, to be sure, hit and miss. My dad made me try liver once, and on another occasion, I accidentally drank his buttermilk. To this day, I can't quite get those grotesque taste sensations out of my stored memory. But the rather mundane point is that it required experimentation to discover what might be great sources of gustatory pleasure, and those who aren't prepared to do the experimentation needlessly run the risk of missing out.

Similar things can obviously be said about other aesthetic pleasures. I'm relatively confident that my road to happiness does not involve a detour into the land of rap music. I've resigned myself to the fact that I will forever be one of those troglodytes who will never appreciate many forms of modern art. I will happily live forever without watching mimes perform, and I can only stand to attend (some parts) of about three operas. But I learned to love many forms of classical music, impressionistic art, and improvised jazz.

BALANCING THE ARGUMENTS FOR AND AGAINST CENSORSHIP

We haven't talked at all yet about issues concerning societally created opportunities for communicating one's thoughts and expressing one's aesthetic vision—issues that critically involve resources and considerations of space and time. But before we discuss those matters, we should look more carefully at considerations that might count as *prima facie* considerations in *favor* of censorship.[13]

When we talked about the harm principle, we became very concerned that one might never find real-world controversies that the principle could settle on the side of freedom. And nowhere is this more evident, I think, than controversies concerning censorship. I said that Mill's harm principle is conspicuous by its absence in his discussion of freedom of thought and expression and suggested that it is probably a good thing that he didn't rest his arguments against censorship on the grounds that the material proposed for censorship never harms or increases the probability of harm to others. There are, in fact, indefinitely many ways in which controversial or extreme political views, flawed scientific views, hateful speech of various kinds, and obnoxious art have the potential to harm others.

Readers of Plato's *Republic* are often shocked to discover that if Socrates (as portrayed by Plato) had his way, the ideal state would engage in massive censorship of everything from poetry to political debate (1974, 377b–ff.). But Plato gave reasons in support of his views, some of which are obviously relevant to any debate over the wisdom of censorship. Plato, like virtually everyone who has thought about such matters, believed that people in general, and children in particular, are highly impressionable. He didn't like the fact that Odysseus, one of the heroes of stories about the Trojan Wars, was portrayed as winning the crucial final battle through trickery and deceit. He wasn't thrilled that the children of Athens might admire a protagonist whose long delay in getting back to his wife was caused, at least in part, by one adulterous dalliance after another. Plato was particularly incensed that the gods were portrayed by the poets as petty, jealous, narcissistic, vengeful, deceitful, adulterous monsters. Children need the right sort of role models to maximize their chances of growing up with the values we want them to have, and if the poets can't understand that, then those poets need to be banished. The future of Athens, Plato thought, was tied to the future character of its citizens, and Athenians (collectively) should do everything necessary to bring about a society comprised of individuals with the best character. If censorship is necessary to guarantee that result, then so be it.[14]

One can only guess what Plato would think if he was somehow resurrected and watched today's cable television and electronic games, or listened to the lyrics of contemporary rap music. He would surely wonder how a society obsessed with the Kardashians has any chance of survival. And while there is a grain of truth in the idea that many of the older people of each generation think that their society is going to hell in a handbasket, there are some very real "Platonic" concerns contemporary Americans might have about today's world. People don't read nearly as much as they once did.[15] The rate of children having children, young mothers having to raise children on their own, a general political illiteracy, an obsession with Facebook as the vehicle to let the world know every trivial and boring detail of one's life, a shockingly high percentage of the population who don't have a job and have no intention of trying to find one—all these must surely be a bit alarming to anyone who thinks about the direction in which the country is going.

To identify problems with contemporary culture is not, of course, to identify the cause of such problems. And it would surely be more than just a stretch to suggest that our woes are primarily caused by not following Plato's advice to control, more closely, potentially negative influences on people as they mature. But there are correlations. When I was a kid, there were exactly four channels on television, and the stories told could have been written by Plato himself. Westerns were all the rage, good guys wore white hats, bad guys wore black hats, and the good guys almost always won the day (most of the time without engaging in behavior any more violent than shooting the gun out of the villain's hand). We know for a fact that there are at least isolated examples of people who "copy" violence that they see in films. Hinkley saw *Taxi Driver*, identified with DeNiro's character, the character's obsession with Jodie Foster, and his plan to impress her by assassinating the president of the United States. To be sure, such people are usually mentally unstable (to put in mildly), but one must wonder whether there aren't more widespread, much less obvious, but still pernicious effects of repeated exposure to violence and sex without affection.

Some feminist philosophers are concerned with the effect that pornography, particularly violent pornography that depicts degraded or subjugated women, has on the behavior of men who consume such pornography.[16] Other feminists cast their net more broadly in search of cultural villains who have a negative impact on society. Louise Antony told me in conversation that she was actually more concerned about the effect cartoons have on children than she is about negative consequences that flow from exposure to pornography. I assume she worries about the classic Disney movies (to which my grandchildren are addicted), movies that often depict women as princesses waiting to be saved and cared for by the handsome princes that come their way.[17]

Examples like these rest on empirical hypotheses about what causes what (and with what frequency). Such hypotheses need to be tested, but the empirical evidence is difficult to get. Several of the perpetrators of recent mass shootings were, apparently, almost obsessed with violent video games. That might suggest a causal link of some sort. But, of course, huge numbers of people play such games and exhibit no antisocial behavior. It may well be the case that whatever causes people to commit horrific acts of violence also causes people to take an interest in violent video games.[18] The connection may be like the connection between the behavior of a barometer and a storm, where both are effects of a common cause. The same sorts of concerns no doubt plague any attempt to establish a causal connection between the consumption of pornography and violence against women. Causal connections of this sort are difficult to establish. Serial rapists often have tattoos, but I seriously doubt that the tattoo is what *causes* the rapist to rape. It is far more likely that there is a slight (*very* slight) probabilistic connection between whatever causes someone to get a tattoo in the first place and other sorts of aggressive behavior.[19]

I noted earlier that I was raised in an era where television Westerns were all the rage. There is very little doubt that exposure to such television caused my sisters and me to have a bit of an obsession with toy guns. Every kid I knew at the time owned at least one holster and practiced their quick draw on a regular basis. When we got tired of wearing a cowboy hat, we would, if lucky enough to have been given one, put on our Davy Crockett hat and pretend that we were defending the Alamo from an onrushing Mexican army. But I suspect my generation was no more violent than any other generation—the same kids who played with toy guns were a significant part of the "make love not war" generation of the 1960s. I personally loved the Greek myths that so worried Plato, and I don't ever recall thinking that it would be good idea to castrate my father or swallow my sisters whole.[20] My own guess is that children are really good at distinguishing fantasy from reality and are perfectly capable of enjoying the fantasy, while they live a life that is quite different from that fantasy.

My granddaughters (whose mother is adamantly opposed to sexist stereotypes) really do love Disney princesses. They have princess dresses, princess t-shirts, princess nightgowns, princess towels, and they sing princess songs. But they are strong, self-confident, and quite opinionated children who would never be intimated by a boy (let alone their grandfather). They like to imagine being a princess, but they also like to imagine being pirates, goddesses, doctors, orphans who need to fend for themselves, and any number of other characters that involve drama of one sort or another. They too know, or so it seems to me, the difference between a game or make-believe, and reality. But none of these hypotheses can be tested through anecdotes. One must at least allow for the *possibility* that Plato was right, at least with respect to the effects that our culture has on at least some people who live within that culture.

On the political front, we know that people have been influenced by radical political treatises, written and oral, to behave in grotesque ways. Most ancient religious texts (the Talmud, the Old Testament, the Torah) are hardly inspirations to be civil and tolerant. "Blessedly," most Christians don't follow the Old Testament's advice when it comes to stoning the members of this or that group for "crimes" that we would take to involve no real offense. Unfortunately, however, the followers of God's self-proclaimed messengers were quite willing to begin genocide at the hint of an "order" from God or one of His self-proclaimed messengers. Given the number of people who profess to take very seriously the wisdom of these texts, it's almost a miracle that there isn't more violence done in the name of religion. And, of course, the world is living with the current scourge of a significant population dedicated to obliterating from the face of the earth all those unwilling to become part of a new caliphate.

Hitler's *Mein Kampf*, the various manifestos of right- and left-wing extremist groups, and the call for a new caliphate aren't taken seriously, perhaps, by huge numbers of people, but it doesn't take very many people to cause a great deal of harm, to blow up, for example, a government building in Oklahoma, or to bring down the Twin Towers in New York. And while Mill might be right that a good many people will benefit from intellectually defending their own views against such extremism, it is surely also true that at least some people will be influenced to adopt views that might lead to horrific violence. Even if the American Nazi Party doesn't engage in actual physical violence against others, its marches through the streets of a Chicago suburb surely produce enormous emotional trauma.

None of the above is intended to be an argument for censorship, but if we are resting our success in arguing against censorship on a careful consideration of consequences, there are often many actual and possible consequences of allowing freedom that must go on the negative side of the ledger.

WEIGHING THE POSITIVE AND NEGATIVE VALUES

So where should we land once we recognize that there are both benefits and risks involved when we fail to regulate certain sorts of speech? It's worth emphasizing one more time that we don't want to use anything like the harm principle if we are arguing against censorship. That argument will almost never work—at least it will almost never work if what we are arguing about is genuinely controversial. Our opponent will almost always be able to find some direct or indirect harm that *might* come to another as a result of our failure to censure the controversial speech (or work of art). And you will recall that any plausible version of a harm principle (or any other view about moral or rational action) must view as relevant *possible* consequences, even those that are extremely unlikely. So, if we are going to win an argument against censorship it will be on the basis of an argument that claims that the sum of the adjusted value and disvalue of the consequences of allowing freedom outweighs the sum of the adjusted value and disvalue of the consequences of censorship. And in making the argument we should, of course, keep in mind that in some situations the best of alternatives open to us might have largely negative consequences. There is no opting out of choice in life—again, doing nothing is a choice that can have disastrous consequences. When faced with a bad situation, a rational person chooses the "least of all evils."

In the approach I favor, one also doesn't need to endorse sweeping generalizations about whether or not one should engage in censorship. When such issues are discussed in the classroom, most of our students start out adamantly opposed to censorship of any kind under any circumstances. But once they start thinking carefully about certain sorts of situations, some real, some hypothetical, many start abandoning this sort of unequivocal opposition to all censorship. Let's start with a couple of hypothetical examples that would, I suspect, convince most that there are possible circumstances in which one should censure (even if that censorship happened to be illegal).

Freedom of the press is a concept that for many is a bedrock principle that defines a commitment that any country makes if it is to be genuinely free. But imagine that some intrepid reporter for the *New York Times* somehow gained possession of the Allies' detailed plans for the invasion of Normandy twenty-four hours before the invasion was to begin. In the real world as it existed back then, the *Times* wouldn't have printed the story. If the U.S. government found out about the situation, they would have pleaded with the reporter not to publish until well after the invasion, and the reporter would have complied. But imagine that the newspaper was opposed to the war, that the reporter wanted to make one of the biggest splashes in news history, and that despite all government pleas the evidence indicated that the story would be printed. Let's suppose there also isn't time to take legal action.[21] What do you think the government should do under such circumstances? The answer seems pretty obvious to most people. You use whatever authority seems most plausible, lock the reporter up until well after the Normandy invasion, and use force, if you must, to shut down the *New York Times* until the release of the relevant news is harmless. And this answer seems right to me. The costs of allowing this particular hypothetical press freedom so prohibitively outweigh any upside that one simply does what has to be done.

The real world is always more complicated than hypothetical situations in which the philosopher can simply stipulate the relevant facts, however unlikely it might be that those facts will ever materialize. But we certainly do run into situations where people like Snowden get information that, if made public could endanger the lives of many people. And real people in the real world need to make decisions about how to handle the possibility that people in possession of such material will make it public and will jeopardize not just lives but undercover operations that might be crucial to the safety of our country. The problem is exacerbated in the age of the internet. Once, it was relatively difficult to disseminate information to huge numbers of people. Now it is easy. Every other day, YouTube has a posting of some bizarre event that millions of people watch. It is harmless enough if it involves just the antics of inebriated or stupid people desperate for their few moments of fame. But when national security is at risk, difficult decisions need to be made.

In light of earlier discussion, it is important to stress the distinction between trying to devise *laws* that will allow one to act in certain ways, and the rationality of a decision to *ignore* the laws that exist. It wouldn't be that difficult to imagine situations in which, despite having made a perfectly sensible decision to pass laws that prohibit certain sorts of actions, people in a position to act would also rationally reach the conclusion that they should ignore the relevant laws. Juries may also reach rational conclusions not to punish such people should they be caught. So, one might conclude that our country should legally prohibit certain sorts of actions, while one also (rationally) hopes that there are individuals and agencies in place that are perfectly willing and able to act outside of the law.

We have been talking about situations in which one might rationally engage in legal or illegal censorship of the press. It has also been my experience that most people get cold feet about extreme anti-censorship principles when it comes to the depiction of the most graphic and horrible examples of violence and pornography. For example, most people draw a line at child pornography. To be sure, the immediate enormous disvalue that comes to mind is the harm done to the exploited child. But one can make the thought experiments more complicated by stipulating that the pornography in question is simulated. And in this day and age, simulation can be extraordinarily realistic. The same is true of so-called snuff films—films in which people are depicted as tortured and eventually sadistically killed. To simplify the situation, we might again suppose that no actual person is *directly* harmed in the making of the film—indeed that everything that seems to be occurring involves only computer-generated images. But still, are we not at least sympathetic to Platonic worries that exposure to this sort of material is likely to cause at least some people, specifically the kind of people who are inclined to watch such material in the first place, to engage in violent acts against their fellow citizens? Is there really any reason to support freedom to produce and distribute this sort of "art"?

Our law, of course, makes a distinction between the legality of work (prose or artistic) that is *directly* inciting people to act immediately in a violent manner and work that might only *indirectly* have such effects. But as consequentialists (or even those who think that consequences matter), we must surely be skeptical of the importance of such distinctions. As we noted earlier, directness is extraordinarily difficult to define, and unless the relevant "directness" translates into probabilities (which will always be relevant in sophisticated cost/benefit analyses), there is no reason to think that the relevant directness or indirectness of consequences would be relevant to a rational person trying to make a rational decision.[22]

So, we are still left wondering how and where to draw the relevant lines. In thinking about the question, however, I stress again that we must remember that decisions about what the *law* should be are quite distinct from decisions about how people in positions of power should act, regardless of what the law allows.

Pragmatic Consequences of Legal Prohibitions

We've talked a fair bit about the costs and benefits of allowing certain sorts of freedoms. But we haven't talked enough about the costs associated with attempting to make the expression of certain views or art forms illegal. Some of these are obvious. Once we engage in censorship, we'll need to collectively decide how we will determine what should be censored and what should not. Then we'll need to formulate laws that capture the class of material or expression that we will prohibit. After that, we'll need an effective way of capturing and punishing those who violate the law. Each step in this process is difficult, time-consuming, and fraught with dangers, including the danger of whether the laws will be interpreted the way the collective wants them to be interpreted, and enforced the way the law envisioned. This, by itself, cannot be a reason for not passing laws with the expectation that they will be enforced. After all, these costs are present *whenever* we pass a law prohibiting or requiring *any* sort of behavior. But we also know that the problems are exacerbated when the subject matter of the proposed laws is as nuanced and abstract as when and how to silence people who are determined to be heard.

You will recall that Mill cautioned against trying to pass laws forcing people to benefit others (in contrast to laws that prohibit people from harming others). While he thought that he could imagine circumstances severe enough that we might correctly decide to legally require people to take action (in contrast to laws requiring them to refrain from acting in certain ways), he emphasized that those circumstances would be exceedingly rare. While we noted that Mill's remarks were highly cryptic, we speculated that he was worried, in part, about just how to formulate such laws. How broad should be their scope? In circumstances where we could identify countless thousands of people who could have benefited others and who didn't, how far should we reach in punishing those "guilty" of inaction?

Similar questions will inevitably arise as we contemplate preventing people from expressing themselves as they choose. Let's suppose we are getting worried about the extent to which people are exposed to gratuitous and explicit violence in films, video games, television, and novels. We really are worried that such exposure is starting to numb people to the pain and suffering of others and that it is leading to a general coarsening of society. We're thinking about doing something about it. We're thinking of voting for legislators who promise to pass "Platonic" laws to restrict what people can market to others in the name of "artistic freedom." Just imagine how difficult it would be even to get started. The category, work of art that contains explicit and graphic violence, is obviously far too broad to capture the kind of work we are thinking about banning. *The Old Testament, Titus Andronicus, Macbeth, Othello, The Wild Bunch, Bonnie and Clyde, A Clockwork Orange, Silence of the Lambs, Pulp Fiction, Dirty Harry, Raging Bull,* and *Taxi Driver,* to give just a few random examples, are all works of art that contain scenes of gore and graphic violence. But few among us would have the slightest interest in banning these "classics." Of course, one might complain that such stubbornness ignores Plato's insights. You can't make an omelet without breaking a few eggs, and to save society from the degeneration caused by exposure to violence, we'll need to cast our net widely enough to catch the odd violent work that we didn't really want to censure. We are still employing cost/benefit analysis and the cost of losing the odd "masterpiece" might be worth the benefit of not coarsening the people whose character will make or break the quality of our future.

Why do I personally care that much about losing the odd play, movie, or television show I like to a practice of censorship that might also have very real benefits? One very crude answer is that I *really* like the plays and movies that I fear would disappear in the name of censorship. People value, and value intrinsically, all sorts of phenomena. But one of the great pleasures that people value is *aesthetic* pleasure. The dark side of human nature has always fascinated people. Literature and other art forms that successfully engage the imagination in a way that creates aesthetic pleasure often does so precisely by focusing on the worst aspects of human beings. The depths of depravation make the triumphs over evil that much more exhilarating. But we are also so constituted that many of us get considerable pleasure from being caused to be very sad, or horrified, or disgusted by the description or depiction of sad, horrifying, or disgusting acts. One can certainly wonder *why* we are the way we are. One can wonder why we enjoy watching a movie that leaves us in tears even after we leave the movie theatre. But whatever the explanation is, it's just an undeniable fact about us that we are this way. Now to be sure, a society that censures, say violent art forms, is going to succeed in eliminating a

lot of trash—plays, novels, movies, and the like—that only the most degraded among us would enjoy. So again, am I really not willing to risk
the loss of a few aesthetic "treasures" for the sake of a refreshing "cleans-
ing" of the aesthetic world? Am I really willing to trade off the health of
society, perhaps even the loss of innocent life caused by the saddest and
most impressionable of people who might be influenced to act out in real
life the fictional violence to which they are exposed? Yes, I am. Life is, of
course, valuable (on just about anybody's account of value). Even the
radical subjectivist will concede that most people, by nature, value the
life and happiness of others. But aesthetic pleasure has enormous value
also, and cold though it may seem, I'm willing to trade lives so that we
can live in a rich, textured world of exotic, aesthetic pleasure.

Let me offer the following analogy, one that might horrify some.
Think about some of the great aesthetic treasures that have survived
through generation upon generation. Think about the experience of seeing the pyramids, the Great Wall of China, the beautiful skyscrapers that
grace some of our most exciting cities. All of these structures were built,
in part, on suffering and death. While people still debate the details of
how the pyramids were built, there is little doubt that their construction
involved enormously hard labor and countless accidental deaths over
large tracks of time. We don't dwell a whole lot on the fact, but until very
recently the building of a skyscraper usually involved at least several
fatal accidents. We didn't know precisely who would die in the construction process, but we had a strongly justified belief that *someone* would.
But in the final analysis we concluded, correctly I think, that the benefit
was worth the cost. In the case of the pyramids, the benefit I'm talking
about is almost exclusively aesthetic. In the case of some of our most
beautiful buildings, the benefit includes not only an effective use of
space, but also the sort of enormous aesthetic pleasure one gets as one
tours the architectural wonders of a city like Chicago. Again, many are
upset at the idea that we would even think of trading human life for
something as intangible as aesthetic pleasure. Still others argue that lives
aren't the kinds of things that one can treat as if they can be sacrificed as a
means to some end.[23] But such views are extreme. We trade lives so that
we can legally drive faster on interstate highways, so that we can drive
cars that are lighter (and more fuel efficient), so that we can enjoy certain
sorts of privacy, free from the probing eyes of government. We don't
know *which* lives we'll lose by raising the speed limit on Highway 80
from Iowa City to Chicago, but we do know that there will be more lives
lost on average in a given year as a result of having the higher speed
limit.[24] Nevertheless, it's worth it to most of us so that we can get the
extra pleasure of arriving at our destination a half-hour sooner than we
otherwise would. If we can rationally trade lives for *that* sort of payoff,
how much more would a rational person risk for the exquisite aesethetic
enjoyment that comes from watching a classic film noir?

The above focuses mainly on censorship of art. When it comes to controversial ideas, including those that might advocate for the violent overthrow of political systems, I think one simply must rest one's case with the arguments I discussed in connection with Mill. But as with our example of a free press, we will need either to carve out exceptions in our law or to occasionally act outside of the law if we are to always act as rationality requires. It may be that we ought not try to write a law that envisions circumstances in which our government can legally stop a press from writing something that is unacceptably dangerous to others. It may be that we ought to settle for law that has a general prohibition against such censorship, and count on someone in government exercising the good judgment to act outside the law in order to prevent the relevant harm from occurring. I'm inclined to think that there probably should be laws and international agreements prohibiting torture. I'm also certain that there are hypothetical situations in which we should engage in torture. The wisdom of having laws prohibiting torture might be just like the wisdom of laws prohibiting censorship of the press.[25]

OPPORTUNITY, MANNER, PLACE, AND TIME

Let us suppose that we are convinced, at least as a general matter, that we should err on the side of allowing people to say what they want to say and express themselves artistically however they want. More specifically, and more precisely, we decide we won't have laws that place many, if any, restrictions on the content of speech, writing, or artistic expression. We would then live in the "land of the free" when it comes to freedom of expression, right? Maybe. But there still remains the concern that a legal freedom that provides no or limited opportunities for people to reach an audience is a spurious freedom. So in the United States, those on the left often complain that in the realm of politics, the voices of the poor and various racial and ethnic minorities are "silenced." The rhetoric will even go so far as to characterize these groups as disenfranchised. I assume that the complaint is not that the laws of the land prohibit poor people or minorities of various kinds from saying what they want to say. Nor is there a really serious complaint that states that require voter identification are *literally* engaged in disenfranchising voters. You can support or oppose contemporary voter ID laws, but I've never even heard of one that makes it anything but a bit harder for someone to get on the voter registration rolls. Rather, the complaint, louder since the Supreme Court decision in *Citizens United v. Federal Election Commission*,[26] is that wealthy people, in virtue of their wealth, have far greater opportunity to express their views in *ways* that most do not. Political action committees (PACs), for example, can spend huge amounts of money buying commercials on television and radio. To be sure, almost everyone has a remote control these days and one can quickly turn off the message if one doesn't want to hear it. Nevertheless, there is surely a greater probability that the wealthy who want to be heard on political matters will find a way of reaching at least some of their intended audience.

When it comes to venues for publication of research, one can extoll the virtues of free speech all one wants, but decisions must be made as to which submissions get published and which do not. In many, if not most, academic fields, the popularity of various kinds of views tends to ebb and flow. The fact is, if you are writing on the cutting edge of this decade's fad, you are far more likely to get published than if you are taking a largely unpopular position on the same topic. It is very difficult to publish a play, a novel, or a piece of music. In the arts it is even more difficult to get your material performed, at least in a venue where significant numbers of people will see or hear it. So, in general, what steps can we take and should we take to ensure that in "the land of the free" citizens not only have a legal right to free expression, but also have opportunities of various sorts to reach an *audience* with the views and art they want expressed?

The issue is more than a little difficult for, as we stressed earlier, a proper respect for liberty includes a proper respect for all sorts of different freedoms. Most of us value enormously our freedom to do as we please. Indeed, when we do our consequentialist calculations about whether to respect someone's freedom, the potential loss of freedom would almost always go on the negative side of the ledger (much more about this later). One of the freedoms I treasure is the freedom to be left alone in peace and quiet. As I relax in a local park, walk down a public street, or try to enjoy a drive in my convertible, I don't want to be harangued with this or that group's latest political thoughts. And I think my values are not idiosyncratic. While we neither want to place general constraints on the content of people's thoughts, nor even their legal freedom to express those thoughts, we obviously do want to place constraints on how, when, and where they exercise these legal rights.

In one sense this is hardly controversial. You may feel passionate about some alleged social injustice and decide to go door to door asking for permission to talk to people about the problem. As I noted earlier, when you knock on my door, I take it that almost no one would support a law that forces me to invite you in and forces me to listen to you for an hour or two. We have good reason to structure a society in such a way that it defines private property, property that I control as long as I am not directly interfering with some legally defined freedom of yours. One of the most important functions served by legally delineating what is yours and what is mine is that behind the privacy of my walls I can do whatever I please. That includes kicking people out of my house who won't stop talking to me about some issue I don't want to discuss. To be sure, if too many of us exercise our freedom not to listen to others, we aren't going to get those benefits Mill thought to be associated with freedom of expression. You will recall that Mill thought that confronting the views of those who disagree with us will force us to get clearer about what we believe and why we believe it. Allowing people to freely express views that disagree with ours could have that effect, but it presumably wouldn't if we steadfastly refuse to listen to others. But we surely don't want to live in a country that uses legal sanctions in an attempt to force people to listen to those with whom they disagree.

We began with a relatively straightforward question, the answer to which is obvious. Does our support of freedom of expression require us to let people into our homes to lecture us on various matters? The answer is obviously "no." But the issue gets more complicated when we move to *publicly* owned property. Again, in our society, public space is collectively owned space and we collectively make all sorts of decisions concerning what we want to allow people to do on the property we collectively own. I suggested earlier that it is hard to see how such decisions can be made other than through something like majority rule. That's not to say, of course, that we might not engage in a great deal of bargaining and compromise in the course of lobbying for what we want. I want a tennis court in the park. You don't play tennis and would prefer a pool. My wife doesn't play tennis and doesn't swim and would much prefer that we use the space for children's playground equipment. If the park is big enough, we can probably agree to find space for all of what we want. If the park isn't big enough, we might agree to use this park for a pool, another park for the tennis courts, and yet another for the playground equipment. Even when we are in the majority, with respect to what we want, we might be induced to compromise on various issues if for no other reason than we know that we won't always be in the majority on other controversies that will arise, and our negotiating power might be increased in these future decisions if we have demonstrated a willingness to compromise in the past.[27]

So how does free speech fit into all of this? We are still going to want to impose time and place restrictions on speech and artistic expression. Public universities are just that — public. But we don't want an individual or group to have the legal authority to march into any classroom and disrupt it with a speech or a performance. We don't want protest groups to be able to disrupt marriage ceremonies in the local chapel. I would want to make it illegal for such groups to disrupt lunchrooms or to protest loudly after midnight outside dorms, and my list goes on and on. As I indicated earlier, I'm not a big fan of ordinances that allow protest groups to close streets or highways. I understand that the whole point of a protest is to grab attention — to try to almost force people to listen. But again, I want the freedom not to pay attention to people when I am completely uninterested in their cause. The issue is, of course, complicated. Most concede that we should have some legal rights to protest in at least some public spaces. In the recent protests over the way in which George Floyd died, a great many celebrated the way in which many people "took to the streets" to force the world to pay attention to their grievances. Many of the protests were described as peaceful even when the protestors prevented people from using public space that they have a perfectly legal right to use. The proposals I make below will, no doubt, be considered far too conservative by many who want the ability legally to force the attention of even those who don't want to listen.[28]

One obvious solution to all of these problems associated with manner, time, and place is to set aside certain places and certain times for people to express themselves. We can also reasonably impose restrictions on how they express themselves—maximum decibel levels, and the like. London has its famous Hyde Park corner. It's a place set aside for people to hold forth on whatever topic they choose. I assume that one needs to get in some sort of queue for purposes of coordination. The idea is perfectly straightforward, and many variations on the theme are possible. One might advertise through internet postings the topic of the day so people can make a more informed decision about whether or not they want to show up.

But a society worried about opportunities for people to communicate their views to others has other ways of trying to make such potential communication easier. Most everyone in the United States has access to television, and almost everyone has access to all sorts of channels on their television. Many cable companies, either as a matter of choice or as a requirement for obtaining their license, make at least one or two of their channels "public access" channels. It is just "Hyde Park Corner" on cable television. Access would again need to be coordinated, and modest efforts could be made at publicizing what the day's programming schedule looks like.[29]

In a similar spirit, it seems to me that a libertarian society might well allow that the government that carries out our collective instruction on what to do with our collective resources should ensure ample opportunity for public political debate before elections. We may or may not want to allow groups to use the public streets for protest or for artistic expression. If we do, we almost certainly will want to solve coordination problems by requiring permits. We don't want all of our streets closed at the same time, and some streets are too important for commerce to allow them ever to close.

If we have a healthy appreciation of the importance of free speech, would we at least insist that restrictions concerning manner, time, and place be independent of *content*? The natural answer is in the affirmative, but I think most of us would favor at least some relatively harmless exceptions. On my campus there was a significant controversy a while ago concerning an artist who put up on the University's Pentacrest a statue that looked like someone dressed in Ku Klux Klan garb. Ironically, while it upset some minorities on campus the most, the statue had all sorts of news stories pasted on it that were supposed to be supportive of claims of various sorts of oppression. In any event, the statue was taken down by university authorities because the artist didn't seek appropriate permission to put up the display—perfectly legitimate requirements of the sort we discussed above. But suppose that a different artist goes through the relevant bureaucracy and asks permission to put up Nazi propaganda, pro-Communist propaganda, anti-Israel propaganda, art that many would view as obscene, and so on? As I understand it, my university has a sensible and obvious policy concerning the last item on the list. Artists, particularly young artists at universities, like to push the limits. Realizing this, but also wanting to give their students opportunities to show their work, the art school makes a judgment about whether a work of art falls into the controversial category, and, if it does, it finds a place that allows the student to more discretely put the artwork on display. The display is clearly marked for what it is.[30] People who want to see the artwork can; people who don't, can avoid it.

Would a similar approach work for political expression that many will find offensive or obscene? I'm not sure why not. Once we set the relevant precedent, we could insist that the most controversial of messages be clearly labeled as controversial and set in an area that minimizes exposure to those who do not want to be confronted by messages they take to be genuinely obnoxious. The difficulty, of course, is how and where to draw the line. Illinois decided that it would let the Nazi Party march in the streets of Skokie where there lived survivors of the Holocaust who would need to choose between reliving the horrors of that experience or staying in their houses with the curtains closed. But once one gets involved in the business of deciding whose political views get the relevant permit and whose do not, one will encounter no end to headaches. Particularly when it comes to speech, it seems to me that the best solution is again to be relatively restrictive on place and time but almost completely permissive with respect to content. Taking this approach will cause us to lose many of the benefits that Mill expected to flow from freedom of expression, but the desirability of protecting privacy is a good that needs to be balanced against the good of confronting the views of others.

At least some of the controversies discussed above have been significantly mitigated in the age of the internet. It costs next to nothing to start a web site or a blog. On that web site, you can publish what you want. You can't make people read or watch what you self-publish, but it is out there for the world to see. When you start publishing state secrets that might cost lives, you had probably better worry about someone taking extra-legal steps to prevent you from continuing, but that worry is nothing really new. Fifty years ago, the aspiring geniuses who were frustrated at those refusing to publish or produce their works of genius had little recourse. Today, one can perform one's music, read one's poetry, get some friends together to put on a play, or do just about anything else one wants via a venue that can *potentially* reach millions of people. And there have been notable examples of people who have literally brought fame to their writing and art through taking advantage of the relevant opportunities. If, collectively, we are concerned with providing people opportunities to express themselves, we could certainly have outreach programs helping people to learn the ins and outs of taking full advantage of cyberspace.

I suspect that the opportunities described above are not going to satisfy those who claim that their voices are "silenced." People can find just about anything they want to find on the internet, but the sheer vastness of cyberspace makes it difficult for one to get the audience one might want. And there is still going to be a significant disparity between the likelihood that the very wealthy, as opposed to the very poor, will get the attention they want. This, however, is something we shouldn't try to remedy. To attempt to use collective force to even the playing field would require a government that is so heavy-handed and intrusive that we would end up killing the very freedom we were trying to promote. At least that is true if, as we shall argue later, we want to live in a society that allows significant disparity of wealth.

The whole premise of supporting freedom of expression is that we want to encourage people to say what they want—certainly say what they want in places that they own or control. Wealthy people are going to have far more opportunity to successfully engage their fellow citizens than will poor people. And there is nothing that we can reasonably do about it. The wealthy have more opportunity to buy advertising. They have more flexibility with respect to their schedules, a kind of flexibility that allows them to make the circuit on television shows (and the clout that will get them such invitations in the first place). Even if they were having trouble buying advertisements in print media, on television, or on radio, the wealthiest have enough money to buy their own print media, their own networks, and their own radio stations. That's the inevitable price one pays for a free enterprise system that allows people to succeed and profit from that success. As we shall see later, there is no viable (rational) option other than to support a system in which significant inequality of wealth is legally prohibited. Once financial inequality exists, it is a foregone conclusion that those with more resources will have advantages of many kinds over those with fewer resources. The wealthy will get better health care (because they can afford specialists who have opted out of government-subsidized systems). They will probably be more educated (should they want to become educated) because they have unlimited resources to secure education. They will have greater influence on the political system because they have resources to buy advertisements in many different media. They have more leisure time to devote to politics. They also know other people who might share their political interests and whom they can influence. Because of their ability to contribute to the campaigns of others, they will directly or indirectly have a disproportionate say in the political views of those to whom they contribute. At the very least their position of power will give them "face" time and all the potential advantages of persuasion that come with that face time. All this and more are true, and to try to do something about it is folly.

We have already talked about how we can make modest efforts to level the playing field through public access. If people can put an idiotic post on YouTube of someone falling off of a diving board, a post that gets two million hits, then they might be able to put on the internet a compelling video containing a political manifesto that affects the attitudes or beliefs of millions of people. I wouldn't count on it, because I suspect more people enjoy watching someone fall off a diving board than they appreciate a compelling argument for a political point of view. But that's not the fault of a legal system. If anything, it is the fault of people who these days have extraordinarily short attention spans and a penchant for the most superficial of news items. We could try to change *that*, but the only real prospects are to go with a heavy-handed Platonic dictatorship (led by the supposed enlightened) that will "force" people to think about what we want them to think about, pay attention to "important" issues, and stay away from "entertainment" that is vacuous and probably destructive to a healthy character. The Platonic ideal is a dictatorship run by intellectual elites. I'm sure I would be a perfect choice for the Philosopher Ruler, but the trouble is that I know a lot of others who would vie for that same position, and many of them haven't had a commonsense thought in their life. Once we decide to live together and gain the advantages of cooperation that come from pooling our resources, we need to choose a government, and I can't really think of anything but some form of democracy that is likely to get us the sort of people we want in leadership. The older I get, the less sanguine I am that democracy will make the best, or even marginally good, choices, but, as the old cliché has it, what is the relevant alternative?

"CENSORSHIP" WITHOUT LAWS OR RULES

The previous discussion of freedom of thought and expression focused primarily on the question of whether we ought to endorse laws, rules, or regulations that place limitations on speech and artistic expression. As we noted earlier, Mill was also concerned with less formal sanctions that society can employ in an effort to control, if not freedom of thought, then freedom of expression. So, let us suppose that arguments against censorship have convinced us that we should impose no *formal* sanctions on those whose views or artistic expression we find distasteful, disgusting, grotesque, and perhaps, even dangerous. We might nevertheless worry that an appropriate respect for freedom will still allow us to associate with whom we please and hire whom we please. Do the arguments against formal sanctions also support the conclusion that we should individually avoid more informal sorts of "discrimination" against those whose views we find abhorrent?

I talked earlier about the setting of academia and the importance of securing, at least *there,* an environment where we not only tolerate but encourage people to put forth views that are highly controversial, or perhaps even repugnant to others. But I also noted that there is a very real worry that the trouble those in power can cause for others who are "politically incorrect" can easily succeed in "quieting" those who would otherwise challenge some of the received views. It is relatively hard for a tenured faculty member to get fired, no matter how outlandish that faculty member's views might be. But untenured faculty members need to worry about gaining tenure, and those applying for positions need to worry about not getting hired. Students need to worry about politically incorrect thought that might earn them poor grades, or, in extreme cases, dismissal from a university. I describe universities because I know them best. But similar pressures on people to "conform" exist in many other areas of society.

If we truly embrace the value of freedom of thought and expression, we surely want to discourage practices that look for "micro-aggression" allegedly exhibited by words that implicitly demean this group or that or dismiss the legitimacy of this cause or that.[31] We want to allow political philosophers or political scientists to say the harshest things about Israel, Palestine, ISIS, capitalism, socialism, communism, religion, and anything else about which they might feel strongly.

All this sounds good, but I suspect that while we do and *should* worry about discriminating in various informal ways against people whose views we disagree with, we also will, and should, engage in such practices when we encounter a person whose views go "beyond the pale." Consider again hiring practices. If ever there were a field where intelligent people hold widely diverse views, philosophy is one. And most of us do try to control our own biases—even welcome the chance to hire someone who brings to our department importantly different perspectives on philosophical views and even the methodological question of how best to do philosophy. But some candidates for positions hold views that we find unintelligible and/or indefensible. We won't hire them. We might acknowledge the plausibility of Mill's fallibilism. We might readily agree that we might be exercising faulty judgment or are even driven by hidden biases, but, in the final analysis, we have no alternative but to make the best decision we can, relying on our best judgement (informed, of course, by due diligence in trying to find out as much as we can about the candidate, and even ourselves, when it comes to worries about biases).

Now consider a much more difficult decision. Imagine that we have found a candidate for our position who seems perfect. The person seems intelligent, her research and teaching seem impeccable, her interview went wonderfully—we are about to make an offer. Then a member of the department discovers, by randomly surfing the net, that our prospective colleague is a well-known Holocaust denier and is someone who advocates wiping Israel off the face of the earth. These views are completely unrelated to the areas in which the prospective colleague will teach and do research for the department. Should this discovery change our attitude toward the potential hire? I'm inclined to think that it should. Such views suggest to me an intellectual defect so serious that I think it could spread into other areas of that person's life, including the kind of collegiality that we value in departmental life.

So, if we make a decision based on this sort of information, what has become of the value we place on freedom of thought? Our candidate freely expressing her views are going to cost her a job. But we have already noted that there is no obvious connection between placing no formal restrictions on the content of speech and ensuring that people have all of the opportunities that they might crave to express their views. Nor have we ever suggested that because we defend freedom of thought and expression, we will ensure that there are no *costs* to those who express controversial and, to some, even repugnant views. Freedom is a two-way street. I'll defend your legal right to say what you want about politics or religion, but if you hold views that I find hateful or disgusting, I'm not going to hang out with you, and I may not hire you if I'm in a position of power to control it. You won't pay a *legal* price for holding your views, but you should know that there are other prices to be paid.

Recently, some university students traveling on a bus rented by a fraternity to take them to a party began singing overtly racist songs. Another student on the bus videotaped the event. The president of the university put some of the students on probation and dismissed others. In one way of thinking about the president's action, it was an overt attack on freedom of expression. The students were not on university property, and it was not obvious that they were creating a hostile work or learning environment. They were acting like objectionable idiots. But don't we want students to be able to express views that we find racist or sexist without having to fear dismissal from a university? The case is difficult. I've already said that I wouldn't hire people who have expressed similar sorts of sentiments. If a student's application to college included an essay with overt racist statements, my guess is that admissions wouldn't admit the student.

Hiring, however, isn't the same as firing, and once we give someone a job or admit someone to a university, we might well want to give that person a special assurance that they don't need to worry about what they say or do when they are not on the job. Once we start firing employees or dismissing students for behavior unrelated to their work, there will inevitably be a dangerous, slippery slope that will be nightmarishly difficult to navigate. One person's abhorrent racist is another person's fervent prolifer. One person's neo-Nazi is another's radical socialist or leader of the Tea-Party movement. We justifiably worry about how to make these sorts of decisions when firing someone from a job, particularly *after* that person has shown that he or she can do the job well and that whatever that person's extreme social and political views might be, those views haven't inappropriately crept into how they do their job. Here we may have located the obvious difference between using information about someone's extreme views in deciding whether to hire that person and using that same sort of information in an effort to get that person fired. The distinction may be primarily epistemic. In a field where we take rationality to be important, it is not foolish to worry that irrationality in one area might be an indicator of potential irrationality in another. From my perspective, the kind of irrationality that a Holocaust denier exhibits would lead me to think that there is an unacceptable risk that such a person has an intellectual defect that would eventually manifest itself in some other important area related to the job that person is expected to do. If I have been working with that person for a while and I've seen no evidence of "irrationality creep," I don't need to worry *as much* and can err on the side of freedom. One might want a more principled answer than this to the question of why we might reach different conclusions about hiring and firing, but the price one pays for a consequentialist defense of freedom is that there are all sorts of distinctions that we might make based on highly nuanced consideration of the probability of many different possible consequences.

Boycotts, Protests, and Other Societal Pressures against Freedom of Speech

We talked above about how practices concerning hiring, firing, and promotion are pressures one can exert on those of whose views we disapprove. But, of course, there are many other ways that we can individually and collectively "punish" people for saying things we don't like. Donald Trump says something that many construe as outrageously denigrating illegal immigrants, and Macy's pulls his line of ties. Other groups urge a boycott of his casinos and golf courses. The CEO of Chick-fil-A, a restaurant chain, says he is adamantly opposed to gay marriage, that he thinks such relationships are morally wrong and should be illegal. The company at the time also contributed to PACs supporting socially conservative candidates. All sorts of groups urged a boycott of his restaurants. Are these attacks on free speech or an exercise of freedom on the part of those who want to protest the free speech of others?

Again, there seems to me no real debate about whether we want to make illegal boycotts or calls for boycotts. The legislation couldn't be written and enforced even if we wanted to have it. Would we attempt to force people to buy certain products against their will? Are we going to tell Macy's when it can decide to drop a line of clothes? Hardly. But we can use speech to talk about whether we should use such methods to put pressure on people to keep their political views to themselves. And for all of the reasons we have been discussing, it seems to me that it is a measure one should consider only with respect to the most egregious of actions. If we are really serious about the advantages of open debate that Mill stresses so much, why should we try to hurt people who are engaging in the very debate that we think is good for the country? It can only be that we are collectively afraid of hearing an argument that might persuade people. But if you are convinced that it is a bad argument, it is taking quite a condescending attitude toward your fellow citizens to suppose that they would be incapable of realizing what *you*, in your wisdom, have been able to discover. On my view, if the Chick-fil-A chicken is good, buy it. If the arguments of its CEO are bad, present effective responses.

I don't for one moment pretend that recommendations of this sort will be followed. Unfortunately, we live in a country where disagreement over political issues, for example, turns into dislike for the person who holds those positions, and it is human nature to reward those we like and do little or nothing for those we dislike. Worse than that, as we pointed out earlier, many tend to hang around only those whose views they agree with. Many people *like* others to agree with them, to tell them how brilliant their arguments or their positions are. We'd probably be much better off if we were bored easily by agreement and interested more in vigorous debate.

NOTES

1. Jacobson (2000) agrees that Mill doesn't make use of his harm principle in defending freedom of expression but suggests that Mill implicitly relies on a rights-based view instead. As subsequent discussion will make clear, I don't agree with that idea. Mill will sometimes talk *as if* he thinks that there are moral rights, but in the end, I think that he is a confirmed act utilitarian who has room only for the "rules of thumb" we talked about earlier in this book.
2. I have argued earlier that one should be wary of the talk about rights in the context of morality. Yet here I am introducing the term "right" into my discussion. I am using the term as shorthand to refer to a right we might want encoded in law.
3. Mill himself recognized the common law principle that one can silence one who presents a clear and present danger (first formulated in the United States in *Shank v. U.S.*). But I'm also referring here to the many restrictions we place on where and when one can express one's views.
4. Hurd (2001) presents subtle and sophisticated arguments against the legitimacy of so-called hate crimes. Jacobs and Potter (1998) also worry that building the psychological causes of already criminal behavior into the definition of a different kind of crime involves an illegitimate and unconstitutional infringement on the rights of people to hold politically incorrect views. Streiker (1999) disagrees.

5. The movie *Minority Report* has a plot that focuses on a future in which three beings could predict with near certainty what people were going to do before they actually did it.

6. See Cohen-Almagor (2017) for interesting examples of people punished for holding "heretical" views.

7. Perhaps philosophy shouldn't be on the list. We noted earlier that it might be better for many people if they don't know the truth about the correct metaethical theory. Consequentialists who try to act as consequentialists might be very bad at calculating consequences—they might make the world a mess. We might be better off if they embraced some mistaken rule-governed conception of morality (as long as the rules happen to get them the correct conclusions most of the time).

8. See Judith Curry (2017) who reports the obstacles she faced as an academic defending unpopular views about climate change.

9. There is extensive research that one can often stave off the effects of aging by keeping one's mind active. Brink (1992, 2001) is eloquent in defending the Millian view that *certain* sorts of debate and argument are critical to human development. He is less sure that some sorts of hate speech serve the same sorts of purposes (and should deserve the same sort of protection).

10. Though again, some would argue that to serve any sort of valuable purpose, the positions one considers should be at least "colorable" (to use a lawyer's expression). Haworth (1998, 42) has no interest in defending Holocaust deniers—people whose views only obscure the truth by ignoring evidence that is there for everyone to consult. The difficulty, of course, is how and where to draw the line. The libertarian is going to argue that one should take great care to err on the side of freedom.

11. Compare with arguments advanced by Schulzke (2016).

12. See again Curry (2017).

13. For a detailed discussion of arguments against free speech, see Leiter (2016).

14. Ironically, Plato seems to violate many of his own rules concerning what people would be allowed to read. He thinks, for example, that people who represent lies or untruths should not be allowed to speak in their own voice—they should only be described through indirect speech. But Plato's own dialogues allow characters like Thrasymachus to vigorously defend views that Plato takes to be pernicious. Plato seems adamant about not allowing authors to lie, but he specifically suggests that the rulers of his ideal state lie through their foundation myth, and even fix the lotteries that will determine who gets to mate with whom.

15. See Moore (2005) and Perrin (2019).

16. See Catherine MacKinnon's (1989) classic essay.

17. It is actually interesting that the heroines of more recent Disney films are often much more assertive and aggressive than their predecessors.

18. For a sophisticated discussion of the probabilistic connections, see Huesmann (2010) and Anderson et al. (2010).

19. Lamberg (1996) discusses a talk by Philip Resnick in which he argues that mental health practitioners should screen patients for their propensity to violence based on whether or not they have tattoos. See also Carroll et. al (2002). The claim is that such people are more likely to use drugs, engage in criminal behavior, and act violently.

20. Behavior that some myths attributed to Zeus.

21. So, in the United States the Supreme Court has decided that even the most fundamental of legal rights enumerated in the Constitution can be abridged by the government under extreme circumstances (the kind of circumstances that would satisfy what the court calls a requirement of strict scrutiny). I'm not sure where the court found this authority to apply different levels of scrutiny, but I suspect it was just something it made up, given that commonsense requires *compelling* interests to outweigh even constitutionally protected freedoms. The actual case introducing the distinctions was *U.S. v Carolene Products Company* (1938).

22. For a discussion of controversies concerning the relevance of unforeseen consequences, see Fumerton (2017).

23. The most famous philosopher associated with the view that you can't treat a person as a means to an end is, of course, Kant (1993). See also Anderson (1993).

24. One estimate suggests that in the past twenty-five years nearly 37,000 additional people died in traffic accidents due to higher speed limits (Barry 2019). For a detailed discussion of such analyses, see Castillo-Manzano et. al (2019). As I complete final revisions of this manuscript, the world is in the middle of a fight against the corona virus. People and politicians are really quite divided on how to approach the problem. On the one end of a spectrum, some recommend that the United States impose nation-wide "lock downs." People wouldn't be allowed to leave their houses and exercise their freedom of association except for absolutely essential activities. The economy will suffer enormously. On the other end of the spectrum, some suggest that we just exercise a bit more caution than we usually do, practice good hygiene and moderate social distancing, try as best we can to take care of our elders and those with underlying conditions, and get our economy back to work. Be prepared to take what comes (where "what comes" will certainly include more people dying). It is easy to embrace the bumper sticker slogan "every life is precious." If we can save a single life by shutting the economy for two or three months, or two or three years, then that's what we need to do. But as some have pointed out, if you can trade the ease of getting from point A to point B a bit faster for a few lost lives, why can't one trade the enormous benefits of a healthy economy for several thousand lives? I'll talk more about this in chapter 6.

25. Derschowitz (2002) would be sympathetic, I think, to the overall point I am making, but argues that the law itself ought to allow (with appropriate judicial warrant) torture.

26. A case in which the court held that First Amendment considerations prohibited the government from imposing spending restrictions on so-called PACs (political action committees). For an argument against the way we allow corporate political spending, see Alzola (2013) and Lessig (2010).

27. The probability that this is so depends, in part, on a view about how farsighted people are. If we want to be able to secure compromise with others in the future (and we probably do), we should realize that the likelihood of success depends on how willing we were to compromise in the past.

28. I'm about to discuss what the law should permit. Obviously, anyone can make the choice to get attention by acting illegally. I might agree that in certain circumstances, that is precisely what it would be rational/moral to do.

29. In my community, there doesn't seem to be a huge demand to take advantage of public access (though there are occasional attempts at "entertainment" that are breathtakingly horrible).

30. One might object that requiring someone to admit to something as being controversial is itself an objectionable infringement on speech—this time a requirement that people say something they might not want to say. One might make the same argument against universities whose policies require professors to give so-called trigger warnings when they are about to cover controversial material, or material the might offend students or cause students emotional trauma. The AAUP, predictably, argues that policies requiring trigger warnings are an infringement on academic freedom. Wyatt (2016) has a nuanced discussion of the issue and suggests that such warning probably should sometimes be given but also that probability shouldn't be a matter of policy. As I'll argue later in discussing economic issues, clear disclosure of the known dangers of a product might be a reasonable compromise in protecting the freedom of people to choose a potentially dangerous product. In the same, way, clear disclosure of the content of a course, including the content of some particular lecture in the course, might be a small price to pay to liberate professors to present controversial and potentially offensive material.

31. For a representative sample of those who stress the negative impact of so-called micro-aggressions, see Sue (2010).

SIX

Social Libertarianism

In the United States, we tend to view the political landscape on a continuum from right to left, from conservative to liberal. But it has become obvious that we need a much more subtle array of continua if our labels are going to be at all usefully descriptive. No matter how many distinctions we make, however, it may be difficult to find the consequentialist endorsing all the policies most commonly associated with various factions. In any event, it is not at all uncommon these days to encounter politicians, or, more generally, politically interested citizens describing themselves as fiscally conservative but socially liberal (or libertarian). The distinction is somewhat artificial. At least some of the social controversies we will discuss in this chapter revolve around liberties that have obvious economic consequences. As such, they could just as easily be discussed in a chapter on economic freedom. Nevertheless, we will proceed as if we can make a distinction between various controversies concerning freedom of lifestyle choices and controversies that more explicitly involve how we should structure our economy.

We can probably guess the positions that the self-described social libertarian will take, but it will be a bit harder to discover what all or most of these positions have in common. It might be useful, though, to start with the positions.

SOCIAL LIBERTARIAN PHILOSOPHY

The social libertarian is likely to endorse some combination of the following policies:

1. We should let people marry any adult (combination of adults?) they please regardless of religion, race, sexual orientation, or anything else that the acronym LGBTQ is supposed to capture.
2. We should make legal the use of recreational drugs for adults.
3. We should allow people to risk their own lives and limbs (drive without seat belts, ride motorcycles without helmets, swim in fast currents, take experimental drugs, order all the 32-ounce sodas they please), at least if they have been informed about the relevant risks. We should also allow people to end their lives as they choose and allow them to seek aid in doing so (perhaps, though, only if certain conditions obtain—soundness of mind, genuine consent, and so on).
4. We should continue to respect the right of people to own and carry firearms.
5. We should endorse most of the freedoms of thought and expression discussed in the previous chapter.
6. We shouldn't stigmatize people for their religious beliefs.
7. We should legalize prostitution for adults.
8. We should generally remain as neutral as we can with respect to alternative "life styles"—we shouldn't disparage couples who live outside of legally recognized marriage, couples who decide not to have children, couples who decide to have children but who use day care and after-school activities to look after them, couples who decide to raise children communally with other couples, and so on.
9. We should legalize most abortions.
10. We should be vigilant against allowing a government to intrude on our privacy through various forms of expansive surveillance.

The list isn't intended to be exhaustive. But it might be long enough to look for common threads in arguments for the respective freedoms.

Obviously, Mill's prediction (discussed earlier) of a future that would be very much concerned with issues involving freedom seems to have been accurate. Controversies concerning freedom did indeed characterize a good part of the political future that he foresaw. Each of 1 through 10 can be put in terms of a position about what people should be free to do without interference, either by formal sanctions imposed by the state or the informal sanctions that people are perfectly capable of imposing to make the lives of others miserable. A consequentialist would need to look at each of the controversies in turn, evaluate the pros and cons of allowing the relevant freedom, and reach a tentative conclusion about what one ought to do, all things considered. Let's illustrate that process of evaluation with some examples, and let's start with the most controversial item on the social libertarian's list, the so-called pro-choice commitment concerning abortion. As we have stressed before, when considering any controversy concerning freedom, we need to distinguish the question of what people ought to do from the question of what we ought to make illegal.

Abortion

Put bluntly, the abortion controversy is an *outlier* with respect to the controversies concerning freedom that separate libertarians and their critics. To be sure, the pro-choice side explicitly frames the issue in terms of freedom. Their mantra is that "a woman should be free to do with her body as she chooses." But no one who has the slightest interest in being charitable, however, would interpret the slogan literally. Women shouldn't be free to strap explosives to their bodies and detonate them in the midst of rush-hour crowds. Women shouldn't be free to use their index finger to pull the trigger on a gun aimed at an innocent bystander. Women shouldn't be free to use their bodies to obstruct traffic on a critical thoroughfare. There are countless legal restrictions any rational person would put on what a woman may do with her body. So, if the slogan is to have any plausibility, one needs to modify it significantly. And the most natural modification takes us all the way back to some version of a harm principle: A woman ought to be free to do with her body as she pleases as long as she isn't harming anyone else (against that person's will) with that decision.

We had occasion to wonder how plausible the harm principle is, but even if we turn to consequentialism, we'll probably almost always reach a conclusion supporting someone's freedom to do as he or she pleases when there are no, or only negligible, identifiable negative effects produced by the action in question. But therein lies the rub. The pro-life side of the debate is convinced that a fetus is a person who can be harmed by having its life terminated. Pro-lifers are adamant that an abortion is inappropriately described as having no harmful impact on anyone else.

It's very difficult to use argument to get beyond the stalemate that so often characterizes attempts to resolve the abortion controversy. We can, of course, make important verbal distinctions. Philosophers will correctly distinguish "value-laden" language from "value-neutral" language. When we describe Jones as *murdering* Smith, it is plausible to suppose that we are not *merely* describing Jones as killing Smith. In addition to asserting that Jones killed Smith, we are also asserting that the killing was wrong.[1] "Murder" is not a *value-neutral* description of killing. There are indefinitely many examples of words that have a value judgment embedded in their meaning. And certainly, if we characterize a fetus as a *person*, we are probably implying all sorts of conclusions about what we morally or legally may or may not do with respect to the fetus. Most human beings are persons, but as Locke suggested (1959, chapter XXVII) we would very naturally extend the concept of person to any number of living creatures to which we assign the same sort of value as a human. So, if we are going to discuss the abortion controversy, we don't want to use language in such a way that we beg questions from the outset. Value-neutral descriptions are readily at hand. It is uncontroversial that a fetus is a living organism, and, perhaps more importantly, it is uncontroversial what it has the *potential* to become if left to develop under certain conditions. It will become a human being with all the properties that most of us think make human beings valuable. The mother whose body is the "home" to the fetus is also a human and doesn't just have the potential to develop capacities that make her life valuable—she also currently possesses those properties.

But this is utterly trivial. Everyone knows all of this. In a skillful rhetorical move made during a presidential debate, Reagan once argued that there is at least some doubt as to whether a fetus (at any level of development) should be viewed as having the same sort of value as a child or an adult, and went on to suggest that when in doubt we should err on the side of caution. He used an interesting analogy. If you were about to demolish a building and just learned that there was a one- or two-percent chance that someone was still in the building, you surely wouldn't proceed with the demolition. You would conclude that the demolition involves an unacceptable risk. His idea was supposed to be that the fetus about to be aborted has *at least* that sort of outside chance of having the relevant value. Just as we should check the building more thoroughly before demolishing it, so also, we should do more research on whether the fetus is a person before allowing it to be killed.

The analogy, however, is clearly problematic in a number of respects. First, those who talk as if we are still awaiting more empirical data to weigh in on the abortion controversy are seriously misguided. We surely know as much as we need to know about a fetus to reach the relevant conclusion about what we should or shouldn't do and what we should or shouldn't legally allow. For example, a fetus (at various stages) may or may not be capable of feeling pain, but that is hardly what is particularly relevant for most of us when it comes to a conclusion about whether or not we legally ought to be allowed to kill it. Most of us are carnivores and anyone who isn't in the grips of a theory understands that the animals we kill and eat are perfectly capable of feeling pain. We think it is OK to kill them because we think that the pain of their death (and their captivity) is outweighed by the benefits we "higher order" beings get from killing them and preparing them to eat in ways that give us enormous aesthetic pleasure. So, if our "pro-life" position rests on the claim that a fetus is on a par with a pig or a cow, then the "pro-choice" group is home free. The moral to draw is that one shouldn't be trying to make an argument based on characteristics a fetus has, but rather on the *potential* a fetus has to become something quite different from a pig or a cow.

Philosophers have argued in imaginative ways for a women's right to choose. Some of those arguments don't deny that the life of a fetus has value, perhaps even the kind of value that a normal adult human being has. Thomson's famous thought experiment (1971) involves a brilliant violinist in desperate need of a transfusion from someone with a rare blood type. The transfusion would need to continue over an extended period of time. Being the kind of fantastic thought experiment that philosophers often use, we are to imagine that only you can provide the transfusion and that a group determined to save the violinist drugged you and hooked you up to the violinist where you will need to stay for about nine months if the violinist is to survive. Whatever you *ought* to do, Thomson argues, you certainly have the moral *right* to rip out the tubes and go on your merry way. And a legal system should respect that moral right by making such a choice legally permissible.

Notice that once again we are arguing using the language of moral *rights*, a language with which the consequentialist isn't that comfortable. Given *my* assignment of the relevant values, it seems to me that consequentialist reasoning will probably force me to the annoying conclusion that I ought to stay connected to the violinist despite the fact that I'd rather be doing something else with my life. That conclusion, of course, is quite independent of what I might rationally conclude with respect to what the *law* should allow me to do. Thinking about Thomson's thought experiment probably forces us to make all sorts of other distinctions that seem relevant to many when it comes to the morality, and what the legality should be, of abortion. In Thomson's first iteration of the case, you were forced into a situation in which the violinist's life is dependent on you. Most cases of pregnancy are not forced choices in that way. But cases of rape are. And accidental pregnancies that occur despite careful precautions seem to many a bit like a decision that is "forced" (by fate or really bad luck) on someone who wanted no part of the situation in which she finds herself.

So, are we getting anywhere in an attempt to decide whether a pregnant woman's freedom to choose is one that we want our law to recognize? It does seem to me that for most people a fetus's life has value—the value that derives from a potential to develop in the wondrous ways that create a human being with a rich conscious life. The value of potentiality, however, is usually not thought of as equal to the value of actuality. If I purchase seeds to grow an exceedingly rare rose bush and you do something to destroy the seeds, a court will probably award me far less in damages than I would have been awarded had the plants grown to maturity and had you destroyed them then. Similarly, one might argue, as a fetus develops it gains more and more value.[2] But it is hard to say what precisely it is about the developing fetus that makes it more valuable as it progresses other than that it is simply closer to the time at which various potentialities become actualities. Certainly, a day-old baby doesn't seem to me all that much different from a fetus in terms of what would give it value.[3] There is a "cuteness" continuum, and, frankly, I suspect that something like cuteness plays an enormous role in explaining one's judgements about the value of a newborn compared to a fetus in the second or third trimester. There is nothing irrational about that. We are more likely to eat cows and pigs than we are to eat puppies. One can search around for a reason to value the survival of puppies more than cows, but I doubt one will find it once one leaves the realm of the aesthetic.[4]

There is no shortage of proposals for what marks the critical distinctions between fetuses one should be allowed to kill and those one shouldn't, and fetuses in general in contrast to new-born babies. Some think that the critical test is whether the fetus could survive outside the womb, but it is surely odd to think that tomorrow's advance in science would change our conclusion about whether it is now OK to kill the very thing that it is wrong to kill tomorrow. It is true that the inconvenience to the mother of carrying a child to birth is not insignificant, however, and I suppose that if one isn't assigning all that *much* value to the life of that fetus, it wouldn't take all that much inconvenience to outweigh the value of life.

It is precisely this sort of cost–benefit analysis that makes it much harder to insist that a woman who is pregnant as a result of rape or incest still carry the pregnancy to term. The woman has been victimized once, and there is every reason to believe that the pregnancy would be a constant reminder of the horror, fear, and disgust that is hard enough to deal with without having a constant reminder of the event in the form of a pregnancy carried to term. Even *most* on the pro-life side of the abortion controversy think that if a woman had to choose between her own life and the life of the child she is carrying, she shouldn't be legally forced to sacrifice her own life. But there is life and there is *quality* of life. If a woman had to choose between the life she is carrying and her life filled with wounds that are constantly being reopened, it is again hardly clear to most that she should be forced to choose the former.

In the end, the abortion controversy is so difficult to resolve precisely because most people are genuinely torn in opposite directions. To be sure, each side vilifies the other. The pro-lifers want to "enslave" women. The pro-choicers are committed to mass murder that makes history's examples of genocide pale in comparison. Neither side in the controversy is guilty of anything other than trying to find their way through genuinely conflicting values that make maximizing expected value difficult.

In thinking through the controversy, we still must keep distinct the two quite different conclusions that need to be reached. One concerns the question of whether abortion is morally wrong. The other concerns the question of whether we ought to make abortion illegal. As we have seen earlier in this book, an answer to the one question doesn't dictate an answer to the other. *Whenever* one is contemplating the possibility of making any activity illegal, one must calculate the costs associated with enforcement and the probability that the enforcement will successfully achieve one's goal. We know from past experience that making abortion illegal won't stop all people who want abortions from having them. There will be a huge underground business that thrives on providing expensive, and often unsafe, abortions to desperate adult women and teenagers. Of course, that, by itself, cannot be a decisive argument against making abortion illegal. As we also noted earlier, making theft, embezzlement, insider trading, rape, murder, assault, going through a red light, and the like illegal doesn't entirely stop any of these types of actions from occurring, though it does, we hope, reduce the rate at which they occur. But the list I just gave involves uncontroversial examples of action kinds that we need to make illegal if we are to survive in society together. While we earlier rejected Reagan's suggestion that until we are sure whether a fetus is a person, we should err on the side of protecting the fetus, we might find more attractive the decidedly libertarian idea that unless we are sure we will make the world a better place by making some act illegal, we should err on the side of liberty. *The tie breaker is, trivially, the value almost all of us place on freedom — not as a means, but intrinsically.* As we shall see, this tie breaker might be crucial in trying to decide a great many other controversies concerning freedom.

Marriage Equality

Let's move from one of the more intractable of controversies concerning freedom to a controversy that in the United States is quickly ceasing to be a controversy — marriage equality. While there are still pockets of the country adamantly opposed to the idea of gays marrying, the tide of public opinion has clearly swung in favor of allowing people the legal freedom to marry whomever they please.[5] More generally (and perhaps more importantly), there seems to be a growing indifference to people's sexual orientation, unless, of course, one is actively thinking of a particular person as a prospective sexual partner.

There still are people who feel very strongly about the issue and are, no doubt, enormously upset at the idea that the courts now allow people to marry who, in their view, shouldn't be married. As I argued earlier when discussing Mill's harm principle, I don't think that there is any point in denying that affective responses can count as a kind of harm (broadly understood). And almost all of us assign negative value to harm. The empirical question is how great a harm it is. And as far as I can tell, when people are upset at the mere knowledge that people are behaving in ways they find objectionable, they are also perfectly capable of "getting over" that sort of initial response.

As always, in a debate of this sort it is helpful to clarify terminology. At least some candidates running for political office were clearly formulating their official views on marriage rights based on careful polling. I'm not sure anyone really believed at the time, or believes now, that despite their official positions Hilary Clinton and Barack Obama were opposed to gay marriage when they ran for political office.[6] But they were worried about the vote in certain key swing states. It became clear, however, that many opposed to gay marriage had little or no complaints about gay people drawing up contracts that looked suspiciously like marriage contracts. The primary differences, of course, between the official marriage of two people and two people entering into a "marriage-like" contract are federal and state tax benefits that go with the former.[7] We'll talk more about tax codes in the next chapter. It is not clear to me why we want a tax code that rewards people for the mere fact that they are married (as opposed to helping people who have various sorts of dependents). In any event, the more one thinks about marriage as a contract, the more obvious it seems to a lot of people that there is no reason, in principle, to restrict various people from entering into these sorts of contracts.

We do want freedom of religion, at least when the practice of that religion does not have strongly negative consequences (more about this later), and it is hard to see why anyone would care if various religions want to put a superscript beside their use of the term "married" so that it means "a marriage officially sanctioned by such and such a church." So Catholics could say even after Jane and Samantha were married that they are nevertheless not married. And members of Islam could say they are not married. One of the easiest freedoms to defend is the freedom for someone to superscript terms as they please. (How would one even try to stop it?) We would then be left with the question of whether tax benefits should go only to people who are correctly described with a superscripted "married," or whether there is an official government document certifying marriage that gets all the work done. Again, we'll need to talk about tax codes and how rational decisions are made about such matters later.

Those who worry a great deal about broadening the legal (as in recognized by government) understanding of marriage, will sometimes bring up all sorts of other possibilities, like the worry that this would be a slippery slope leading to the recognition of various forms of polygamy. The reaction to this worry is, ironically, quite divided. One group is horrified at the suggestion that one should associate gay marriage with anything as morally problematic as polygamous marriage; the other (probably the significant minority) are content to allow any number of people to enter into a marriage contract.[8] If two people can fall in love and want to live together with legal protections afforded by a marriage contract, why can't three, or four, or five people love each other and enter into the kind of contract that gives them those same protections? It is certainly a good question, and if there is an answer, it has to do with the sheer practical difficulties of writing the relevant contracts, particularly once there are children that issue from the polygamous marriage.[9] As it is, divorce is a nasty enough business. There are often hard-fought and ugly legal fights over custody. Almost any humane person worries about children caught in the middle of such disputes, children who end up spending some of the time with one parent and some of the time with the other. One can only shudder at the prospects of legal fights concerning the custody of those children raised by the polygamous, five-parent family.[10] Problems concerning the "division" of custody would be paralleled by problems concerning the "division" of property. Prenuptial agreements in polygamous marriage arrangements and attempts to figure out which funds were co-mingled, and which were not would keep lawyers in business for years, should polygamous marriage become common. Complexity of contracts is not, in itself, a reason not to recognize them as legally binding, but again, children can't look after themselves, and we collectively may well want to do what we can to minimize their exposure to serious potential harm.

Other consequentialist arguments against allowing gay marriage, or, for that matter, polygamous marriage, would need to identify the relevant bad consequences that are supposed to result from this change in our legal system. It is most natural to assume that with the legal recognition of marriage comes the legal opportunity to adopt children. The literature seems to indicate that children raised by gay couples do just as well as do children raised by heterosexual couples, so it is hard to see what the problem is.[11] There is less research on children raised in polygamous households. As we pointed out above, however, the process of adoption obviously has as one of its primary responsibilities the protection of children, and without the relevant research one could easily worry that allowing adoption rights to those involved in polygamous marriage poses unacceptable risks. The difficulty, of course, is that there is no way of preventing people from living in such arrangements, and there is no plausible way of stopping people in such relationships from producing children. The question then returns to whether the collective wants to provide any sort of *encouragement* for such families by providing tax benefits.

Drugs

The hardcore social libertarian leans toward legalizing the sale and use of just about any sort of drug, no matter how potentially addictive or self-destructive the use of the drug might be. One can hold such a position, of course, and insist that those who sell the drug make readily available any known information about the probability of its addictive nature or dangerous side effects. When it comes to most controversial drugs, the *costs* of making them easily available by making their sale and use legal are undeniable. To be sure, we can try to make something like

Mill's distinction between direct and indirect harm. But as I argued earlier, it is not clear why we should care that much about such a distinction. The form of consequentialism I defended includes, among the costs that dictate what one ought to do, *possible* consequences, even those with a very low probability of occurring. As we noted, we don't let people celebrate their favorite sport team's victories by discharging firearms in the air because we think that there is relatively low benefit and a potential (though perhaps fairly unlikely) high cost.

There are all sorts of important differences between kinds of drugs. Some drugs one can now legally buy over the counter—others one needs a prescription to buy. Some one can't get legally at all. Alcohol is clearly a kind of drug and one to which adults have ready access and to which they can easily get addicted.[12] And one doesn't need to be addicted to alcohol to get drunk. Drunk people often make unwise decisions, decisions that hurt other people. Every year, more than 10,000 residents of the United States die as a result of people driving while intoxicated.[13] Many more are seriously hurt. On college campuses, there is a very strong connection between abuse of alcohol and various forms of sexual assault.[14] And these are only the most obvious sorts of negative consequences associated with the consumption of alcohol. You will recall Mill's admission that those who wreak havoc on their own lives can hurt both those who are near to them and those who depend upon them, but also, indirectly, society as a whole. There are decidedly negative possible consequences to allowing people access to and use of alcohol.

What is true of alcohol is true of almost every other drug to which one can become addicted. There is a longstanding debate as to whether marijuana is more or less addictive than alcohol, and whether people are more less likely to behave in harmful ways when they are "high" on pot, but it is surely undeniable that there are possible negative consequences of people using marijuana similar to those of their consuming alcohol.[15] And the stronger the drug is, the more obvious the risks are. One only needs to see a heroin addict on an episode of *Cops* to realize how devastating the use of that drug can be on those who become addicted to it. All sorts of people become addicted to pain killers and when they can no longer get prescriptions from a doctor they will often turn to an underground market.[16]

So again, one hardly even needs to make the case that on consequentialist criteria for evaluating actions, there are both reasons not to use certain sorts of drugs and reasons to make their use illegal. But the real question is whether those reasons are *outweighed* by other considerations.[17] What are the potential benefits from both the use of, and the decision to make legal the use of, various sorts of drugs, even those that are potentially addictive.

Most everyone thinks that most pleasure has positive intrinsic value and most pain has negative intrinsic value. As we discussed earlier in this

book, some have famously argued that *only* pleasure has intrinsic positive value and *only* pain has intrinsic negative value. Whether or not that
is true, it seems plausible to suppose that most drugs that people want to
use either produce pleasure or help people avoid various sorts of pain.
The claim is not completely uncontroversial. In *The Republic*, Book IX,
Plato argued that many of the so-called physical pleasures (pleasure associated with what he called desire or appetite) are a kind of illusion (1974).
He suggested that desire or appetite (the kind of desire satisfaction of
which is associated with physical pleasure, e.g., hunger, thirst, sexual
desire, but also desire for luxuries of various sorts) is a kind of suffering
or pain, and that often when the desire is satisfied, all that happens is that
we move into a "neutral" state (a state that is no longer pain but is also
not a genuine pleasure). He further argued that we *confuse* the neutral
state with genuine pleasure because it seems so good *by contrast*. Even
worse, according to Plato, the more we satisfy certain sorts of desires and
appetites, the stronger they get, so all we really obtain from our pursuit
of their satisfaction is more and more pain and suffering. Again, one can
get a bit of a feel for Plato's view by thinking about the severe alcoholic or
the heroin addict. There probably does come a time in the lives of addicts
where all they really get from the drug to which they are addicted is
freedom from the intense suffering that comes from their not receiving
the drug.

It doesn't seem likely that Plato's view is the *whole* story about pleasure and the satisfaction of desire and appetite. The alcoholic and the
heroin addict may reach a point at which they no longer get any real
pleasure from satisfying their desire, but it is difficult to see how the
addiction would get started without positive reinforcement of some kind.
And the idea that there is nothing genuine about the pleasure associated
with the satisfaction of sexual desire, or desire for a fine wine or a fine
meal, seems almost bizarre. Sexual desire, thirst, and hunger may involve
an element of suffering but one can obviously get rid of the suffering in
ways that are better or worse. Eating stale bread will get rid of hunger,
but it won't give one nearly as much pleasure as eating filet minion
grilled to perfection. Still, even if we take Plato's warning with a grain of
salt, there is a genuine concern that some desires are unpleasant and do
grow stronger the more they are satisfied. The pleasure associated with
satisfying them may eventually be offset by a desire that becomes more
and more painful with its growing strength.

Whatever benefits accrue to an individual seeking pleasure (or the
avoidance of pain) from taking drugs, the cost–benefit analysis of making
illegal the sale and use of various drugs is considerably more complex.
We have already had occasion to note that the enforcement of law and
the punishment of those who break the law always brings with it substantial costs. And we also acknowledged that this, by itself, cannot be a
decisive reason against having a law. It is an empirical question as to

which laws are effective in actually modifying behavior, how expensive the laws will be to enforce, and how expensive the cost will be of imposing sanctions on those who break the law once they are apprehended. The United States did try once to enforce laws prohibiting the sale and consumption of alcohol. The results were decidedly mixed. While the percentage of people who drank alcohol actually did go down substantially under prohibition, there also developed a huge industry built on the illegal sale of alcohol.[18] And with that illegal underground came all sorts of violence that affected not only those vying with each other for control of a market, but bystanders who became victims of an increasingly powerful criminal underworld. One can make a strong case for the conclusion that we should have learned from the experiment with prohibition that we would encounter precisely the same problem with the attempt to enforce laws against the use of other so-called recreational drugs. There is obviously a huge and violent criminal industry associated with the transportation, sale, and consumption of marijuana, cocaine, heroin, opioids, and other drugs. When we try to get serious about the enforcement of such laws, our prisons become depressingly full of the economically worst off of our citizens — people who turned to the sale of drugs to make easy money and people who turned to the use of drugs to help themselves deal with their horrible situations.

With all of this in mind, more and more mainstream politicians are urging that we begin to emphasize treatment instead of incarceration as a way of dealing with the large numbers of people faced with addiction. But it is not at all clear that this will change very much the costs we are worrying about. We will need to decide whether we are going to *force* people to get treatment or merely make treatment *accessible*. If the former, we will still need laws and something very much like due process to carry out the enforced treatment. And my guess is that the recidivism rate wouldn't be all that much lower than it is for those who we currently put in prison. After all, most of those who serve a prison term have a forced detoxification program, and most of them also return to their habits when they leave prison.[19] One will also need to decide whether various attempts at treating those with addictions should be "on record" so that the history of such people would show up when they apply for a gun permit, or, for that matter, a job. It is all well and good to want to maximize the chances of those who kick an addiction to get gainful employment that might turn their lives around, but there are all sorts of jobs where one would surely want to know whether the applicant has had an addiction that might well resurface.[20]

Those who feel that they are perfectly capable of using recreational drugs responsibly will, no doubt, argue that they should not be penalized for the fact that there are all kinds of people who do vile things while under the influence of drugs. While there is the danger that someone's use of alcohol might lead to that person becoming addicted or behaving in dangerous ways after getting drunk, we don't want to lose sight of the fact that many people enjoy a cocktail (or two) before dinner and a couple of glasses of wine with dinner. Why should they be forced to alter their behavior to prevent the possibility of poor behavior by others who can't drink responsibly? And what we say about alcohol would presumably apply, *mutatis mutandis*, to other drugs. To respect the relevant distinctions, we should do the obvious: criminalize certain sorts of *behavior* (whether it is caused by drug use or caused by anything else for that matter) and leave people alone who aren't hurting anyone through their conservative and harmless use of drugs.

In chapter 4, we have already had occasion to note that the notion of an act that does not hurt anyone else is difficult to define, and we will face inexorable pressure to expand the relevant concept of harming another until just about anything remotely controversial that one does will fail the relevant test for not hurting anyone else. Certainly, one can't insist that one's actions are benign just because they are taken in the confines of one's home. Parents, for example, may be risking the wellbeing of young children under their care if they overuse drugs (including prescription pain medication) while they are supposed to be looking after the kids. But then we already have laws protecting children from endangerment, and if we make the distinction between using drugs and acting dangerously while using the drugs, we just need to be prepared to enforce vigorously the relevant law in cases where endangerment is caused by people in too toxic a state to make rational decisions.

Even when one is alone in one's house and one has taken mind-altering substances that render one irrational, there is still the risk posed by the fact that there is no telling what a wildly irrational actor might do. But here one must calculate the risk and weigh it against the cost of living in a society where the state is so intrusive that it can dictate in this sort of detail what an individual with no assignable responsibilities is doing, either on his or her own, or with other adults who have decided to engage in the same activity. One might think about framing laws that take into account a person's history of behaving irresponsibly while using drugs. Probabilities matter, and the fact that I get drunk every night but have no history of doing anything but watching old movies while in such a state makes me a much lower risk of causing mischief to others than someone else who has the same pattern of getting drunk, and who has a long history of heading downtown to engage in all sorts of obnoxious behavior. But it wouldn't be easy to draft such legislation and, intuitively, it doesn't leave appropriate room for people who actually succeed in changing for the better. Their past history, while still showing up in statistics that are relevant to probability, is no longer relevant to the kind of person they are now. One can also try to write all of *that* into law, but it won't be easy.

I have been talking mainly about so-called recreational drugs — drugs whose original purpose at least included various sorts of pleasure associated with their use. As a matter of fact, their use by some is also a form of self-medication. One can cut the edge off boredom, depression, and physical pain, at least initially, with recreational drugs. But there is also a huge problem with the over-use of prescription pain killers, anti-depressants, sleep aids, and the like. As with every other sort of self-destructive behavior, the harm will almost always reach others. The hard-core libertarian might insist that we can afford to let people destroy themselves when we have done what is necessary to ensure that they have detailed information (or as much as we know) about the product they use. The price is worth paying to ensure that we live in a land that respects privacy and private property. That may well be true, but we must be clear about what precisely the price is that we are paying.

Ever since we started talking about the harm principle, it has been a recurring worry, one raised by Mill himself, that one can't destroy one's own life without hurting others, at least indirectly. He talked about the fact that those engaged in self-destructive behavior will often render themselves unable to benefit others — they become guilty of harming society through their inaction. But importantly, he also talked about such people becoming a burden on the affections of others. Society or, more accurately, the collective that makes decisions in a given society, will need to decide what to do with those who are in the chains of addictions that are not only destroying their ability to work for a living but, in some cases, are slowing killing them. The problem is that they typically don't just die. Rather, they get very sick and need care, sometimes long-term care. And such care is expensive. In our current health-care system there is a decent chance that they are uninsured.[21] When such people show up at a public hospital, we could, of course, ask for the insurance and turn them away when they don't have it. That's a hard thing to do, though. That is the burden on our affection about which Mill talked. And the problem isn't solved even were we to turn to a something like a single-payer health-care system. The costs of our health care don't show up in the form of premiums we pay, but it is a cost, nevertheless. It might be perfectly rational to conclude that people who so abuse themselves that they require extensive health care are simply a drain on our resources. Again, the collective could refuse to spend its resources on people who have a demonstrated pattern of substance abuse, or force them to rely on the mercy of various charitable organizations. But the psychological burden on normal people to help those in need is enormous — one I think we would always be willing to pay.

The bottom line, I think, is that one can't make a case for the legalization of drugs based on the observation that drug users aren't going to hurt anyone but themselves. Society does have an interest in such matters, even if it decides that on balance it would be better to err on the side of legalization and take the money saved to spend on treatment and health care, or anything else that improves quality of life in such a way that it might make drug use less desired by many people.

Living Dangerously

What was said about the controversies involving the legalization of drugs applies more generally to all sorts of other dangerous activities that many would restrict by law. Consider two relatively trivial issues: laws requiring people to use seatbelts when driving a car, and laws requiring people to wear helmets while riding motorcycles, bikes, skateboards, and so on. All states now require the use of seatbelts. Ironically, although riding a motorcycle without wearing a helmet is far more dangerous than driving a car without wearing a seatbelt, a number of states do not mandate the use of helmets. For all I know, riding a bicycle without wearing a helmet is more dangerous than driving a car without wearing a seatbelt, but, again, far fewer states try to mandate the former.

We are not here talking about the wisdom of driving without a seatbelt or not using a helmet while doing things that could easily involve an accident resulting in a serious head injury. I must confess that I don't like wearing a seat belt. I grew up not using one and I still find seat belts uncomfortable. I suppose, however, I'm inclined to agree that I'm at least slightly irrational for being willing to take such a risk. I used to ride a motorcycle without a helmet, but even as I was doing it, it did occur to me that I was behaving idiotically. I simply cannot get used to the idea of riding a bike while wearing a helmet. Again, this attitude is no doubt traceable to the fact that when I was a kid you would have been laughed off the planet had you shown up at school wearing a helmet while riding a bicycle. But again, let's not debate how foolish it is to take various sorts of risks. The question at hand is whether even if such behavior involves irrational risk, we should make it *illegal* for people to take the risk.

What I said about the cost of allowing people to engage in potentially self-destructive drug use applies even more obviously to those who engage in risky behavior. The hopelessly addicted may easily become a burden on our affections. But the motorcyclist who becomes a vegetable after his motorcycle skids on loose gravel presents the same problem. In the spirit of freedom, we might suggest that this sort of behavior is a problem for insurance companies. They could issue policies that are null and void should an accident victim suffer injuries while driving without a seatbelt or riding a bike without a helmet. But someone will still drag the now uninsured person to the hospital and we (collectively) must still decide whether to spend a potentially huge amount of money caring for that person. If we become the kind of people who can bring ourselves to refuse that person care, we might also become the kind of people who become calloused in a way that spells trouble for our interactions with others in society.

It is difficult to think through many of these issues clearly and consistently. We gave examples above of actions that one might consider dangerous and that might involve direct or indirect harm to others. But the list of foolish, dangerous, and unhealthy choices that people are currently allowed to make goes on indefinitely. Given the amount of beef and fried chicken wings I eat, I'm sure I'm doing a pretty good job of hardening my arteries, raising my blood pressure, and increasing the risk of a debilitating stroke. My insurance will probably cover such matters, but the cost of insurance rises for everyone the more people there are who are like me. On a single-payer plan, the distribution of costs to others is even more straightforward. Insurance companies (private or state) could write policies designed to take into account differences in lifestyle of this sort. I've heard, for example, that if you are young, you will pay more to insure a red car than another car of the same value but painted a different color. The insurance company has statistics that show an increased correlation between the kind of person who buys a red car with the kind of person who has accidents. But the more insurance policies are written in such a way that they are invalid when the insured does not comply with various conditions, the more often we face that problem of what to do with someone who suffers serious injuries and who can't pay for the relevant treatment.

People, at least a lot of people, don't like to live bland lives. Most people like to do at least some things that are risky. Sometimes the risk is short term—sometimes, it is long term. As I indicated earlier, I have a good friend and colleague whose sport is climbing. As I understand it, climbing is one of the most dangerous hobbies one can have (per capita). I know others whose life-long dream is to climb Everest, an endeavor that is, as I said earlier, a bit like playing Russian roulette. It's not a terribly difficult climb (in terms of what it requires by way of technique). Your success depends largely on your body's ability to cope with the high altitudes and luck with respect to weather systems that can come screaming in so quickly that one can't do anything about them. I played hockey and I personally know people who play professional football. Both sports are fun, and both sports are dangerous in various ways. The fact that most of us do want to add a little color and texture to our lives is probably what explains the rationality of our willingness to "subsidize" risk by implicitly agreeing to look after those whose gambles go badly. To be sure, my first reaction to kicking in resources to pay for the long-term care of the rock climber might be negative. But I also know that there are things I do, that my children do, and that my grandchildren will probably do, that might leave us in a similar position. I'll no doubt be encouraging those I love not to take the most foolish of risks that seem to me to carry little in the way of possible reward, but they'll probably take at least some of those risks anyway. Given the way of the world, the vicissitudes of fate, and human nature that seems to have remained rather constant over at least thousands of years, I can see the collective that makes up a society deciding to deal with the situation with a kind of compromise. I'll back your stupid decisions that turn out badly if you'll do the same for me.

In the next chapter, we'll talk more about how plausible it is to suppose that policies and law come into being as the result of a kind of implicit contract. The view has had many proponents and equally many critics. But as we pointed out earlier, if we have decided to own things collectively and to achieve great goods by acting together, we need some decision-making procedures for what to do with what we own and what actions we want to take collectively. It is hard to see how some conception of bargaining won't fit into a plausible story.

Guns

I'm not concerned here with the legal issue of how to interpret the Second Amendment to the U.S. Constitution. That issue is certainly difficult given the amendment's preamble about the need for a well-ordered militia and the general context in which the amendments were written.[22] There are also larger issues concerning what constraints there should be on a plausible interpretation of the Constitution.[23] Even if we embrace the basic idea behind original intent as a guide to interpreting the Constitution, one must surely allow that the framers couldn't have had specific intent with respect to what they wanted the *future* to include under the extension of the expression "arms." The most one could do is try to figure out what they *would* have wanted to include *were* they to know something about advances in technology. And it is notoriously difficult to speculate intelligently about such matters. In any event, as we noted earlier, the court has created various standards of scrutiny. Even if we could resurrect the framers of the Constitution and we discovered that they would have included nuclear-tipped missiles in one's backyard as a firearm in precisely the sense that they intended, the Supreme Court would no doubt have decided that there is a "compelling state interest" to prohibit a private individual from owning a "firearm" of that sort. For present purposes, let's talk about the issue as if we had the ability to alter significantly the law as it is. The Constitution, after all, is difficult to change, but it isn't impossible to change. If a good argument can be made for restricting the legal freedom to own firearms, then we ought to seriously consider taking the steps necessary to make that happen.

By now, the consequentialist refrain for how to approach controversies like this may be becoming tiresome for the reader. There are costs to allowing people to own the kind of guns that can easily be bought on the open market. Some people get angry enough to want to do violence to others; some people go crazy and imagine all sorts of insidious plots against them, plots that lead them to engage in some sort of misguided, preemptive self-defense; some people get caught up in the grips of wild theories—theories that involve accomplishing goals through attacks on others; a depressingly large number of people in large cities are members of gangs whose lives are defined by hatred and acts of violence toward others; some people turn to a life of crime and are sometimes prepared to carry out those crimes with violence. Typically, violence is easier to carry out by people with guns. A gun is the proverbially great equalizer. You can be twenty years younger than I am and outweigh me by fifty pounds of solid muscle, but if I'm carrying a Glock and you are carrying a knife, I'm in the driver's seat.

Just as some people can become dangerous to others, some can find themselves in the depths of depression—a depression that can cause them to entertain thoughts of suicide. There are all sorts of ways to kill oneself, but if one is acting on impulse, the use of a gun is one of the easiest and surest way to accomplish the goal. Finally, there will always be some incidence of tragic accidents when people own firearms. Some of those accidents involve children. To be sure, people who practice proper gun safety can minimize those accidents, but children can be innovative in getting what they want, and even adults with the best of intentions can forget to lock a drawer or a gun case.

Just as there are costs involved in allowing people to own guns, there are also benefits. The most obvious is that people can defend themselves against attack by others.[24] In a well-ordered society, the need to use a firearm in self-defense is exceedingly rare, but there are well-documented cases in which innocent people have saved their lives because they were able to defend themselves against people bent on doing them harm. There are examples of even more dramatic cases in which people have saved others from harm through a well-timed use of firearms.

There are also those who claim that there is strong evidence of a connection between areas of the country in which there are permissive right-to-carry laws and reduction of violent crime (Lott Jr. 2010). Establishing *causal* connections when there are so many variables for which it is difficult to control is challenging at best.[25] But there certainly is no established connection between gun ownership or right-to-carry laws and *increased* crime. Apparently, in the "wild" West, when there were very few restrictions on carrying a firearm, the per capita instance of death or injury due to firearms was lower than it is today.[26] The guns weren't as good back then and even at short range it is surprisingly difficult to hit what you are aiming at with a Colt revolver, but knowing that your use of a firearm might well be matched by someone else's effective response might also have been a deterrent. In today's world, it is almost common sense that if one's business is crime, one wouldn't set up that business in a neighborhood where large numbers of people are carrying weapons. To be sure, crimes of passion probably aren't affected by such calculations. All sorts of studies suggest, again unsurprisingly, that in the heat of passion people just aren't thinking much about consequences, one way or the other.[27]

Self-defense is only one consideration that leads many to feel passionately about having a legal right to own weapons. Like many other countries, the United States has a long tradition of people who hunt for sport. It would be more sporting, I suppose, if hunters used bows, and bows are far less likely to be used effectively in causing harm to other people. But trying to kill a pheasant with a bow and arrow would be an exercise in frustration for most people. You need a shotgun, and a shotgun is precisely the sort of weapon that can do a lot of damage in the hands of someone who is deranged or otherwise bent on violence. The argument that freedom to own guns is necessary for the sport of hunting is, of course, highly controversial. Increasing numbers of people think that killing animals, even for food, is immoral. The number of vegetarians and even vegans is on the rise. And they probably aren't that impressed with the hunters' plea that they be allowed to blow birds out of the sky with a shotgun. With very few exceptions, hunters (in the United States) can hardly make the argument that they *need* to hunt for food. These days, it is almost always more expensive to get food through hunting than it is to wait for the next sale at your local grocery store.

The most controversial argument for allowing people to own guns, even sophisticated automatic weapons, returns to the idea of self-defense. This time, however, it is not the desirability of defending yourself from other *individuals* acting lawlessly. It is, rather, the fear that one's government could go rogue and begin tyrannizing its own people. The thought is that a well-armed populace would make such a government's ability to achieve such an end much more difficult. It is not wildly implausible to suppose that the Second Amendment's prominent place in the Bill of Rights reflects precisely the concern that people should be in a position to defend their freedoms from all possible threats, including threats from a government that turns to tyranny.

This argument is ridiculed by many. They argue that it is only the fringe elements of a libertarian movement that indulge in these sorts of paranoid worries. Our country is the paradigm of a stable democracy that has a Constitution and respects it. There is a justifiable sense of pride every time a president loses an election, makes a gracious speech, and turns over power to the person who won. It is, however, worth remembering, once again, that if we are consequentialists, we do need to take into account possible, even if highly unlikely, consequences of actions in deciding what it is rational to do. Though we have fought the deadly Civil War, two world wars, the Korean War, the Vietnam War, and the ongoing war on terrorism, we have been relatively lucky to avoid facing the kind of economic disaster that can lead people down the darkest of paths. As it is, we haven't always behaved in admirable ways. The fear that gripped us in World War II caused the government to intern more than one hundred thousand Japanese living in the United States legally. Many were U.S. citizens. And that decision was supported enthusiastically by the vast majority of Americans.

History should teach rational people lessons, and one of those lessons is that desperate people act in desperate ways. Although he didn't win a majority, Hitler came to power through election. His country faced the ravages of hyperinflation. It was literally cheaper to wallpaper your house with currency than to buy wallpaper. When people feel that kind of desperation, they sometimes look to the most bombastic and "patriotic" of politicians for salvation. And those politicians are sometimes truly dangerous people. It is obviously unclear as to what a well-armed populace might have been able to do once it became evident what a Hitler, a Stalin, a Castro, a Mao, or an Assad was going to do to gain power and try to keep it through force, but it is clear that you would have a better *chance* of fighting for your freedom if you had a decent weapon and ammunition. So, at the risk of aligning myself with the paranoids, I don't think that this argument for having a Second-Amendment right to own sophisticated weapons is *frivolous*.

If one were arguing as a deontologist, one might worry that acknowledging a "right" of this sort would force one to the untenable position that private citizens should be allowed to own literally any sort of weapon. After all, if we are worried about the possibility of defending ourselves against our own government, shouldn't we allow people who can afford it to buy and deploy ballistic weapons in their backyard? But consequentialism allows one to make subtle distinctions. There are slippery slopes, but along these slopes the probabilities and potential disastrous consequences continue to change. We noted earlier that the existence of *sorites* paradoxes doesn't imply that we can't make perfectly useful distinctions, even while we concede that there will be grey areas. It is already bad enough that allowing people to own guns forces us to live with the risk that some lunatic will force his way into a school and randomly shoot the most innocent of the innocent. Perhaps we can conclude that this is a risk with which we should live. But it is surely not the case that we would be willing to live with the possibility of a potential lunatic unleashing the devastation of a missile aimed at the center of one of our largest cities. Am I prepared to draw a clear line? Will I tell you which weapons we should allow people to own and which we shouldn't? No. We would need to take each example on a case-by-case basis. We would also almost certainly want screening of potential owners of dangerous weapons, screening that needn't be the same for ownership of *all* kinds of weapons.

Really hard-core libertarians are worried that the government will eat away at Second-Amendment legal rights by gradually increasing restrictions on who can legally own firearms. A rational consequentialist, however, won't give much weight to this concern. The American people, it seems to me, have it more or less right. We see the Sandy Hook killer and justifiably wonder why we don't have mental health background checks that would prevent *that* person from ever legally purchasing a gun. There are very real practical concerns here. As the slogan goes, mental health problems should be treated as an illness like any other. And once one treats mental disease as a health issue, one surely wants to allow for the possibility that a person can get "better." Those who propose effective background checks for the legal purchase and ownership of a gun, however, will probably be justifiably skeptical about people who claim to be "cured."[28] As a result, it may well turn out that rational gun laws will prevent at least some now perfectly rational people from owning a gun. But that, I would argue, is a sensible price one should be willing to pay for the freedom most of us will have to own and even carry firearms. And, as I suggested earlier, I do think that the "tests" one needs to pass for the legal ownership of weapons should probably vary depending on what the weapon is. One can do a lot of damage with a shotgun, but one can do far more with an AK-47. One can do even more with grenades. I don't see why one shouldn't ratchet up the tests one needs to pass in order to purchase and legally own more deadly weapons. To be sure, I suppose such an approach might lead some to worry about seeking psychological help early in life. If such records are going to follow one through life, stripping from one legal right that others enjoy, then there probably will be some who forgo treatment that would help them. But the likelihood of this is small. And when we are doing cost–benefit analysis, it will probably not factor heavily in our ultimate decisions about what it is rational to do.[29]

Prostitution, Gambling, and Other Controversial Lifestyle Choices

Defenders of the harm principle trying to use that principle to find illegitimate interference with decisions that adults might make have often turned their attention to prostitution, gambling, and related lifestyle choices that people might make. We have argued against using the harm principle to decide controversies over freedom, but we have also allowed that consequentialist reasoning will often favor a conclusion on the side of freedom when we can't identify serious and relatively close harms associated with someone's choice. When we search for victimless crimes, prostitution always comes up as a potentially plausible candidate. Prostitution is typically nothing more than a contract between two people where one agrees to have sex in exchange for money, or something else of value. We'll talk more about contracts in the next chapter. At least some current restrictions on what will count as a valid contract seem more than reasonable. It is not difficult to imagine enormous harm that comes from allowing minors to enter into contracts that they are not equipped to evaluate. But let us stipulate that the kind of prostitution we are considering here involves the acceptance of relevant contracts between consenting adults in full possession of their reason.

It is not difficult to identify various benefits that result from allowing legal prostitution. The most obvious is that at least one party to the contract presumably gets sexual pleasure. And pleasure is surely a good candidate for something that has value. The prostitute may or may not receive any pleasure but does receive payment that can in turn be used to purchase various goods and services. There are always two sides to the ledger, however, and one can legitimately fear that prostitution has a coarsening effect on virtually everyone involved. It is hard for some of us to understand what sort of person would get much pleasure from a physical act involving another person who has no interest in you as a person. I wouldn't deny, of course, that there is an element of pleasure, but the pleasure would be so much more enhanced if there were at least some degree of intimacy involved. One can't help but worry that legalized prostitution makes it that much easier for people to turn away from a path that leads to deeper and more lasting pleasure.

There is also no getting away from the fact that the life of a prostitute is often a nasty, gritty, life. The money may be relatively easy to make, but the cost of making that money in terms of any sort of positive self-image is dear. It is also a dangerous life. As with abortion and drugs, it is clear that making prostitution illegal won't stop it. And however dangerous the "profession" is when legal, it is even more dangerous when illegal. At least if prostitution were legal it could be regulated so as to minimize such concerns as the spread of STDs. But every time we discuss this particular concern, we need to emphasize that whenever we make the sale and distribution of some product or service illegal, there will almost always be an underground, often a dangerous underground, that will still sell the product or the service. That, therefore, can't by itself be a conclusive reason to refrain from passing laws. But it is always a cost that must be factored in along with other costs and benefits.

In the final analysis, one of the reasons to err on the side of liberty with respect to prostitution is the difficulty of even making clear conceptual distinctions between prostitution and other contractual or quasi-contractual arrangements that aren't all that dissimilar from prostitution. It is no great secret that at least some people marry for money. They don't particularly like their spouse or enjoy the relevant sexual companionship. But they are willing to "sell" their companionship and sexual services for a financially comfortable existence. I suppose it is a bit less seedy than soliciting a prostitute online for a weekend of sexual activity, but it really isn't a whole lot different from legalized prostitution. The practical difficulty of preventing such relationships, even if we wanted to do so, would be insurmountable, but given that this is so, why would we want to stop people from seeking their own short-term financial gain from engaging in feigned intimacy? We took note of the fact that being a prostitute is probably almost always a nasty way of making a living, and we might think that it is an act of kindness to remove the temptation to make easy money that way. But it is not as if there aren't thousands of jobs that are equally nasty and that we not only legally allow but encourage people to take. I wouldn't want to be a garbage man, a dentist, a mine worker, a maid, a gardener, a roofer, or a policeman working in vice. We do, however, need people to do such things, and we wouldn't dream of saving such people from the temptation to take jobs that might wear on them but also pay their bills. It is hard to see where we will go if we start placing restrictions on the kinds of jobs people can take when there is an obvious market for their services.

Almost everything that we said about prostitution applies to other attempts to make illegal various forms of vice. People do get addicted to gambling. Like a drug addict, a gambling addict can destroy his or her life, and with it the lives of the addict's dependents. There are real costs to a society that makes gambling easy, particularly for those who aren't in a position to deal with their losses. But there are also benefits. I know gamblers, probably addicted gamblers, who can afford their losses and who do get considerable enjoyment from their gambling. And even the patrons of local stores who purchase their lotto tickets no doubt get short-lived pleasure from the fact that they hold in their hand at least the dream of a brighter future. When the dream becomes an obsession, problems loom on the horizon. But for many, the occasional purchase of a lottery ticket is a relatively cheap, harmless distraction from an often-dreary life.

As with prostitution, there is an element of dissonance in the attempt to make illegal certain forms of gambling when it is literally impossible to live one's life without gambling. Every time one gets on a plane, one gambles with one's life. Winning the gamble is getting to one's destination quickly with minimal wear and tear. One way of losing is dying in a fiery plane crash. It is a good bet given the relevant probabilities. Driving a car, walking on a sidewalk, and getting married all involve risks, but the relevant gambles are usually pretty good.

One might complain that the above comments torture the ordinary meaning of "gamble." I don't really think that is true, but even if there were some danger of equivocating on the notion of a gamble, almost all of us make investments as part of our retirement plans. These investments are classic examples of gambles and are *described* using the language of gambling. One's investments can be more or less risky. Some of the most lucrative possible gains are matched by equally heavy losses. But I take it that no one, at least no one who broadly buys into the American political and economic system, would contemplate laws prohibiting people from investing in housing, the stock market, securities, and the like.

There are differences among different forms of gambling and I'm not suggesting that one couldn't try to capture those differences in deciding what to make illegal. The kind of gambling that has been targeted by many states is typically "all or nothing" in terms of winning or losing. If you bet on a football game or buy a lottery ticket, there is almost always a good chance that you will lose your entire "investment."[30] As a matter of empirical fact, it is also probably the case that those who can least afford this sort of gambling are particularly inclined to make the relevant bets. It's easy to do and it doesn't require much in the way of planning or prior investigation. It is *designed* for those who make impulsive decisions based on little or no thought about the future. And it is probably more addictive than investing in land or a stock market.[31]

When all is said and done, however, it does seem to me that the vast majority of people are perfectly capable of enjoying all sorts of gambling and are perfectly capable of keeping it under control. It seems no more reasonable for us to collectively deny ourselves the pleasures of gambling and the good of making a free choice about whether to gamble or not, than it is to deny ourselves the option of buying a doughnut for desert just because there are people who are obese and have difficulty controlling their desire for sweets.

Safety and Surveillance

Not long before I wrote this part of the book, controversies concerning the extent to which we ought to allow the government to engage in surveillance were on the proverbial hot burner. After Paris was attacked by terrorists, the French government wanted broader powers to conduct surveillance on its citizens. The United States crossed that bridge after 9/11, when it passed the Patriot Act.

As with some of the other controversies discussed above, I want to separate the questions with which we are primarily concerned from questions about the current constitutionality in the United States of taking various sorts of actions. The latter debate often centers on subtle distinctions between "block" data gathering (surveillance that allows the government to monitor where calls and e-mail are sent and received), and surveillance of the specific *content* of an individual's calls or e-mail. When the framers worried about illegal search and seizure, it is hardly clear what precisely they would or wouldn't object to in today's technological age.

The potential harm of not engaging in the kind of surveillance that the United States currently does is clear. It is sometimes through monitoring patterns of calls that one discovers leads that eventually allow the government to foil potential acts of horror that could kill and maim sig-

nificant numbers of innocent people. The harm of allowing intrusive surveillance is also clear. Almost of all us do value our privacy. We may not
want others to know with whom we are communicating or the subject
matter of our conversations. Even if the government says it is not interested in the content of 99.9 percent of the communications it has the
potential to access, the possibility of abuse of such programs is certainly
real.

Some of us have more of a vested interest in such privacy than others.
My conversations by phone or by e-mail tend to be boring, and I can't
honestly say that I would be that bothered by the fact that someone could
potentially eavesdrop on such conversations. As I understand the current
law, such eavesdropping would be illegal without a court order. But the
probable cause that secures such an order might be something as vague
as odd patterns discovered with respect to my calls, both here, but espe-
cially, overseas. I imagine that if I am talking frequently by cell phone to
certain people in Syria or Iran, there is an increased chance that a court
will allow government agencies to monitor my calls. I also imagine that if
I have an obsession with internet sites containing instructions on how to
make home-made bombs and where to plant such bombs so as to cause
maximum injury, I might again be the subject of a court-ordered investigation.

Many no doubt fear a slippery slope and erosion of the constitutional
concern with policing methods that might get out of control. But in the
final analysis, it seems to me that the compromises currently in place in
the United States strike a reasonable balance between our justifiable concern for privacy and an equally rational concern for safety. When police
start investigating a crime, they can't barge into your home and start
searching through your possessions. But they can ask questions of both
you and others. You don't have to answer the questions, and neither do
others, but if they get answers that start making it likely that you committed the crime, our system will allow the more intrusive investigation. To
be sure, in this case we are imagining a crime that has actually been
committed. In the surveillance involving terrorism, our goal is often to
prevent a crime before it occurs. Again, one can understand why you
would not want to be investigated in *any* sense of investigation without
the investigator having some reason to suppose that you were involved
in some specific crime. However, one is sometimes legitimately investigated for conspiracy to commit a crime before the crime actually occurs,
and I don't really see that there is all that much difference between the
kind of surveillance that bothers so many people and the kind of surveillance that always has been routine police work.

The devil is always in the details, and if it becomes evident that our
government is monitoring the content of actual conversations without
court approval, we will need to strengthen safeguards and, probably,
penalties against its doing so. That is not a practice we want legally to

allow. But I'll end this very brief discussion with a reminder of conclusions we reached earlier. There may be very good reason to have in place strict laws with harsh penalties, while there are also sometimes very good reasons for certain people to violate those laws. It is not that hard to imagine circumstances in which an emergency dictates that information be gathered very quickly, so quickly that one shouldn't wait even for an expedited court order.[32] The person who rationally violates the law may or may not benefit from prosecutorial discretion or jury nullification. It may seem odd that we would even countenance the possibility of punishing someone for behaving in precisely the way we think they ought to have behaved, but our long-term goals might dictate exactly such a response.

Freedom of Association, Freedom to Take Risk, and Pandemics

As I make final revisions to this manuscript, the world has found itself in the middle of a global pandemic. COVID-19 is in the process of killing hundreds of thousands of people. Countries, including the United States, are desperately trying to figure out how to slow and eventually stop the spread of the virus. While I write this sentence, many U.S. states are trying to enforce some sort of "stay in place" policy. They are, presumably, relying on the proposition that we face dire circumstances and that even after we take care to employ strict scrutiny, it is time to curtail such treasured freedoms as freedom of association. There are strong disagreements about what our policy should be, and that's because whatever we do, there will be enormous costs that need to be compared to possible benefits. The economic shut down devastated the economy of the United States. The economic pain will probably be felt for years to come. The current consensus is that the price we pay is worth it for the lives we save. But throughout this manuscript, I have been emphasizing the importance of careful cost–benefit analysis, a kind of analysis that will often strike many as cold and calculating. How should we approach the challenge presented by a serious pandemic?

One thing is clear to me. We can't rely on slogans. One very popular governor repeated at briefings the mantra that if we can save a single life by putting into place a given policy, then that's precisely what we ought to do. It all sounds very noble. Human life is priceless, isn't it? No. Not if the suggestion is that loss of life doesn't fall on a continuum where its disvalue can't be compensated for by enough benefits. Earlier in this book I have an endnote referencing the many thousands of people who die each year because we have raised speed limits on our interstates (chapter 5, note 24). The statistic could hardly come us a surprise to anyone. When an accident occurs involving cars traveling 75 mph, there is obviously going to be a higher chance of mortality than if that same kind of accident had occurred when the cars were traveling more slowly.

Back in the Carter years, when a severe oil shortage led the government to reduce maximum speed limits to 55 mph, we saved not only gas but also lives. And people traveling the interstates were bored out of their minds. Are we really going to sacrifice lives to avoid boredom and save a little time traveling to our destination? I actually think that the answer is "yes." We don't like to think about it, we cringe a bit if we are forced to think about it, but in the end, we will shrug our collective shoulders and live with increased risk.

The dilemma is interesting for a number of reasons. If a being we knew to be omnipotent promised us that we could travel as fast as we like on the interstate, and that being would ensure that we lost only half of what we currently lose in traffic fatalities, we would probably agree to the deal. But many of us would get cold feet if we had to select the ten thousand or so people who would face certain death. We do treat the certainty of a particular person's death quite differently from the high probability that someone or other will die. But that, I suspect, is just a fact about human psychology. I'm not sure it has anything to do with rational behavior.

Perhaps after reading the above, you will rethink societal commitment to high speed limits on interstates. But it doesn't take much imagination to extend the analogy. We require people to wear seat belts when driving. We don't require them to wear helmets. Helmets aren't that expensive and head injuries are one of the most common ways of dying in a car accident. You don't wear one and I don't wear one. Why? We have decided we will live with the risk. Still, you might argue, it is your own life you are risking when you refuse to wear a helmet and that makes a difference. It is true that it is your life you are risking directly, but we have already talked about how harming oneself involves all sorts of indirect harm to others.

In the case of draconian restrictions designed to curb the virus, those who want to risk becoming infected are told that they aren't just risking their own health, they are risking the health of others—particularly the old and those with underlying conditions. It is an empirical question as to whether we could tailor less drastic solutions to our problem in order to protect the most vulnerable. I suspect we could. But I also suspect that if we open up society and with it the economy, more people will die, including people who haven't "volunteered" to take the increased risk.

I have no particularly insightful conclusion to draw about what we ought to do in the face of this extraordinarily nasty situation. The best a philosopher can do is take a position on the kind of reasoning that should be employed. It just can't be right that the correct policy is necessarily the one that saves the most lives. Examples we have talked about throughout this book make that point painfully obvious. To be sure, a politician will get crucified in the press if that politician supports a policy that will probably cost, say, ten thousand lives and argues that a booming economy is worth that horrible price. But the idea that one needs to balance the benefits of a healthy economy against the horrors of death and the infringement of all sorts of other freedoms is not absurd. Indeed, it is the only sensible way to think about the decisions that need to be made.

NOTES

1. There is probably still an ambiguity concerning whether the "wrongness" that is part of the meaning of "murder" is moral or legal. There is certainly a sense in which we can, without contradiction, conclude that someone has committed murder even though the law allows the killing. The Nazis murdered millions of people and the immoral killing was legally permitted.

2. It is worth reminding the reader that all of this talk about what has value can be translated by the subjectivist into talk about what is valued.

3. McMahan (2007) argues that there is no moral difference between a fetus and a newborn. He also argues that some moral philosophers are hesitant to take this suggestion seriously for fear of backlash—yet another example of pressure that academics sometimes feel to limit candid expression of their views. Bermudez (1996) argues that newborns have a kind of self-awareness that fetuses cannot have. It's hard to know how one could be very sure of that, and, in any event, I doubt that it would distinguish newborns from cows and pigs.

4. Where we would all surely concede that our aesthetic reactions are often conditioned in large part by our cultural environment.

5. And that public opinion is also finding expression in legal opinion. See, for one example, *Obergefell v. Hodges* (2015).

6. See McCullom (2007) and Feldman (2011) for critical assessments of the political calculations that went into Clinton and Obama's decisions not to support marriage equality.

7. There are others that vary from state to state. Visitation rights in hospitals, the fact that there are all sorts of default legal rights that come to partners in a marriage, and so on. On the rather large list of federal benefits of marriage, see US GAO-04-353R Defense of Marriage Act (2004).

8. For a powerful defense of the view that we should broaden legally defined marriage to include polyamorous groups and even just good friends, see Brake (2012). Cheshire Calhoun (2005) argues that as a matter of contingent fact most actual polygamous marriages leave women with diminished power.

9. See Metz (2010) for a defense of the view that we should just replace state recognized marriage with contracts of various sorts.

10. For a discussion of various issues involving the well-being of children raised in various sorts of families, see Garrett (2013).

11. For an extensive survey of studies that seem to overwhelmingly support this conclusion, see https://whatweknow.inequality.cornell.edu/topics/lgbt-equality/what-does-the-scholarly-research-say-about-the-wellbeing-of-children-with-gay-or-lesbian-parents/.

12. Sher (2003) argues that consistency would require one to treat alcohol the same as almost every other drug to which one can become addicted. He concludes, however, by suggesting that, all things considered, we should continue to make alcohol consumption legal (and by parity of reasoning, make most other drugs legal as well).

13. See Expert Center blog entry "DUI Statistics" (n.d.).

14. See Reed, et al. (2009) for a survey of various forms of violence connected with substance abuse, and data on the connection between alcohol use and sexual assault (212). See also Bryan et al. (2016).

15. See Weiss and Wargo (2017) and Gorelick (2014).

16. As I work on this manuscript, the opioid "crisis" is front and center in political dialogue.

17. For a nuanced discussion of these issues, see Husak (2007). Among other things, Husak casts doubt on the claim that criminalizing drugs has a significant deterrent effect. He also argues that many of the deaths attributed to drug use are actually caused by other diseases associated with those who use drugs.

18. And even on the empirical issue concerning the effect on consumption, studies don't agree. Blocker (2006) argues that alcohol consumption did go down under prohibition. Miron (1998) argues that there was no substantial change.

19. See Binswanger et al. (2007) for depressing facts about the deadly consequences of recidivism among those released from prison.

20. You wouldn't want a pilot who was a recovering drug abuser, and the same sort of consideration applies to anyone whose work has life and death implications.

21. For statistics, see Pollack (2013).

22. See Barnett and Kates (1996) for a discussion of this particular interpretive question.

23. For a survey of these sorts of issues, see Waluchow (2012). And for a discussion of how to understand plausibly "original intent), see Barnett (1999).

24. For an excellent discussion of this and other issues related to controversies over whether we should restrict gun ownership, see Huemer (2003).

25. Dixon (2011) argues that ownership of guns do not make people safer. Berstein et al. (2015) argue the opposite.

26. See DiLorenzo (2010). The story is complicated, however. Parts of the "wild" West weren't so very wild, and many towns had restrictions on carrying firearms.

27. The evidence is clearly not unequivocal. There are too many variables to control them effectively and too many differences between people to suggest that it never deters. For an extensive study, see Nagin and Pepper (2012). See also Van Den Haag (2010).

28. Diseases such as paranoia or schizophrenia are notoriously difficult to control. Drugs certainly help, but the victims of such diseases often go off the drugs, and the dose of the drugs needed to control these diseases can vary significantly, depending on a wide range of conditions.

29. Once medical records are kept and potentially made public, there is probably a much more serious concern about one's medical records affecting one's potential to get certain sorts of jobs. The pilot who killed hundreds of people by crashing his plane into the side of a mountain was receiving care for psychological problems. The airline that hired up may well have, probably should have, fired him were it to become aware of that information.

30. This oversimplifies actual gambling. In sports gambling one can "push." If the spread is ten points, the winning margin might be exactly ten points and the bet is essentially "off." Even some lotteries have a range of prizes, some equal to the price of the ticket. But the point is that the gambler has a good chance—in lotteries a very strong probability—of winning nothing and losing everything. And "day trading" on the stock market can become remarkably addictive. For some it is exhilarating (but also dangerous).

31. Though in the internet age, it is not that hard to get addicted to something like day trading.

32. There is a wonderful scene in the movie *Dirty Harry*. Harry has just shot in the leg a contemptible human being who buried a child alive in the hope of securing ransom. Harry tells his partner to walk away and begins to torture the suspect by running his gun up and down the open wound. One's first reaction is probably revulsion. But the camera then pans away from the scene and slowly focuses in on the coffin in which the horrified victim is experiencing unimaginable terror. Most viewers want Harry to ratchet up the torture until he gets the crucial information.

SEVEN

Economic Libertarianism

I'm not an economist and *consequentialist* defenses of various sorts of economic freedom will inevitably rest on a host of controversial empirical claims. As I indicated in chapter 1, the only hope for a *philosopher* is either to rely on what economists say or, alternatively, to argue only for conditional claims (claims about how we ought to organize society if such and such causal connections obtain). As I suggested in chapter 1, the former approach would be as problematic as a non-philosopher trying to partner with a philosopher to gain relevant philosophical input on an empirical project. Philosophers don't agree with each other all that much, at least on fundamental philosophical issues. Without being in a position to assess philosophers and philosophical views, one wouldn't be in a position to know whose views to trust and whose views to ignore.[1] One could, I suppose, just choose a philosopher based on that philosopher's reputation and hope for the best, but if we gathered five of the best philosophers who work on rational action, for example, we would probably get five significantly different approaches on how to understand and apply the relevant concept.

A similar problem would afflict any philosopher trying to partner with an economist to evaluate arguments for and against various forms of economic freedom, such as freedom from high taxation or freedom from complex regulation. Economists may not disagree with each other *quite* as much as philosophers do, but one doesn't need to do much reading in the field of economics to realize that Nobel Prize–winning economists disagree, sometimes radically, with each other about the effects of implementing various policies. So, without studying economics, how am I supposed to make an intelligent decision about whom to trust? As I indicated earlier, there are some claims about the impact of economic policies that strike me as bordering on commonsense. Even here, howev-

165

er, I will always be careful to make it clear that if I am wrong concerning an empirical claim about consequences, that error could easily affect the overall plausibility of a position I'm inclined to defend. Before we get to empirical claims, however, there is much that a philosopher can contribute simply by making careful distinctions.

PROPERTY

A great deal of the rhetoric concerning economic policy, particularly at the popular political level, invokes, either directly or indirectly, some notion of property.[2] When citizens complain about taxation, for example, they often complain about the government taking *their* money—taking something that *belongs* to them. But as we have had occasion to note earlier, but only in passing, there are a number of philosophers who would argue that the concept of property—in Hobbesian terms, the concept of *mine* vs *thine*—can exist intelligibly only in the context of a legal system that *defines* what belongs to you and what doesn't.

One can write an entire treatise critically evaluating various conceptions of property and the even more abstract notion of a justified state that often goes hand in hand with a political philosopher's views about property. The most we can hope to do in this context is clearly define the issue and make clear what hinges on the conceptual framework we endorse.

We noted above that many philosophers think that the concept of property is *legally* defined or, more cautiously perhaps, legally defined by a *legitimate* state. But there are others, like John Locke, who would reject that idea. Locke started with the intuitively plausible idea that, at the very least, each of us "owns" our own body.[3] If we are trying to find a pre-legal notion of property, after all, it might make sense to look at natural uses of possessive pronouns. These are *my* hands that I'm using to type, *my* eyes with which I view the keyboard, *my* foot I'm tapping up and down, and so on. While there is actually considerable philosophical debate about how exactly to understand the previous assertions, it does seem initially plausible, if not obvious, that their truth-makers have nothing to do with society and its legal dictates. I suppose even here, however, complications could arise. I might be one of those wretched, addicted gamblers we talked about in the last chapter who made the rather drastic decision to bet my left eye on a hand of poker. The person with whom I was playing was in desperate need of a transplant. One could probably make sense of my losing ownership of the eye once I lose the bet. The person to whom I lost it might caution me to take good care of *his* eye until he can arrange for the transplant to occur.[4] Still, even in this case, there is the thought that prior to any legal decision there were these facts about me and the body parts that are *mine*.

Looking at the use of possessives to get a pre-theoretical grip on the notion of what *belongs* to me in the sense that my property belongs to me is, at best, merely suggestive. We also feel perfectly comfortable describing someone as *my* enemy, *my* best friend, *my* favorite actor, and so on. Yet it would be absurd to infer from these natural uses of possessives that the enemy, friend, and actor should be included among my *possessions*. So perhaps Locke was assuming a great deal in taking as his starting point that each of us "owns" his or her body.

Nevertheless, however controversial, that *was* Locke's starting point (again leaving out what was probably crucial for Locke—the religious underpinnings). Beginning with this idea, Locke tried to extend the idea of my property/possessions beyond my body itself to what I produce through my body—through my labor. Initially, the idea doesn't seem absurd. I'm whittling away on a piece of wood until I produce a lovely bowl. I mix paints and produce a wonderful painting. I find some land that isn't being used by anyone, put a fence around it to keep animals out, and grow some corn on the plot of land. Isn't there some intuitive notion of property, such that the wooden bowl, the art I painted, the land I found and developed, and the fruits thereof are all mine?

It is not difficult to see philosophical clouds on the horizon. The "just so" story told above imagines a world where one could just come upon land that isn't already claimed by someone else. Obviously, in a real word inhabited by many people, disputes will arise quickly concerning whether the land you decided to use for some purpose was really "unclaimed" or "unused" land. This sort of issue becomes particularly problematic when the dispute is among people who use land for different purposes. When the Europeans came to North American, they found that at least some native tribes relied heavily on hunting for their survival and well-being. How much land is a Native American tribe "using" in the context of hunting? One possible answer is: as much as they need, a matter contingent on how difficult it is at a given time to find game. The deer that used to roam near a settlement might have moved substantially farther away, for example. When the hunters of one tribe run into the hunters of another tribe, decisions will be made—they could compromise, try to reach agreement concerning future rough and ready boundaries for their respective hunts, or start fighting with each other. But the problem doesn't just arise for hunters. Farmers typically have plans to expand their farming, perhaps to rotate crops, and perhaps to allow some of "their" land to lay fallow as a way of building up the soil's nutrients. It's not all that hard to build a fence. If I am ambitious at fence building, do I thereby possess as mine all the land I've enclosed?[5] Water has always been a particular concern to those trying to build settlements. It may be that there is a sense in which no one is using part of a river that runs far north of a given settlement, but if I claim the unused river as my own and divert the water to my land and away from yours, that will often cause an outright declaration of war. Similar hostility arises to this day when one nation feels that another is about to deprive it of waterways that it uses for transporting goods.[6]

Locke himself puts restrictions on how much land someone can claim through use of that land and how much of what is produced on that land the "owner" can legitimately claim as a possession. Locke's suggestion is that one can claim: "As much as anyone can make use of to any advantage of life before it spoils, so much he may by his labour fix a property in. Whatever is beyond this, is more than his share, and belongs to others" (1993, 130). It doesn't take subtle thought to realize that Locke's restriction isn't much of a restriction at all, particularly when one moves to a more sophisticated conception of benefits that include *possible* benefits. But consider first the obvious. I plant some apple trees and eventually I am in a position to harvest a great many apples. I can't eat them all or use them myself, at least directly, but I can sell them to those who want apples. And the more I have, the more I can sell. The Lockean principle might suggest that at the very least I should leave for others those I can neither consume nor sell, but, again, one doesn't need to be a sophisticated economist to realize that if I adopt such a policy, it might cut down on my sales. Our local grocery store Hy-Vee used to sell its unsold fresh bread for a dollar after 7 p.m. It didn't take many of its customers long to realize that it might be rational for them to wait until 7 to get their bread, and the sale of full-priced bread earlier in the day plunged.[7]

There is another way of trying to extend the idea of one's "owning" one's own body that we could easily have discussed in the previous chapter. Among the most obvious examples of things that we produce are our biological children. Certainly, we feel perfectly comfortable using the possessive in connection with them. Rob is *my* son and Tara is *my* daughter. Of course, the reverse is true as well. My children will refer to me as *their* dad. In neither case is it obvious that we really intend the use of the possessive to indicate that the person "possessed" is some kind of property. Nevertheless, some with strong libertarian leanings do seem to think that in a genuinely free state we ought to be free to raise our children as we see fit—at least within certain limits. So, in the United States most states will defer to the parents' desire to homeschool their children, albeit within a framework containing fairly strict state regulations. Most states lean toward allowing parents to make certain sorts of medical decisions concerning their children—whether or not to give the child various vaccines, for example. And it is tempting to think that in these and other matters there is at least a hint of the idea that until children become of age they *belong* to their parents, and those parents have considerable latitude with respect to what they will do with those possessions.

All this might seem initially plausible, but only if we understate the circumstances in which the rest of us will not, and should not, turn a blind eye to how a child is being raised. These days we won't let parents discipline their children in whatever manner those parents decide is best. And, at least in some states, we won't let parents deny their children medical treatment necessary to save their lives.[8] We value the lives and well-being of children and will only tolerate so much from those parents who choose to risk that well-being, even if we decide to grant them special legal rights as the guardians of those children. And, again, that is surely how it should be.

The State, the Law, and the Concept of Property

Many have this deep Lockean intuition that there is some pre-legal, pre-conventional idea of what *belongs* to us. We can give initially plausible examples. But we soon must confront the fact that there will be much disagreement as to what belongs to whom and without law *defining* what is mine and what is yours, we will face chaos. How, though, are we supposed to decide these critical matters of law? It is at this point that it is difficult to avoid an excursion into the deepest of theoretical questions concerning the nature and purpose of a rationally constructed state.

One tradition, going all the way back to a suggestion considered in Plato's *Republic,* is that society and the rules that we call law (and morality) emerge out of self-interest. In *The Republic* (1974, Book II), Glaucon suggests that rational people will quickly realize that a short-sighted, dog-eat-dog existence will frustrate at least their long-term goals. The trouble with living in a dog-eat-dog environment is that there is a decent chance that you will get eaten by a dog. Almost two thousand years later, Hobbes argues that the greatest of powers that people have is the power that they can exercise through coordinated and cooperative action (1994, 50). We can create great things, things that make life comfortable for all of us, only if we act in concert. Realizing that this is so, Hobbes argues, if we are rational agents interested in getting what we want, we will need to find ways to cooperate with one another. Glaucon's view was a mere sketch; Hobbes filled out that sketch with significantly more detail. For Hobbes (1994, 80), the specific solution to the problem of how to cooperate involved the selection of a sovereign to whose directives we agree to submit (with one crucial exception).[9] Both Glaucon and Hobbes are associated with what has come to be known as a social contract theory of the state and its authority over individuals.[10]

Social Contract Theory

There are many importantly different kinds of social contract theories. They differ with respect to what they are theories *of,* and they differ with respect to what the details of the theories are. The primary purpose of some social contract theorists is to explain the alleged obligation people have to obey the dictates of a state. In one very crude view, the idea is that we already have a fairly good grasp of obligation that is created by agreements or contracts. This version of the view starts with the idea that if you and I are rational adults who, in full knowledge of what we are doing, agree to do something, then each of us has at least a prima facie obligation to do what we agreed to do. We then seek to understand the obligation we have to obey laws, including laws that define property, in terms of either an explicit or implicit agreement that we have made to obey the dictates of some person or group of people (provided that the person or group was selected in an agreed upon way). We might call this version of the social contract theory one that is *derivative*. It is derivative in that obligations to obey the state are derivative of the more general obligations we have to keep contracts.[11] One might, of course, hold that obligations to obey contracts are *themselves* derivative. So, an act consequentialist might conclude that as a rule we ought to act in accordance with the agreements we strike, but only because in the long run we will be better off doing so. It is useful, one might argue, to be able to *assure* people that we will act in certain ways and get assurance from others that they will act in certain ways, and it is through the conventions of promising, contracting, and agreeing that we provide those assurances. Depending on the nature of the promise, contract, or agreement, the sanctions associated with breaking it might be legal. Alternatively, the sanctions may be the more informal sorts of "grief" one will get when one doesn't do what one explicitly promised or agreed to do. Once I *promise* to help you move, there is an implicit understanding we have that I can expect you to react in a hostile manner should I renege on the promise. You might, of course, accept various excuses, but at least I know I'd better be fairly creative in the excuses I give. If anything like a consequentialist justification for the rationality of keeping promises, even those that are not legally binding, can be given, then a contract theory of obligations to the state would be doubly derivative.

Despite his reputation as a social contract theorist, I suspect that Hobbes wasn't quite endorsing either of the derivative models sketched above for understanding obligation to obey law. Hobbes was very explicit (1994, 9–92) that there might be no reason to act in accordance with agreements or contracts made absent an existing state *with a sovereign to enforce those agreements or contracts*.[12] The reasons people have to obey the law once a sovereign is in place are constituted solely by the threat of the sovereign's sharp sword descending upon the neck of those who violate the sovereign's directives—directives that presumably will involve keeping contracts or agreements. It is true that Hobbes talks as if the commonwealth, and with it the sovereign, will come into existence (when a commonwealth is "instituted") *as a result* of a pact people make with one another. But the agreement that creates the commonwealth and with it the sovereign is, by hypothesis, an agreement that is made without there already being a sovereign in place to enforce contracts. Thus, by Hobbes's own lights, it is an agreement that isn't binding on rational subjects. To be sure, we might individually and collectively have good reason to go along with what we agreed to do (just as we might individually or collectively have good reason to go along with some particular agreement we make in the "state of nature"—the hypothetical state of our existence without society). But, for Hobbes, that would be contingent on whether or not acting in such a manner was in our best interest. I don't really think it matters from a Hobbesian perspective how a sovereign gets in the position of power. That is precisely why he thinks that you can end up in a satisfactory position even if your sovereign gained power over you through force. What matters is that there is in place a person or group of people (the sovereign needn't be a single person) willing to enforce laws that allow for rational, self-interested people to cooperate. Of course, this will only work if the sovereign body itself concludes that it is in *its* self-interest to put in place and enforce such laws. And here Hobbes can really only count on the assumption that a rational, *far-sighted,* sovereign will see that his, her, or their interests lie with the general well-being of the people. After all, the sovereign will only be as rich and prosperous as the people are generally well-off. And because Hobbes allows that people can rationally attempt to overthrow a sovereign if they are being mistreated in such a way that their lives are threatened (and this includes not just direct use of force, but deprivation of food and medicine), a prudent sovereign will presumably ensure that few (if any) people are in such a predicament. [13]

So, as I read Hobbes, the contract that creates a commonwealth (when one is instituted) is at best a means (and an uncertain one at that) to the end of having a sovereign in place. If an appropriate sovereign determined to enforce rational laws with a sharp sword were to drop from the heavens, *that* would achieve the relevant goal just as well. In that sense, I don't really think that Hobbes is a social contract theorist, at least in the sense in which such a theorist seeks to *ground* reason to obey law in reason to keep contracts.

Let's not worry for the moment about the details of any particular contract theory. You will recall that the fundamental problem to which the contract theorist seeks a solution is the problem of finding a way for rational people to act in concert to achieve their goals or ends. As we noted earlier, Hobbes thinks of people as essentially egoistic—as having as their sole goal or end their own "ease and sensual delight" (1994, 68). [14] But we can allow that people are more complicated than that. As a matter of contingent fact, it seems to me that people value intrinsically the happiness of at least those close to them, and perhaps even people in general. I do think it is equally obvious that people value much more (again intrinsically) their own happiness, the happiness of their family members, the happiness of their friends, and (to a gradually decreasing extent) those to whom they feel "close" in their community and even their country. They may value intrinsically the happiness of faceless people in foreign lands, but not so much that a typhoon that wipes out thousands will even interfere that much with their enjoyment of dinner. However we describe our goals or ends, the Glauconian and Hobbesian idea that we can get much more accomplished when we act together seems almost obviously right. And we do need some account of how rational cooperation of the relevant sort is to be achieved.

It does seem to me that what is needed is something like an agreement that rational people can enter into and that it is rational for all or most people to keep all or most of the time. Earlier in this book, we talked about how groups make decisions. We talked about a very simple but familiar problem—the family outing. In our example we imagined a relatively large family deciding that they wanted to go to some restaurant for dinner. Again, in the view that was defended, a group can want to do something only insofar as all or most members of the group want to do that thing. So, to say that my family wants to eat out this evening is to say that each member of the group wants to participate. Some may want to participate primarily because they want to eat at a restaurant with the others. Some might prefer to stay home with the family, but once they realize that most want to go out, their desire to do something with the group is stronger than their desire to stay home, and they apply a cost–benefit analysis to conclude that it is worth it, all things considered, to put up with going out for the sake of being with the others.

So, the group wants to go out. But they still need to make that painful decision about where to go. It is not as if there is always or usually some explicit contract or agreement made that every member of the group will abide by the decision of the majority (though that is one way the decision could be made). *Bargaining* occurs. People start making suggestions. Some of the suggestions are rejected strongly by others. Some are protested, but only weakly. If all goes well, a choice that allows people to achieve their end of eating together is agreed upon. All needn't go well. The majority may strongly desire to eat at a vegan restaurant that doesn't serve wine, and if they determine that as their destination, the family may lose me as a participant. In the example we are considering, that is an option and it isn't the end of the world (though families being what they are, my behavior might not easily be forgiven and forgotten).

I realize that it is a bit of a stretch, but it seems to me that our model for the family's group decision-making really does apply, with some important qualifications, to the crucial decisions that societies need to make. Again, as Hobbes says, there are things we can do together that we couldn't do on our own. I like to play golf, and to play a decent round of golf you need a decent golf course. Sadly, with the resources I have been able to accumulate, I can't afford to buy my own private golf course. I can't afford to build my own roads, my own electrical grids, my own water supply system, my own tennis courts, my own swimming pools, or any of the other "publicly owned" property that makes my life and the lives of people I care deeply about go much better. Most of you reading this can't afford such items either. But if we pool our resources, we can afford to put these all in place to make our lives happier and more enjoyable. Again, in this respect it is no different from the family that decides it wants a summer home on the lake, but where no member of the family can, on his or her own, afford such a home. One solution (not to be entered into without considerable thought) is to pool resources to purchase the home, a home that will be shared in some way upon which the individuals agree.

All of this might seem relatively unproblematic. But again, the devil is always in the details. None of us living in the United States were part of the process that created the country, its Constitution, or the laws that were in place when we were born. There is a sense in which it seems preposterous to suggest that our current mode of cooperation resulted from some agreement or contract that each citizen signed on the dotted line. I'm arguably an exception. I'm a naturalized U.S. citizen. I did sign an oath and explicitly agreed to abide by the laws of the United States. There is no sense in which I was forced to do so. My native country was Canada, and I hardly qualify as a refugee forced to seek protection elsewhere. Contract theorists will sometimes claim that even if citizens born into a country didn't *explicitly* agree to live by certain laws or make decisions in certain ways, they *implicitly* "signed on" by deciding to live in the country, or even by actively securing a social security card, or refusing to officially renounce their citizenship.[15] A Humean would argue that, for many, deciding to leave one's country isn't a realistic option and that, as in law, one can hardly view someone as agreeing to do something if that person has no realistic choice.[16] It would be a bit of joke for the man who robbed me at gunpoint to claim that I gave him the money of my own free will—after all, I had the option of refusing and taking the risk of being shot.

It's not clear to me, however, that the proponent of the view that we have made implicit agreements to live in a certain way would need to concede that Hume's objection is decisive. Determined people can get out of this country and probably succeed in living elsewhere. The decision might involve enormous cost. The cost would usually include financial loss, but also loss of cultural "identity." And the "choice" people have is now limited. There might have been a time in which people could literally strike out on their own—claim new land as theirs and begin their own lives, alone or with others who are of like mind. Today, most inhabitable land is taken, and if you don't like decisions that are made in the United States, you'll have to settle for some other country whose constitution and laws you would prefer.

I won't press the idea of implicit agreement, however. I do think that the situation most people are in is more realistically likened to the family members who have casually decided to go on an outing together. There is no need for each to formally agree to abide by some outcome or even some way of determining the outcome. One waits to see what happens. If one dislikes the outcome enough, it may well be, all things considered, that one will opt out. In the case of citizens who don't like the way things are going in their country, the "opting out" gets a bit more problematic. One can leave the country for another country. One can head for the wilderness of the Northwest Territories—it's officially "owned" by Canada, but if you find the right place to pitch your tent or build your cabin, no one is going to bother you. You can also try to be a free-rider—refuse to participate while enjoying whatever benefits come your way. But this, as we shall see, is easier tried than accomplished.

So, we are born in the United States. The people who literally created the country through certain decisions and agreements cared a great deal about freedom. Those of us who care a great deal about freedom lucked out when we were born here and now. We obviously didn't craft the Constitution, nor did we explicitly vote to adhere to it. As we saw above, one could try to make the case that we have tacitly agreed to abide by the terms of those original agreements (including laws that were established in a constitutional way) by accepting citizenship and continuing to live here—we have, so to speak, voted with our feet. We have already discussed the wisdom of some of the provisions in the Constitution that were designed to protect various freedoms. But the Constitution leaves it up to legislators to decide whether they want to place other restrictions on human freedom. And while the constitutionality of the details is not completely uncontroversial, the tax system and various regulations on business and commerce are among the areas of human life upon which elected legislators have imposed their will. We have argued that Locke's view of property might have been overly simplistic. In the end, it is probably best to construe the concept of property as legally defined.[17] But in our attempt to define property, we in the United States probably still start with something like the idea that Locke put forth. We have a system that encourages people to produce (in a broad sense of produce) goods and services. The people who produce may use the goods and services themselves, but in sophisticated economies they barter them. While once they may have bartered them for other goods and services, we obviously now rely on currency as way of giving ourselves maximum flexibility with respect to what we want to purchase. In our society, we have decided that the lion's share of what we earn, through producing goods and services and risking money through investment, we get to use as we would like (at least within the limits of the law).

As Hobbes emphasized so strongly, however, we have collectively decided we want to produce many things that we, individually, cannot afford even if the law allowed us to keep everything we make. There are many ways to pool resources. Earlier we talked about that summer cottage that neither my other family members nor I can afford to purchase on our own. But there is nothing to stop us from pooling our resources to collectively purchase the desired home. When we do, we might engage in some fairly intense bargaining with respect to how much each person contributes to the cost of the cottage. One of us may have accumulated much more wealth than any of the others—not enough to buy the cottage on his or her own, but enough to afford a larger contribution to the pooled resources. If the rest of the family asks that person to contribute that larger share, he or she may, of course, refuse and pull out of the agreement. No one gets the cottage. On the other hand, fair or not, it may well be that each person gets close to what they want if the relevant sacrifice is made. A more equitable deal might be struck with strangers, but some of us enjoy spending time with family, and that enjoyment will weigh heavily in the cost–benefit assessment.

An interstate highway costs a lot more to "buy" than a cottage, and many of us are very glad that we have collectively decided to build and, of course, pay for the construction of the sort of infrastructure that makes our lives so much easier. Building this sort of thing, though, requires a decision with respect to pooling a great many resources. Really extreme libertarians, obsessed with private ownership, might suggest that each of us could build a stretch of highway and call it our own. Alternatively, smaller communities could pool some resources to build larger stretches of highway. And, of course, we could defray at least some of the cost of building and maintaining the highway through a system of tolls—those who use the highway keep paying for the cost; those who don't, at the very least, pay a much smaller share. But almost everyone gets something from having a healthy infrastructure of roads. I get to arrive at my destinations much more easily. Truckers also get to their destination more easily and that might well result in my paying less for some of the goods I want to purchase. However, not everyone who lives in the United States will benefit in any direct way from the investment. If you have moved to the wilderness of Oregon and are more or less living off the land, you might not get very much from the interstate system. At the same time, you probably aren't contributing very much, if anything, to the pooled resources that allowed the construction in the first place.

What is true of infrastructure is true of indefinitely many collectively owned projects and resources from which most of us benefit. The need to enter into collectives, particularly collectives that involve in some way the *entire* population, will be more controversial in some cases than in others. So, for example, in most developed countries there is a system of public education that is paid for, or at least heavily subsidized by, pooled resources. One could treat schools and universities as projects that people build with the goal of making a profit through the sale of their product—education. Various forms of schools will need to compete with each other. Like other products, some will be better than others. And, of course, as always, we'll need to decide what to do with children who, through no fault of theirs (and possibly no fault of their parents), don't have the resources to purchase this crucially important product. We can either rely on charity or we can make a collective decision that "we" will be charitable and pool resources to provide the benefits more effectively. The latter is essentially how we deal with those who can't afford to pay for other products that are crucial to their well-being—even their very survival.

The above shouldn't be all that controversial, even if the precise method of pooling resources will start serious arguments. Where we have decided that we are going to try collective ownership, we need a systematic way of pooling resources. Our tax code has evolved in such a way that those who earn a great deal contribute *far* more to the pooled resources than those who make very little.[18] Unlike the example of purchasing a cottage, it isn't going to be as easy to engage in the relevant debate, and it isn't going to be as easy for those who have decided that the arrangement is not to their satisfaction to pull out of the deal. In our democracy we decide how to pay for what we want by electing representatives who support various proposals. In making our decision, many of us will be critically interested in which decision is practically most effective—which way of doings things wins in terms of a cost–benefit analysis. There always has been, and always will be, lots of disagreement among perfectly intelligent and well-educated people over these matters. The wealthier among us may care enough about others that we don't mind paying a disproportionate amount that goes toward building infrastructure and education, but most people are only willing to give so much. I love my sisters, but if they wanted me to pay for 95 percent of the cost of that cottage we were interested in getting for our common use, I suspect that I'd walk away from the proposed agreement. In making their proposal, my sisters should have considered just such a possibility.

When it comes to proposals for various sorts of joint ownership and the specifics of a tax code designed to collect what the proposals will cost, we *also* need to worry about people walking away from their acceptance of the implicit agreements with which they have been living. We talked earlier about how difficult it is for *most* people simply to pick up and move to a place that might be more to their liking. But it isn't that difficult for the very wealthy to pick up and leave the United States for the Bahamas, Hong Kong, Montenegro, Luxembourg, Switzerland, or any number of other places where the tax code might seem to them less onerous. Almost all Western nations make a distinction between personal income tax and corporate income tax. For various reasons, the law allows people running a business to incorporate, and to distinguish the income the *corporation* receives from the income the individuals who run the business receive (for example, as a salary paid to them by the corporation). For that reason, even if *individuals* don't want to give up the various benefits they get from living in the United States, they can move their *businesses* to countries where they are required to pay less in taxes. Given this reality, it is all the more important to ensure that the tax law in a given country doesn't give the people making decisions about where to locate corporations too much of an incentive to move elsewhere.

So far, we have been discussing the need to give people an incentive to stay and do business in the United States. Although it would be an extreme decision likely to cause huge and counterproductive pushback, one could try to minimize some of these problems through heavy-handed legislation that simply forbids people from living in one country while serving on the board of a corporation that does business in another. Even more aggressively, one could simply prevent both people and corporations from moving capital out of the country.[19] Most economists would agree that such moves would be counterproductive. They would inevitably be met by other countries behaving in a similar fashion, and if one has the confidence to think that one can make conditions for doing business better in one's own country than in others, one wouldn't want to risk this sort of all-out economic warfare against free movement of capital.

Even if such measures were feasible, there is, of course, another kind of incentive one needs to worry about in setting tax policy. Most investment requires at least a certain amount of risk. Restaurants, for example, are among the most likely of businesses to go belly up. You might start a business that succeeds, but you will usually be risking a significant amount of your money for the chance of making a good profit. If the tax rates are too high, a cost–benefit analysis will almost certainly lead to the conclusion that the potential loss outweighs the potential gain. The point is easy to make if we start with an absurd (or what should be recognized as an absurd) tax code. Suppose we were to decide that above a certain level income earned by either a business or an individual would be taxed at a rate of 90 percent.[20] Now imagine that you are someone who is about to enter the 90-percent tax bracket. Any investment you make still involves a not insignificant risk of loss, and the gain, by hypothesis, is minimal. Why would a rational person take the relevant chance?

There are possible answers to the hypothetical question. There are people who care about such things as their legacy. On the positive side of *their* ledger, they will put fame and glory. Other people genuinely care about others and are willing to risk their own money to improve the lives of others. And some simply enjoy what they are doing and don't really care about rewards in the form of financial compensation and the material comforts such compensation can bring.[21] So we are dealing with contingencies. As we saw in chapter 3, what it is rational for people to do is relative to their subjective goals or ends, and those can vary from person to person.

As I have already admitted, we have couched this whole discussion in terms of the world as it currently exists. There are certainly other possible worlds in which almost none of the above considerations apply. If we lived in a world in which kindly gods would give us whatever we want, we could stop worrying about how to structure an economy. Somewhat more realistically, I suppose that if we lived under a single world government, we wouldn't need to worry nearly as much about people choosing to exit their current situation and relocate elsewhere. There would be no "elsewhere."

There are less drastic changes that would obviously affect decisions that people make when trying to maximize their own well-being. So, for example, when Canada introduced a version of "single-payer" government health insurance, it needed to worry about losing some of its best doctors to the United States.[22] The United States, however, was an "easy" move for Canadian doctors looking for a higher income. The language and culture are nearly identical (apologies to my Canadian friends who would find this observation offensive). If the United States moved to a single-payer system, the options for exodus are significantly more limited. One might still worry that without the financial reward available to U.S. doctors one would have a more difficult time enticing the "best and brightest" into the crucial field of medicine. But the life of a doctor isn't a bad life. Many, if not most, doctors love what they do and take considerable satisfaction in helping other people. Their salaries would still no doubt be high relative to other occupations (just as it is in most countries that have single-payer systems). It is not at all obvious that medicine would face a problematic "brain drain."

Not everyone enjoys their occupations as much as I enjoy mine. Many jobs are rewarding; many are not. When people work hard at unpleasant jobs, one surely should worry about how hard they will work if taxation (over a certain income-level) takes a huge chunk of their gross income. But the problem is probably most severe for individuals and corporations who make money by investing money. We want people to take financial risks. We want people to risk their savings on exploring natural resources, on creating new businesses, on inventing new technology, on inventing new drugs. The risks in question can be significant indeed. With respect to many investments, the reward is close to "all or nothing." If one stands to lose a great deal with an investment, why would a rational person make the investment absent the possibility of a great reward?[23] A tax code needs to take such questions seriously.

Economic Consequences of Tax Policy

The reader might be understandably frustrated at this point. The above discussion of taxation is at such a level of generality, one might worry, as to be virtually useless. There is, after all, already a rather broad consensus that the tax rates for both individuals and corporations should be somewhere between 0 percent and 100 percent! After that things get contentious. Trivially, we need to decide what we want to own or develop collectively, and we need to decide how to pay for it. The more we want, the more we will need to cough up in tax revenue. We also need to decide whether we want a flat tax or a graduated income tax. Most wealthy people I know don't complain all that much about some form of graduated income tax. The number and volume of the complaints rises, however, the higher the tax rate gets.

There are all kinds of empirical questions to which we need answers before we are in a position to make rational decisions about these matters. One concerns the factual question of how much income a given tax policy will actually generate for our collective spending. It's not all that hard to compare tax policies with respect to the revenue they would produce in a given year *holding constant the income people made for that year*. But as we have already pointed out, the relevant empirical questions certainly need to include the effect a given tax policy will likely have on future revenue. Tax policies causally affect the behavior of people who pay taxes. So we want to know how raising or lowering taxes will affect income moving forward. [24]

Still, that is an empirical question that is surely answerable. It's not as if we fell from the sky yesterday with no experience that bears on the relevant answer. We could begin by looking at what happened in the past, both when we raised taxes and when we lowered them. Such a study must, of course, be done carefully, and one's conclusions must be extremely tentative. We have all learned at some time or another about the "fallacy" called *post hoc ergo propter hoc*. It is a fancy way of pointing to the fact that we can discover correlations between phenomena that are not *causally* connected. The rapid fall of a barometer portends a storm, but the barometer's fall doesn't cause the storm. Increase in the sale of ice cream is strongly correlated with an increase in street crime, but one shouldn't be in law enforcement if one tries to reduce crime by outlawing the sale of ice cream.

Reaching a mistaken conclusion, however, is not the same thing as engaging in fallacious reasoning. There are difficult metaphysical and epistemological questions concerning the metaphysics and epistemology of causation. We can't examine in depth those controversies here. But there are many respectable views about what makes one thing the cause of another that would still recognize correlations as indispensable *evidence* for the existence of causal connection. Indeed, I'm not sure that we have made much progress in the epistemology of causation since Mill introduced his famous "methods." It might be worth briefly reminding ourselves of what the methods are.

Mill's Methods

Like Hume before him, Mill argued for a version of the so-called regularity theory of causation. Mill says:

To certain facts, certain facts always do, and, as we believe, will continue to, succeed. The invariable antecedent is termed the cause; the invariable consequent, the effect. And the universality of the law of causation consists in this, that every consequent is connected in this manner
with some particular antecedent or set of antecedents. (1974, Ch. V,
327)

He goes on to note that:

It is seldom, if ever, between a consequent and a single antecedent that
this invariable sequence subsists. It is usually between a consequent
and the sum of several antecedents; the concurrence of all of them
being requisite to produce, that is to be certain of being followed by,
the consequent. In such cases it is very common to single out one only
of the antecedents under the denomination of Cause, calling the others
merely Conditions. (327)

So, to illustrate Mill's point, I might identify as the cause of my house
catching fire that it was struck by lightning. But the lightning strike by
itself was only a part of a complex set of conditions (the presence of
oxygen, the absence of a sprinkler system, and so on) that together was
the *full* cause of the house catching fire. It's no easy task to capture the
informal rules governing which of the many causally relevant variables it
is appropriate to describe as "the" cause of a given event (though often it
seems to have something to do with *change* as opposed to *standing* conditions, and in some contexts, when we are identifying actions as causes,
we seem to take into account where we have decided to assign blame).
The regularity theory of causation faces enormous difficulties as an account of the meaning of causal claims. But here, all that is important is
that we see Mill's methods against the backdrop of his idea that causality
is all about regularities in nature. While Mill unquestionably endorsed
the idea that causation is nothing but regularity, it might be more plausible to suppose that his famous methods *presuppose* only what we might
call a *generality* theory of causation. Like the regularity theorist, the generality theorist insists that particular causal claims presuppose regularities
between kinds of events. Unlike the regularity theorist, a generality theorist leaves open that the relevant laws might themselves invoke some
strong notion of necessary connection.

   With the presupposition that causal connection is underwritten by
regularities, or, at the very least generalities, in nature, Mill introduces his
methods for discovering the cause of some phenomenon we are investigating methods that do seem undeniably to capture certain commonsense considerations we take into account in investigating causes. Again,
the methods are not altogether new. Some of them get at least inspiration
from Hume's (1978, 173–175) "Rules by which to judge of causes and
effects." But Mill's statement of the methods is perhaps the clearest, most
comprehensive, and, certainly, most influential of the early attempts to

set out the epistemology of causal knowledge. All of the methods make more sense if we suppose (as I think Mill did) that the relata of causal connection are best understood in terms of property exemplifications (though he often calls them "circumstances"). The search for causes among antecedent conditions is best understood as a search for which of the relevant properties that have been exemplified are those that are causally efficacious.

The Method of Agreement

The first of Mill's methods he calls the Method of Agreement:

> If two or more instances of the phenomenon under investigation have only one circumstance in common, the circumstance in which alone all the instances agree is the cause (or effect) of the given phenomenon). (1974, Ch. VIII, 390)

The basic idea is simple and familiar. So, if I occasionally get heartburn and am looking for the cause, I can plausibly rule out drinking beer (at least as the sole cause) if drinking beer is sometimes followed, but also sometimes not followed by heartburn. On the other hand, if there is only one circumstance common to all those occasions in which I get heartburn (e.g., drinking red wine), then it is a pretty good bet that the red wine is the culprit.

It is a pretty good *bet*, but as Mill himself concedes (390), employment of the method carries with it a number of often highly problematic assumptions. Perhaps, most obviously, we are presupposing that we have isolated from among the indefinitely many antecedent conditions those that are *candidates* for the cause. We also typically presuppose that we are not dealing with a case of overdetermination. The beer consumed with French fries might have been the cause of that heartburn last Tuesday, while the red wine on an empty stomach might have caused the heartburn last Saturday. It's entirely possible that if we make all of our relevant presuppositions explicit, we might really have a case of enthymematic deductive reasoning, where the real epistemological questions concern the justification we have for the relevant *presuppositions*.

Enthymematic description of reasoning, I would argue, is the norm, even in philosophy. The evidence we cite is rarely our total evidence. When I conclude that I have been robbed after noticing valuables missing and windows broken, I am relying on all sort of information about customs and laws that I don't bother to state. If I make explicit all of those background assumptions, I might be able to construe the reasoning as deductively valid (though it will be no stronger than the evidence I have for the premises). In like fashion, I'm suggesting that the use of Mill's methods might often be best seen as deductively valid reasoning from the observations described in the method supplemented by background premises which if justified allow us to deduce the conclusion in question.

We noted that the method of agreement can easily go wrong (in part because our background assumptions might not be true). Use of the second method, the Method of Difference, can help lessen the possibility of error.

Method of Difference

Mill describes this method as follows:

> If an instance in which the phenomenon under investigation occurs, and an instance in which it does not occur, have every circumstance in common save one, that one occurring only in the former; the circumstance in which alone the two instances differ is the effect, or the cause, or an indispensable part of the cause, of the phenomenon. (1974, chapter VIII, 391)

So, in our example of the heartburn if we find that there are four factors, A, B, C, and D, which are always followed by heartburn, but then find that when we remove D, the heartburn doesn't occur, then we might tentatively conclude that D was the culprit. The method of difference is particularly useful when the candidates for cause are easy to manipulate (as with our example). Of course, if we somehow know *in advance* that the cause was one of A through D, then we can *deduce* that none of A through C is the cause, at least the full cause, once we have those conditions and we don't have the heartburn. The full cause of a kind of event X, you will recall, is that kind of condition or set of conditions which is *invariably* followed by events like X.

There is, of course, nothing to prevent one from using both the method of agreement and the method of difference together (Mills calls this the Joint Method).

Method of Residues

The method of residues is a prescription for how to identify causes against a background of prior causal knowledge. Mill states it as follows:

> Subduct from any phenomenon such part as is known by previous inductions to be the effect of certain antecedents, and the residue of the phenomenon is the effect of the remaining antecedents. (1974, chapter VIII, 398)

So, *if* you find that A, B, and C are followed by X, Y, and Z, and you have *already* established that A is the cause of X, and that B is the cause of Y, then you can justifiably start speculating that C (the residue, that which is left over) is the cause of Z. Again, it seems obvious that the reasoning is highly enthymematic. As Mill himself would emphasize, you would need to antecedently know not just that A and B are the cause of X and Y respectively, you would also have to know that C is the *only* other antecedent condition that is a plausible candidate for the cause of Z.

The Method of Concomitant Variations

Here is how Mill describes the last of his methods:

> Whatever phenomenon varies in any manner whenever another phenomenon varies in some particular manner, is either a cause or an effect of that phenomenon, or is connected with it through some fact of causation. (1974, chapter VIII, 401)

When I began to suspect that the stereo had something to do with the interference with my TV picture, I might investigate further by moving the stereo closer and farther from the set. Suppose that as I move the stereo closer, the picture gets worse, and as I move it farther away, the picture gets better. Commonsense would certainly suggest that I have gained more evidence for the conclusion that the stereo is indeed the culprit.

It is not entirely clear to me that the method of concomitant variation is distinct from the method of difference. The various forms of picture distortion are, after all, distinct events, each requiring a causal explanation (on the supposition that there is a cause of the phenomenon). The method, then, might be construed as repeated application of the method of difference, together with, perhaps, reliance on an inductively justified principle that where we find a certain kind of cause responsible for a certain kind of effect, and we have another presumed effect similar to the first kind of effect, we should look for a similar sort of cause.

Mill's Methods and the Effects of Tax Policy

Any attempt to use Mill's methods encounters the obvious problems one inevitably faces in trying to establish causal connections. One must control for variables. And the more complex the phenomena one is studying the more difficult it will be to control for even the variables that one *suspects* might well be causally relevant. The economy of a country like the United States is incredibly complex. We can certainly go back through U.S. history and find out what has happened to tax revenue in the wake of both rate hikes and rate cuts.[25] I suppose one of the main reasons I *lean* toward economic libertarian policy is that it does seem to me that more often than not tax cuts have been win/win strategies. People get to keep more of their income, and they spend that income in ways that give them and those they care about pleasure. Those who own businesses, both small and large, have more profit that they can use to expand those businesses. Such expansion generates job opportunities, creates more wealth for more people, reduces the amount of money we spend on those who are relying on a social safety net, and so on. And, perhaps paradoxically, the tax cuts haven't typically resulted in *significant* reduction of tax revenue.[26]

Historically, tax rates have been all over the place.[27] In the early twentieth century, the top rate was as low as 7 percent. To meet the expenses of the World War I, they were raised significantly and went as high as 77 percent. In 1925, the top personal rate dropped again to 25 percent. In 1961, the highest tax rate was 91 percent, and the United States was still fighting a significant deficit. In a theory about stimulating the economy, Kennedy cut that top rate to 70 percent. All of the tax cuts just discussed were followed in the immediate or near term by increased tax revenue and increased economic growth. The famous Reagan tax cuts in the 1980s were followed by impressive increases in net tax revenue and a healthy increase in GDP.

The above paragraph states facts. But it doesn't discuss the huge array of other variables any of which might have causally contributed to a growth in the economy, and with it a growth in taxable revenue. Stock markets go up and go down. Every time they do, someone has an "explanation." The explanations sometimes seem comical as they seek to explain not only trends but why Tuesday's market went up and Wednesday's went down. It is certainly hard to resist the conclusion that at least on some occasions we are dealing with something like the "butterfly effect," the idea that the tiniest of changes can have "snowballing" effects that in the end make huge differences. But in addition to market changes, economies have very real growths and setbacks. The tech boom in the United States created enormous wealth and, with it, enormous increases in tax revenue. During the headiest of those high times, the details of tax policy wouldn't have made a whole lot of difference. There were significant parts of the economy that were on a "roll" and nothing was going to stand in the way of at least temporary economic "exuberance."

On the other side of the ledger, there have been significant global changes that affect so-called heavy industry in the United States. It is just a fact that labor is cheaper in many other countries. It is cheaper because workers are paid less and workers have far fewer safeguards in terms of health insurance, retirement plans, and so on. One can engage in "protectionist" trade policies, but in a global economy such policies will almost certainly engender trade wars the outcome of which is, at the very least, uncertain.

It is a dangerous and politically incorrect thing to state, let alone underscore, but there have been significant cultural changes not only in the United States but in other cultures. Attitudes toward what people *deserve* in the way of safety nets and quality of life affect behavior. And trends concerning the stability of child-rearing adults can have the most profound of impacts on not only the lives of children, but on the probability of their eventual success in life.

To state the obvious, many of these changes are taking place at the same time that changes in tax rates are taking place. It is truly hard, perhaps impossible, to decide with any sort of assurance what is causing what. Was Clinton an economic genius whose tax policies and social reforms (both worked out in conjunction with a Republican-led Congress) were the engines that fueled a rapidly growing economy—an economy that created not only expanded tax revenue but decreased reliance on government by millions of citizens? Or did Clinton get really lucky in occupying a presidency that coincided with one of the greatest stock booms in history? Or was it a combination of both? I don't really know.

To write this part of the book, I read work by some of the most respected economists in the country. They don't agree with each other. They don't even come *close* to agreeing with each other. And I'm not about to get my own doctoral degree in economics. So, I'm left trying to sort through opposing views with what seems to me to be "common sense." If tax rates are too high for businesses, they won't take financial risks to make money. They would be crazy to take such risks unless the CEOs of those businesses are motivated by much more than profit (motivated in such a way that they don't even fulfil their legal fiduciary duties). If we decide we want to have a social safety net, we surely also want to decrease the number of people who fall into that net. We want to create conditions under which as many people as possible can find work— ideally, find work that they find reasonably satisfying and that will allow them to advance and make their lives and the lives of their loved ones more satisfying. All this goes on the "benefit" side of a cost–benefit analysis.

On the other hand, we also have collective projects that cover everything from providing social safety nets for the least fortunate—for people who literally can't take care of themselves or their families—to the many forms of infrastructure that can most conveniently be paid for through the pooling of resources that just is tax revenue. And there are parks, tennis courts, golf course, public beaches, community centers, and a host of other opportunities for pleasure that we couldn't afford to build individually, but we can afford to build when we pool our resources. It should be a relatively trivial truth that when we figure out what we want, we also need to figure out how to pay for it. If our pooled resources (the tax revenue) can't pay for everything we want, we either need to give up on some of what we want or we need to find a way of increasing the tax revenue. But as we just noted above, it is hardly obvious what the best way is of increasing revenue. It certainly is *not* uncontroversial that we will achieve that goal simply by raising tax rates on all or some subgroups within our society.

LET'S NOT TALK ABOUT FAIRNESS

At least some of today's political discourse seems utterly obsessed with "fairness." Particularly on the Left, the slogan is that the wealthy must pay "their fair share" of taxes. But we can't even assess such a claim until we have at least a hint of how we should understand all of this talk about fairness.[28] There are, of course, uses of the expression "fair" with which we are all relatively comfortable. When mom is cutting up the cherry pie for dessert and gives her eight-year-old child a piece of pie twice as big as the piece given to the nine-year-old, charges of unfairness will fly at her with fury. When I'm grading exams and give one student an A and another student a B, for answers that are essentially exactly the same, almost everyone will agree again that I have acted unfairly. Of course, the above examples only offer prima facie indications of unfairness. Perhaps the nine-year-old had sweets earlier in the day. The student who was awarded the B might be a graduate student, while the student who was given the A might be a freshman—I might have made clear early in the course that I will expect more from more advanced students. But the examples still suggest that we have at least some grip on the concept of fairness.

When it comes to cutting the pie, fairness seems to have something to do with equality. We are treating two people fairly when we treat them the same way in relevantly similar circumstances. But those who complain about our unfair tax system surely don't want any crude understanding of fairness as equality. The wealthy, after all, pay far more in taxes than the poor. They pay more in terms of total dollars, and they pay more in terms of percentage of their income. The critic of the current system is more likely to insist that the lack of fairness has something to do with the fact that the wealthy can afford to pay much more than they do. If we measure the cost of one's contribution to government revenue in terms of something like sameness of *sacrifice*, then I suppose one might be back in business complaining that the wealthy make far less of a sacrifice when contributing to government revenue than the middle class. (If you are poor enough, you simply don't contribute to federal government revenue in the first place).

But even if we could squeeze the concept of a fair tax code into some concept of equal sacrifice, conceding that such equality would be exceedingly difficult to measure, we also need to keep in mind all of the other potential effects tax policy has on the broader economy. As we noted earlier, one doesn't need to support the much-maligned idea of trickle-down economics to concede that an economy will typically be better off if it expands, and that expansion requires investment of capital. The more money we take from those who invest, the less there is left for them to invest. The higher the tax rate, the less rational it becomes to take risks of the sort that we want entrepreneurs to take.

All of this might seem to beg at least some questions concerning suggestions for more radical changes to our economic system. Individuals and corporations aren't the only forces that invest in ways that benefit almost all. After all, that's the whole point of having a government and finding a way to fund that government. There are at least some things that we think the government can do better than individuals and private corporations. That government still needs to be funded, and when we collectively try to decide how to fund it, we had better make sure that we don't cut off our nose to spite our face, all in the name of fairness.

Some people are smarter, stronger, better looking, more charming, more articulate, and luckier than others. Some of that luck includes the circumstances into which one is born, circumstances that in turn affect one's education and economic opportunities. Given a modest altruism, one might well be inclined to level the "playing field" of life as much as possible. I'm certainly not opposed to devoting enormous resources into making sure that we give all children the best education we can. We should also try as hard as we can to give people a safe environment in which to live. But there is only so much that will be effective, unless one embraces draconian social policy that yanks children away from their parents as soon it becomes evident that those parents pose a serious risk to the advancement of their children. As long as there are people who are smarter and more imaginative than others, those people will have a natural advantage over others. They are more likely to succeed in all sorts of ways. And, however we structure the rest of society, those who are "superior" in certain respects will make it that much easier for their children to succeed. And it would be a serious mistake to try to do anything to put obstacles in the way of those who are lucky enough to have this sort of head start in life. Is it fair that some people have this kind of head start over others? Well, the attributes that contribute to success weren't allocated equally. Some people start out with a much bigger slice of the pie. There is a *sense* in which perhaps that's just not fair, but one doesn't want to destroy one's economy so one can prevent those with natural ability to succeed and to indirectly benefit people as a whole.

HOW MUCH REGULATION IS TOO MUCH REGULATION?

Another unavoidably empirical question that is crucial to resolving controversies concerning economic freedom is the degree to which we will let people conduct business unfettered by federal and state regulations. Many Republicans and Libertarians complain bitterly about the alleged fact that business, in general, and small businesses, in particular, are drowning in a sea of burdensome regulations that increase substantially the cost of producing products, a cost that is, of course, passed on to consumers. And if consumers won't pay the additional costs, the businesses fail.[29]

Given the consequentialism that I have presupposed throughout this work, it will be difficult to say much that is useful at a very abstract level. Essentially, each regulation must be considered and evaluated in terms of its potential costs and benefits. It is worth suggesting, however, that certain sorts of regulation might best be viewed as the friend, not the enemy, of freedom. Some of us are most concerned about maximizing the choices we have in life, and that includes the choice to consume what we wish. But, generally speaking, we would like to have a good idea of what we are about to consume before we make the relevant choice. Knowledge doesn't decrease one's liberty. One might insist that even if that is so, the market will take care of matters. We have a legal system that allows people to sue those who misrepresent products. And we have an economic system that allows consumers to refuse to buy products if the manufacturer refuses to provide the information that they want so that they can make an informed choice. Presumably, if people are half-way intelligent in their choices, they will drive out of business those who won't give them the accurate product information that they want.

There is probably a sense in which that may be a plausible claim. But consumer behavior takes *time* to influence the behavior of those who produce and sell goods. And, as always, we are particularly concerned to protect children as much as possible. We do want to make our own decisions concerning what risks we want to take as adults, but as we just noted, most of us want to know what risks we are taking. By collectively insisting that anyone who sells products label those products with the information we seek, we put ourselves in a much better position, it seems to me, to defend our freedom to take the relevant risks. Those interested in paternalistic intervention can no longer use the excuse that they are protecting "us" from deceptive and unscrupulous producers if those producers have labeled clearly the contents of a product and its known potential risks.

Consider the much-used example of cigarettes. The evidence is overwhelming that cigarette smoking exacerbates the risks of contracting various sorts of disease. And if you already have certain diseases, it can aggravate the symptoms. Given our current laws, cigarette manufacturers are legally obliged to "warn" the consumer of the relevant research. We get two benefits from these warnings. First, we don't need to feel particularly bad for a consumer who decides to smoke and who suffers as a result of the decision. In Mill's terminology, the "burden on our affections" is lessened. But we also could save a great deal of money. Lawsuits are expensive. Even when the loser in a civil suit is required to pay court costs, those payments cover only a fraction of the total cost of a legal system that is already overburdened. Once people are warned of the dangers of using a given product: a) many will be less likely to use the product and b) those who do use the product will be less likely to sue the manufacturer who included specific warnings with the sale of the product.[30] Our system being what it is, lawsuits can be successful even when consumers have been appropriately warned, but that is something that could be, and perhaps should be, changed.

Requiring manufacturers to disclose the contents and known risks associated with the use of a product is only one small fraction of the regulations that govern business. We have a collective interest in preventing various forms of pollution. Again, one could wait for the pollution to occur and attempt to deter future polluters through massive lawsuits, but we surely have a collective interest in preventing the problem in the first place. Some environments are fragile and take a very long time to recover when seriously damaged. Whether our concern for the environment should extend to protecting every species of snail that might be affected by the construction of a dam or a bridge is entirely another matter, and each proposed piece of legislation needs to be scrutinized carefully. People worry, perhaps justly, about delicate ecosystems, but there are legitimate concerns that the delicacy of such systems is overstated. Species of fish in various lakes come and go and the overall quality of the aquatic life in the lakes often seems barely affected. There are changes to be sure, but while some changes are bad, some are good, and some seem to matter relatively little.[31]

Still, serious harm done to the environment is a harm that affects almost everyone. As we contemplate how we want to spend our collective resources, protection of the environment will always be high up on the list of items that will likely survive the cost–benefit analysis. I'm old enough to remember when cities like Buffalo and Pittsburgh were environmental disasters, and when Lake Erie and Lake Ontario were becoming cesspools. As anyone who has been walleye fishing on Lake Erie will tell you, there are dramatic improvements that are in no small part a result of EPA regulations. But one still must consider the costs associated with environmental protection.[32] When polled, most people will be over the top when it comes to what they will spend to protect the environment. But they will be equally over the top on what they will spend on education and any number of other societal projects. And many of those people also complain vehemently about out-of-control government spending. We obviously need to have a realistic assessment of the risks and a realistic assessment of the costs before we pass regulations. According to many, the greatest threat to the environment is human-influenced global warming. Those who favor dramatic collective action to reduce or eliminate the use of fossil fuels are convinced that the science is settled and there is almost no limit to what we should spend to alleviate the alleged disastrous results that will occur. We can't do any sort of justice to this topic here. The most we can do is remind ourselves that when we do cost–benefit analysis we need to take into account *all* of the relevant probabilities and possible consequences of our actions. Philosophers of science sometimes talk about a "pessimistic induction." They are referring to the alleged fact that highly theoretical and abstract posits of science have a really bad track record when it comes to proving true. Whether or not this is true depends greatly on how one defines the relevant reference class of scientific theories. But climatology is still a relatively young science and its track record when it comes to predicting climate change has not exactly been stellar. It seems to me folly to place the almost absolute faith many seem to have in the accuracy of its current predictions. Having said that, one can't ignore evidence and one must make the best estimates of probability that one can with respect to the possibility and probability of climate change, its causes, and its effects.

As we noted earlier, there is no shortage of government regulation of business. In addition to the areas already discussed there are a host of actual and proposed regulations concerning employment and labor. In the United States today there is a minimum wage, for example. It is a matter of considerable controversy among Libertarians as to whether there should be such a requirement, and among the rest of the population there is even more controversy over where the minimum should be set. As always, there are critical empirical questions that need to be answered. Increases in wages are virtually always passed on to consumers, and we need to decide whether we want to bear the additional financial burden. It is worth keeping in mind that the cost to society of providing an increase in minimum wage is at least reduced by the consequences of not providing such increases. When people don't have enough to support themselves or their families, the cost of providing such support will fall to the rest of us. At least it will if we succumb to that "burden on our affections" about which Mill spoke so eloquently. Most of us certainly won't let children go without food, clothing, and shelter, and when their parents aren't making enough to provide such necessities, the rest of us will pay for them.

There are also a huge number of regulations on businesses of a certain size to provide health care and retirement plans to *full-time* employees. Those who worry about the possibility that such regulations will affect the number of full-time employees a business hires (as opposed to part-time employees) are probably right to have such concerns. But again, many businesses will be able to pass the cost of complying with such regulations on to those who consume their products or services, and in many cases, we'll end up paying one way or another for the health-care costs and retirement income of those who haven't had the benefit of the kinds of plans that exist today. At least that is so as long as we aren't going to turn people away from emergency rooms because they can't afford medical treatment, and we aren't going to let people die in the streets because they weren't able to save for their old age.

At least some would argue that we can avoid such dire outcomes by relying on *voluntary* charity. But particularly in difficult economic times it is not clear that people are all that generous, and I'm sure it is more than a bit annoying to those who are generous that they pay disproportionately so that those of us who are not can sleep with a clear conscience. This may not seem in the spirit of libertarian political thought, but then the consequentialist defense of libertarianism that I am offering is not a defense of the more radical of libertarian policies. Once one allows that it makes sense for people to take collective action, and that in most circumstances we won't let people "free ride"[33] on the benefits provided by the contributions of others, then we are going to find a role for our government representatives to play in coordinating our efforts at achieving various goals.

Earlier, we discussed government requirements for truth and accuracy in advertising. I argued that one should probably view such requirements as an opportunity to expand informed choices that one can defend against unwise government intrusion. One might make a similar argument concerning the many regulations that require employers to provide safe workplaces. The concept of safety these days has expanded to cover freedom from harassment and other factors that make a work environment needlessly unpleasant or uncomfortable. Of course, whatever one requires of employers, it is just a fact that some work is more dangerous than others. Although the number of workers who die while building high-rises isn't as high as it used to be, it is still a bit shocking. Many people simply can't or won't work near the top of a skyscraper. Those who can and do are compensated well. But the market doesn't always compensate those whose jobs are inherently more dangerous. The conditions of underground mining have certainly improved, but as long as it exists, there will always be catastrophic accidents. *This* dangerous work is hardly compensated well.

Just as we argued with respect to truth in advertising, it seems to be a relatively small infringement on freedom to require those who hire employees to make clear the known risks associated with a given job. And it probably makes sense to require employers to take "sensible" steps to make the workplace as safe as is practically possible. The sensibility of a given requirement, though, is obviously a function of the cost to the employer of securing the relevant safety, a cost that will be passed on to consumers. While there is an act requiring businesses to make their buildings as accessible "as possible" to those who have various disabilities, that act also recognizes that the costs of doing so in any particular case might be prohibitive, and the owner of the building is free to make the case for an exemption. Cars could be made much safer that they are. They could be built with many of the same safety equipment upon which professional race car drivers rely. The government could also require people driving cars to wear not only seat belts but also helmets. Most of us have decided that we don't want to bear the relevant costs for the benefit of the additional safety.

It is, in the end, however, a cost–benefit analysis. When workplace environments are needlessly unsafe, we'll collectively bear the costs of an overworked legal system trying to deal with additional lawsuits and the costs of looking after those who suffer serious injuries. The costs exist whether the person has relevant health insurance or not. Insurance companies are in business to make money, and the more they pay out, the more they charge their customers. And even if we had a single-payer health-care system, we are still paying for doctors, nurses, and the facilities they use. The more people there are who need care of one sort or another, the more caregivers we'll need and the more we will end up spending.

It is worth reminding ourselves once again, that when we do a cost–benefit analysis most of us will always view as a benefit freedom of choice itself. Personally, and perhaps idiosyncratically, I place a not insignificant value on being able to decide whether or not to wear a seat belt when I drive a car. I grew up riding a bicycle and playing hockey without wearing a helmet, and I would value being able to make a similar decision today. The value of freedom can be outweighed by other values. It is a contingent fact (and almost certainly culturally relative) as to how much people, in general, subjectively value freedom. The more people value various freedoms, the more we can negotiate over whether they are willing to pay the costs of giving each other the freedom to engage in risky activities. If you let me (probably stupidly) drive my car without wearing a seat belt, I'll let you pursue your hobby of dirt-bike racing. If you let me ride my bicycle without a helmet, I'll let you try to reach the top of Mount Everest. Freedom has a price, but the freedoms we just discussed don't have that high a price, and those of us attracted to libertarian thought are willing to pay the relevant price as long as it doesn't get too high.

NOTES

1. As we noted earlier, there is a view that suggests that even philosophers are in a similar position vis-à-vis trusting their *own* judgements. Given that we find ourselves sometimes disagreeing with those we take to be our peers—people just as smart as we are and just as well-read, why should we trust ourselves and our conclusions over our peers? See Feldman and Warfield (2010) for a collection of essays discussing this controversy.

2. Many would argue that some concept of property, not defined by, but reflected in legitimate law, is at the heart of the libertarian's conception of freedom. There are certainly elements of this thought in Nozick (1974), Narveson (1988), and Valentyne (2007).

3. See Locke (1993, 128). This itself is a bit misleading. There is a religious overlay to what Locke says—his view is always couched in terms of God's gifts. I'm going to ignore this part of the view and if the reader would prefer to couch the discussion in

terms of a Lockean view, that would be fine with me. For a more historically based examination of Locke's view of property and the way in which Locke's concept lies at the heart of some defenses of libertarianism, see Mack (2018, chapter 4).

4. I'm aware that present law precludes selling, and I would presume, gambling with one's organs.

5. See Nozick (1974, 174–182) for a detailed discussion of this and related problems.

6. Both Russia and Germany have always longed for a reliable warm-water port and have, from time to time, gone to war to achieve this end. When one party is considering secession, water rights are often on the minds of those from whom the party is seceding. So, for example, Quebec has occasionally considered whether or not to secede from Canada. But as an independent country, Quebec would control a crucial part of the St. Lawrence Seaway, a condition that the rest of Canada might have been willing to fight to prevent.

7. Furthermore, as Locke himself admits (1993, 138), the notion of spoiling doesn't seem to make much sense once we have a currency and begin to trade commodities for that currency.

8. The state of the law on these issues is still murky. The U.S. Supreme Court (*Parham v. J. R.* 1979) seems to give wide latitude to the judgment of parents with respect to health issues concerning their children. But many states seem to make no exceptions to laws prohibiting parental abuse when it comes to failing to provide appropriate medical assistance to a child.

9. As I read Hobbes, he always claims that one retains the right to do what is necessary to preserve one's life, regardless of what other agreements one makes. See p. 79.

10. For a rejection of the very idea that we need a theory that legitimizes political authority and its correlative political obligations, see Huemer (2013).

11. See Rawls (1964).

12. At least that's the way it seems to me. For opposing views, see Taylor (1938), Martinich (1992), Warrender (1957), Rhodes (1992; 2002), and Gert (1991).

13. Hampton (1999) suggests that this "right of nature" points to a kind of inconsistency given that Hobbes also sometimes talks as if the sovereign's power is absolute. I think it all makes sense, though, in the final analysis. The right of nature is an escape clause. We agree to do whatever the sovereign tell us to do . . . and then in fine print there is the *unless* . . . a *rational* sovereign knows that's how we think of things and that's what gets a sovereign to do the kinds of things we want a sovereign to do.

14. Again, not everyone thinks that Hobbes endorsed the view that people are by nature egoistic. See Gert (1967).

15. See Locke (1993, 176).

16. Hume (1987, 475) gives the example of the conscripted sailor who is "free" to leave the ship on which he finds himself to point out the absurdity of supposing that in such a situation there is genuine choice.

17. This position horrifies some, but I think there is potential confusion caused by an equivocation on the term "property." It seems relatively uncontroversial that some expressions are "value-laden" in the sense that there very meaning includes a value judgment. As you will recall, I suggested that to describe an act of killing as murder is to claim that the killing in question is morally wrong. At least sometimes, I suspect when they describe something as their property, they don't mean just that they are *legally* entitled to have it (and that others are legally prohibited from taking it), but that they are morally entitled to it (and that it would be morally wrong for others to take it). And if the view I'm defending here is correct, that claim can in turn be translated into a claim about what the property laws morally ought to be. I can consistently embrace the idea that property is a legal concept and be morally outraged at what some societies have deemed to be property. It was morally outrageous that in the antebellum U.S. South, states would include in the property held by people other people.

18. According to the U.S. Department of Treasury (2018) the top 5 percent of taxpayers pay more than half of the total income tax.

19. Gupta and Sao (2009) explore the legal and constitutional issues such an attempt would face, but also discuss the negative political consequences that would likely ensue from any such attempt.

20. Historically, this isn't absurd. From 1951 to 1963, the top rate in the United States for personal income was 91 percent or higher. See https://files.taxfoundation.org/legacy/docs/fed_individual_rate_history_nominal.pdf

21. Though everyone cares about meeting basic needs—food, shelter, and clothing, for examples.

22. Skinner (2002) investigates the question of whether this sort of worry was realistic or exaggerated.

23. Again, I'm not suggesting that the only rewards in life are financial. I'm sure a successful inventor takes great satisfaction in making the world a better place. And those who successfully build new businesses and create employment opportunities for all sorts of people probably take enormous pride in what they have accomplished. But one can't ignore financial risks in one's business endeavors, and that financial risk needs to be offset by significant profit.

24. Sowell (2012) takes issue with the expression "trickle-down economics," a theory that he notes is relatively recent in the history of modern economic theory and that has pejorative connotations. Sowell examines a number of different tax rate reductions beginning with those put in place in the 1920s. He argues that such tax cuts virtually always significantly increased tax revenue. One of his explanations for this fact is that the wealthy would find ways of sheltering taxable income when rates are high—sheltering that wouldn't make economic sense but for the need to avoid higher taxes. As I indicate in this discussion, however, Sowell's discussion in a way underscores how complicated the relevant policy decisions are. While it might be a horrible mistake *simply* to raise taxes (for many of the reasons Sowell discusses and that I will discuss in what follows), advocates of higher tax cuts could counter by arguing for more extensive tax reform. That tax reform dramatically revises a tax code that allows various sorts of deductions, and might even make illegal movement of capital out of the country.

25. See again Sowell (2012).

26. As I indicated, the literature on such matters is voluminous. And, of course, there are all sorts of different taxes—sales tax, property tax, state income tax, federal income tax, corporate income tax, and so on. For an argument that state business tax cuts don't have a positive impact on gross state product, job creation, personal income, poverty rates, and business establishment, see Prillaman and Meier (2014). But for an almost diametrically opposed position, see Mertens and Ravn (2012). They argue that "Implemented tax cuts, regardless of their timing, have expansionary effects, on output, consumption, investment, and hours worked, while real wages increase" (145), and that "unanticipated tax cuts give rise to major stimulus to the economy, which is reflected in persistent increase in output, consumption, investment, and, to a smaller extent, hours worked. Anticipated tax cuts also stimulate the economy once taxes are cut, but during the pre-implementation period that output, investment, and hours worked drop, while consumption is roughly unchanged" (175).

27. See http://federal-tax-rates.insidegov.com/.

28. In what follows, my complaints about how to understand "fair" outcomes bears at least a family resemblance to Hayek's (1976) complaints about the "meaninglessness" of talk about just or unjust distributions of income and resources. As I understand him, Hayek thinks that it is a kind of category mistake to talk about just or unjust outcomes in a system of economics like ours. Justice or injustice arises only in connection with actions that people take in a competitive arena. I'm not making a claim as strong as Hayek's with respect to fairness. As will become clear, I worry that the expression has become simply a vague term of evaluation used to signal that one

objects to certain facts about how taxes are levied and goods, income, and power are distributed.

29. See Gray (1987), Bosch and Lee (1994), and Dawson and Seater (2013).

30. Van Zee (2009) argues that in general we should require that legalizing of drug use be accompanied by full disclosure of the drug's addictive or harmful tendencies. Failure to fully disclose the addictive properties of opioids is at the center of the current criticism of drug companies "pushing" the drug (a drug was is also enormously helpful to those suffering from certain sorts of chronic pain).

31. One of my sisters lives on a lovely lake in Ontario, Penn Lake. After a year of significantly high waters, northern pike appeared in the lake for the first time in recorded history. Pike are voracious and it, no doubt, affected the populations of other fish in the lake. But the bass and perch didn't disappear, and northern pike are a lot of fun to catch.

32. The EPA's budget for the last fiscal year was $8,058,448,000 and has been higher in the past (U.S. Environmental Protection Agency, n.d.). Perhaps this is a good expenditure of tax revenue but would certainly need to calculate very carefully one's priorities.

33. See Rawls (1964).

EIGHT

Summary

In the previous chapter, I expressed some sympathy for the importance of requiring truth in advertising. After reading this book, I worry that some will argue that there should have been a warning on the title page that "libertarianism" was being used in a rather flexible, perhaps almost idiosyncratic, sense. Certainly, I haven't tried to defend the more extreme versions of libertarianism that find almost no role for a federal or state government other than, perhaps, defense of the country. But to be fair, the goal was to explore the best *possible* consequentialist defense of libertarian policies. As I have emphasized in a number of places, consequentialism will almost never evaluate favorably *every* plank in a political platform that endorses a wide range of various policies. Rather, the consequentialists take their sophisticated cost/benefit (expected utility) analyses to each specific policy. It may turn out that the consequentialist analysis will endorse some policies that are also embraced by self-identified Libertarians, others by self-identified Republicans, and still others by self-identified Liberals or Democratic Socialists.

If one is committed to evaluating possibilities from the perspective of a consequentialist, there will be no avoiding the obvious conclusion that the rationality of one's evaluation will depend on the rationality of conclusions concerning a host of very complicated facts about the possible consequences of actions (particularly legislative actions) and the probabilities of those consequences. And, of course, no evaluation will be possible until values are assigned to those consequences. As we emphasized earlier, an action itself might be valued or disvalued in virtue of the kind of action it is (keeping in mind that each action is simultaneously of many different kinds).

Cost–benefit analysis must be sophisticated. We must never think of it solely in terms of *economic* impact. An ideally rational use of the concept of a benefit is held hostage to an ideally rational understanding of value. One needs a view about the content of judgments about what has intrinsic value and disvalue. I've defended a view in detail elsewhere (1990) that I have summarized earlier in this book. In the final analysis, I have argued, there is no intrinsic value in the world that cannot be reduced to facts about what people and collectives (made up of people) value intrinsically. And while there might be considerable overlap in terms of what people value intrinsically, there are almost certainly also important differences. It seems almost obvious to me that I subjectively value, for its own sake, the happiness of the people I love *much* more that I subjectively value the happiness of strangers. And for reasons that have, no doubt, evolutionary explanations, I value the happiness of those in my city, my state, my country, and probably my culture, more than I value the happiness of those further removed from me. When a group of people is determined to act in concert, however, they need to define goals in terms of intersections of values. They need to find goals that can be used in an understanding of what is rational for the *group* to do. Those goals will still be understood in terms of subjective value, but the values that enter into the definition of those goals involve the process of individuals bargaining and compromising.[1]

In defending freedom, it is a disastrous mistake to leave out of one's calculations the effects of actions, particularly government actions, on freedom *itself*. As I argued earlier, it seems to me that most people in our culture greatly value *for its own sake* the freedom to make choices without fear of coercion by other actors. To get many of these freedoms, they will realize that they need to compromise when it comes to allowing others freedom to act in ways of which they might strongly disapprove. But compromise takes us only so far. When the harm to me and to those I love becomes severe enough, I'm probably going to support efforts to stop you, with force if necessary, from inflicting on us the relevant harm. And, no doubt, you will do the same to me. The desire for freedom, it should go without saying, doesn't trump all other goals we may have. But it is always a *member* of the court that rules on the ultimate rationality of our actions.

If there is another message I want to underscore in this book, it is how very *complicated* these issues concerning freedom are. It is a gross understatement to suggest that the relevant empirical considerations upon which the rationality of action depend are complex. Really intelligent people with the best of educations don't agree with each other on the economic impacts of raising or lowering taxes, eliminating various government regulations, and so on. If academic economists really had the knowledge to make the relevant predictions, they would be hedge-fund managers instead of academics and they would have amassed enormous fortunes. But however difficult it is to make the relevant probability calculations, there is no alternative to our trying to do the best we can with the evidence we have—there is no opting out of decision-making in life. As we emphasized before, the very *act* of doing nothing can have catastrophic results when compared to the alternatives open to one.

In the approach I have been defending, it is also easy to reach incorrect conclusions by failing to consider alternatives. One can do wonderfully choosing among the alternatives one has considered only to discover in horror that one has overlooked an alternative that would have fared much better under the appropriate cost/benefit analysis. And with but a modicum of humility, one should admit that it is more than a little easy to fail to consider all of the critically relevant options when trying to make a difficult decision, particularly when one is under time pressures.

Figuring out what one ought to do is generally extraordinarily difficult. The more variables one needs to take into account, the harder it is to reach the correct conclusion. And when it comes to crucial questions concerning how a state ought to regulate itself, there are a plethora of causally relevant variables. I say all this not to apologize for failing to reach more definitive conclusions on a number of controversies, but as a plea for all of us to exercise a bit more humility when it comes to endorsing the political views we favor and disparaging the political views with which we disagree. In today's political climate, our political foes are often described as immoral or even evil. Or if they are not evil, they are often characterized as stupid, if not crazy. We are obviously right; they are obviously wrong. But in a consequentialist approach to resolving political disagreement, it should be painfully obvious that one should view oneself (and others) as highly fallible. That is not to imply that one shouldn't make judgments and vigorously defend them. Mill was right to suggest that we are most likely to make intellectual progress in the context of vigorous argument—the celebrated marketplace of ideas. But one doesn't need one's vigorous intellectual arguments against the positions of others to lead one to disparage the character or the intellect of one's opposition.

A consequentialist defense of any controversial course of action is almost always controversial in part because the relevant consequences and their probability are so very complex. It would be nice if we could achieve Mill's goal of finding a relatively simple, straightforward principle that we can easily apply to controversies concerning freedom in order to resolve such controversies. Consequentialist principles can be made clear, but their application to the controversies that divide us will almost always involve extraordinarily complex judgments about which reasonable people will often disagree. Such is life.

NOTE

1. Again, this is *not* a defense of a contract theory of rationality or morality. I am not suggesting that we *define* the rational or the moral in terms of what follows from contracts or agreements.

References

Alzola, Miguel. 2013. "Corporate Dystopia: The Ethics of Corporate Political Spend-ing." *Business & Society* 52, no. 3 (September): 388–426.
Anderson, Craig A., Akiko Shibuya, Nobuko Ihori, Edward L. Swing, Brad J. Bush-man, Akira Sakamoto, Hannah R. Rothstein, and Muniba Saleem. 2010. "Violent Video Game Effects on Aggression, Empathy, and Prosocial Behavior in Eastern and Western Countries: A Meta-Analytic Review." *Psychological Bulletin* 136, no. 2 (March): 151–173.
Anderson, Elizabeth. 1993. *Value in Ethics and Economics*. Cambridge, MA: Harvard University Press.
Aquinas, St. Thomas. 2001. *Treatise on Law* (Summa Theologica, *Questions 90–97*): *With a New Introduction by Ralph McInerny, University of Notre Dame*. Washington, D.C.: Gateway Editions, Regnery Publishing, Inc.
Ayer, A. J. 1953. *Language, Truth and Logic*. New York: Dover.
Barnett, Randy E., and Don B. Kates. 1996. "Under Fire: The New Consensus on the Second Amendment." *Emory Law Journal* 45, no. 4: 1139–1260.
———. 1999. "An Originalism for Nonoriginalists." *Loyola Law Review* 45, no. 4: 611–654.
Barry, Keith. 2019. "Higher Speed Limits Led to 36,760 More Deaths, Study Shows." *Consumer Reports*. April 4, 2019. https://www.consumerreports.org/car-safety/high-er-speed-limits-led-to-36760-more-deaths-study-shows/.
Bermudez, Jose Luis. 1996. "The Moral Significance of Birth." *Ethics* 106, no. 2: 378–403.
Bernstein, C'Zar, Timothy Hsiao, and Matt Palumbo. 2015 "The Moral Right to Keep and Bear Firearms." *Public Affairs Quarterly* 29, no. 4: 345–363.
Bentham, Jeremy. 2019. *The Collected Works of Jeremy Bentham*, Volume 2, edited by John Bowring. Edinburgh: William Tait. First published 1843.
Binswanger, Ingrid A., Marc F. Stern, Richard A. Deyo, Patrick J. Heagerty, Allen Cheadle, Joann G. Elmore, and Thomas D. Koepsell. 2007. "Release from Prison: A High Risk of Death for Former Inmates." *New England Journal of Medicine* 356, no. 2 (January): 157–165.
Blocker, Jack Jr. 2006. "Did Prohibition Really Work? Alcohol Prohibition as a Public Health Innovation." *American Journal of Public Health* 96, no. 2.
Bosch, J. C., and I. Lee. 1994. "Wealth Effects of Food and Drug Administration (FDA) Decisions." *Managerial and Decision Economics* 15: 589–600.
Brake, Elizabeth. 2012. *Minimizing Marriage: Marriage, Morality, and the Law*. Oxford: Oxford University Press.
Brandt, Richard. 1979. *A Theory of the Good and the Right*. Oxford: Clarendon Press.
Brink, David. 1992. "Mill's Deliberative Utilitarianism." *Philosophy & Public Affairs* 21, no. 1: 67–103.
———. 2001. "Millian Principles, Freedom of Expression, and Hate Speech." *Legal Theory* 7, no. 2: 119–157.
———. 2013. *Mill's Progressive Principles*. Oxford: Clarendon Press.
Bryan, Amanda E. B., Jeanette Norris, Devon Alisa Abdallah, Cynthia A. Stappenbeck, Diane M. Morrison, Kelly C. Davis, William II. George, Cinnamon L. Danube, and Tina Zawacki. 2016. "Longitudinal Change in Women's Sexual Victimization Expe-riences as a Function of Alcohol Consumption and Sexual Victimization History: A Latent Transition Analysis." *Psychology of Violence* 6, no. 2: 271–279.

Butchvarov, Panayot. 1989. *Skepticism in Ethics*. Bloomington: Indiana University Press.

Calhoun, Cheshire. 2005. "Who's Afraid of Polygamous Marriage: Lessons for Same-Sex Marriage Advocacy from the History of Polygamy." *San Diego Law Review* 42, no. 3: 1023–1042.

Carroll, Sean T., Robert H. Riffenburgh, Timothy A. Roberts, and Elizabeth B. Myhre. 2002. "Tattoos and Body Piercings as Indicators of Adolescent Risk-Taking Behaviors." *Pediatrics* 109: 1021.

Castillo-Manzano, José I., Mercedes Castro-Nuño, Lourdes López-Valpuesta, and Florencia V. Vassallo. 2019. "The Complex Relationship between Increases to Speed Limits and Traffic Fatalities: Evidence from a Meta-Analysis." *Safety Science* 111 (January): 287–297.

Cohen-Almagor, Raphael. 2017. "J. S. Mill's Boundaries of Freedom of Expression: A Critique." *Philosophy* 92, no. 4: 565–596.

Curry, Judith. 2017. "JC in Transition." *Climate, Etc.* January 3, 2017. https://judithcurry.com/2017/01/03/jc-in-transition/.

Dawson, John W., and John J. Seater. 2013. "Federal Regulation and Aggregate Economic Growth." *Journal of Economic Growth*, 18, no. 2: 137–177.

Derschowitz, Alan. 2002. *Why Terrorism Works: Understanding the Threat, Responding to the Challenge*. Yale University Press. Vol. 18, No. 2 (June 2013), pp. 137–177.

DiLorenzo, Thomas J. 2010. "The No-So-Wild, Wild West." *The Independent Review* 15, no. 2 (Fall): 227–239.

Dixon, Nicholas. 2011. "Handguns, Philosophers, and the Right to Self-Defense." *International Journal of Applied Philosophy* 25, no. 2: 151–170.

Donner, Wendy, and Richard Fumerton. 2009. *Mill*. Oxford: Wiley-Blackwell.

Dworkin, Ronald. 1986. *Law's Empire*. Cambridge, MA: Harvard University Press.

Expert Center. Blog, BACtrack. n.d. "DUI Statistics" https://www.bactrack.com/blogs/expert-center/35040645-dui-statistics. Accessed November 11, 2020.

Farley, Melissa. 2004. "'Bad for the Body, Bad for the Heart': Prostitution Harms Women Even if Legalized or Decriminalized." *Violence against Women* 10: 1087–1125.

Feinberg, Joel. 1984. *Harm to Others*. New York: Oxford University Press.

Feldmann, Linda. 2011. "Gay Marriage: Can Obama Stay on Tightrope until 2012 Elections?" *Christian Science Monitor*, June 24, 2011.

Feldman, Richard, and Ted Warfield, eds. 2010. *The Epistemology of Disagreement*. Oxford: Oxford University Press, 2010, 91–111.

Finnis, John. 1980. *Natural Law and Natural Rights*. Oxford: Oxford University Press.

Firth, Roderick. 1952. "Ethical Absolutism and the Ideal Observer." *Philosophical and Phenomenological Research* 12 (March): 317–345.

Fletcher, Joseph. 1966. *Situation Ethics*. Westminster: John Knox Press.

Frankfurt, Harry. 1988. *The Importance of What We Care About*. Cambridge: Cambridge University Press

Fumerton, Richard, and Richard Foley. 1982. "Epistemic Indolence." *Mind* 91: 38–56.

———. 1990a. *Reason and Morality: A Defense of the Egocentric Perspective*. Ithaca, NY: Cornell University Press.

———. 1990b. "Rationality, Act Consequentialism, and Group Action." *Midwest Studies in Philosophy* XV: 296–311.

———. 1996. *Metaepistemology and Skepticism*. Boston: Rowman & Littlefield.

———. 1997. "Relatives and Relativism," with Diane Jeske, *Philosophical Studies* 87, 143–157.

———. 2007. "Open Questions and the Nature of Philosophical Analysis." In *Themes from G. E. Moore*. Eds. Susana Nuccetelli and Gary Seay. Oxford University Press, 227–243.

———. 2009. *The Philosophy of John Stuart Mill*, with Wendy Donner (Mill's Logic, Metaphysics and Epistemology), Blackwell Publishing.

———, and Diane Jeske. 2012 "The Right and the Wrong Way to Think about Rights." In *Readings in Political Philosophy*, eds. Richard Fumerton and Diane Jeske, 311–321.

———. 2013. *Knowledge, Thought and the Case for Dualism.* Cambridge University Press.

———. 2017a. "The Costs and Benefits of Profiling." *Georgetown Journal of Law and Public Policy* 15 (Special Issue): 909–926.

Garrett, Jeremy. 2013. "Marriage and the Well-being of Children." *Pediatrics* 1: 559–563.

Gaus, Gerald. 2001. "What is Deontology? Part Two: Reasons to Act." *The Journal of Value Inquiry* 35: 179–193.

———. 2008. "Reasonable Utility Functions and Playing the Cooperative Way." *Critical Review of International Social and Political Philosophy* 11, no. 2: 215–234. DOI:10.1080/13698230802021371.

Gauthier, David. 1986. *Morals by Agreement.* Oxford: Clarendon Press.

Gert, Bernard. 1967. "Hobbes and Psychological Egoism." *Journal of the History of Ideas* 28: 503–520.

———, ed. 1991. "Introduction to *Man and Citizen (De Homine* and *De Cive*)," by Thomas Hobbes. Indianapolis: Hackett Publishing Company.

Gorelick, David A. 2014. "The Relative Harms of Marijuana and Alcohol." *American Journal of Drug & Alcohol Abuse* 40, no. 6 (November): 419–421.

Gray, Wayne B. 1987. "The Cost of Regulation: OSHA, EPA and the Productivity Slowdown." *The American Economic Review*, 77, no. 5, 998–1006.

Gupta, Amar, and Deth Sao. 2009. "Anti-Offshoring Legislation and United States Federalism: The Constitutionality of Federal and State Measures against Global Outsourcing of Professional Services." *Texas International Law Journal* 44, no. 4: 629–663.

Hampton, Jean. 1999. "The Failure of Hobbes's Social Contract Argument." In *The Social Contract Theorists*, 41–45.

Harman, Gilbert. 1975. "Moral Relativism Defended." *Philosophical Review* 84: 3–22.

———. 1977. *The Nature of Morality.* New York: Oxford University Press.

Hare, R. M. 1965. *Freedom and Reason.* Oxford: Oxford University Press.

Haworth, Alan. 1998. *Free Speech.* London: Routledge.

Hayek, F. A. 1976. *Law, Legislation, and Liberty, Volume 2, The Mirage of Social Justice.* Chicago: University of Chicago Press.

Hobbes, Thomas. 1994. *Leviathan Parts I and II*, edited by Edwin Curley. Indianapolis: Hackett. First published 1668.

Huemer, Michael. 2003. "Is There a Right to Own a Gun?" *Social Theory and Practice* 29, no. 2: 297–324.

———. 2013. *The Problem of Political Authority.* London: Palgrave Macmillan.

Huesmann, L. Rowell. 2010. "Nailing the Coffin Shut on Doubts That Violent Video Games Stimulate Aggression: Comment on Anderson et al)." *Psychological Bulletin* 136, no. 2 (March): 179–181.

Hume, David. 1978. *A Treatise of Human Nature*, edited by L. A. Selby-Bigge. London: Oxford University Press. First published 1888.

———. 1987. "Of the Original Contract." In *David Hume: Essays, Moral, Political, and Literary*, edited by Eugene F. Miller. Indianapolis: Liberty Classics. 465–487.

Hurd, Heidi M. 2001. "Why Liberals Should Hate 'Hate Crime Legislation.'" *Law and Philosophy* 20, no. 2: 215–232.

Husak, Doug. 2007. "Drug Legalization." In *The Blackwell Guide to Medical Ethics*, edited by Leslie P. Francis, Anita Silvers, and Rosamond Rhodes, 238–253. Hoboken: John Wiley & Sons.

Jacobs, James B., and Kimberly Potter. 1998. *Hate Crimes: Criminal Law & Identity Politics.* New York: Oxford University Press.

Jacobson, Daniel. 2000. "Mill on Liberty, Speech, and the Free Society." *Philosophy & Public Affairs* 29, no. 3: 276–309.

Jeske, Diane. 2008. *Rationality and Moral Theory: How Intimacy Generates Reasons.* New York: Routledge.

————, and Richard Fumerton. 2012. "The Right and the Wrong Ways to think about Rights and Wrongs." In *Readings in Political Philosophy*. Edited by Diane Jeske and Richard Fumerton, Broadview Press, 311–321.

Kant, Immanuel. 1993. *Grounding for the Metaphysics of Morals*, translated by J. W. Ellington. Indianapolis: Hackett. First published 1785.

Katz, Leo. 1996. *Ill-Gotten Gains*. Chicago: University of Chicago Press.

Korsgaard, Christine. 1996. *The Sources of Normativity*. New York: Cambridge University Press.

Lamberg, Lynne. 1996. "Prediction of Violence Both Art and Science." *JAMA: Journal of the American Medical Association* 275, no. 22: 1712.

Leiter, Brian. 2016. "The Case against Free Speech." *Sydney Law Review* 38, no. 47: 406–439.

Lessig, Lawrence. 2010. "Democracy after Citizens United." *Boston Review* 35, no. 5: 11–29.

Libertarian National Committee, Inc. 2018. "Platform." *Libertarian: The Party of Principle*. July 2018. https://www.lp.org/platform/.

Locke, John. 1959. *An Essay Concerning Human Understanding*, edited by Alexander Campbell Fraser. New York: Dover. First published 1690.

————. 1993. *Two Treatises of Government*. London: J. M. Dent Publishers. First published 1689.

Lott Jr., John R. 2010. *More Guns Less Crime*. Chicago: University of Chicago Press.

MacKinnon, Catherine. 1989. *Toward a Feminist Theory of the State*. Cambridge, MA: Harvard University Press.

MacDonald, Scott. 1991. "Ultimate Ends in Practical Reasoning." *Philosophical Review* 100, no. 1: 31–66.

Mack, Eric. 2018. *Libertarianism*. Medford, MA: Polity Press.

Mackie, J. L. 1977. *Ethics: Inventing Right and Wrong*. London: Penguin Books.

Martinich, A. P. 1992. *The Two Gods of Leviathan: Thomas Hobbes on Religion and Politics*. Cambridge: Cambridge University Press.

McCullom, Rod. 2007. "Behind the Gay-Friendly Faces. (Cover Story)." *Advocate*, no. 983 (April). 40–45.

McMahan, Jeff. 2007. "Infanticide." *Utilitas* 19: 131–159.

Mertens, Karel, and Morten O. Ravn. 2012. "Empirical Evidence on the Aggregate Effects of Anticipated and Unanticipated U.S. Tax Policy Shocks." *American Economic Journal: Economic Policy* 4, no. 2: 141–181.

Metz, Tamara. 2010. *Untying the Knot: Marriage, the State and the Case for Their Divorce*. Princeton, NJ: Princeton University Press.

Mill, John Stuart. 1956. *On Liberty*. New York: Bobbs-Merrill. First published 1863.

————. 1974. *The Collected Works of John Stuart Mill, Volume VII: A System of Logic Ratiocinative and Inductive*, Books I–III edited by John M. Robson, introduction by R. F. McRae. Toronto: University of Toronto Press; London: Routledge and Kegan Paul. Accessed 11/13/2020. https://oll.libertyfund.org/titles/246. First published 1843.

————. 1979. *Utilitarianism*, edited by George Scher. Indianapolis: Hackett. First published 1861.

Miron, Jeffrey A. 1998. "An Economic Analysis of Alcohol Prohibition." *Journal of Drug Issues* 8, no. 3 (Summer): 741–762.

Moen, Ole Martin. 2014. "Is Prostitution Harmful?" *Journal of Medical Ethics* 40, no. 2: 73–81.

Moore, David W. 2005. "About Half of Americans Reading a Book" *Gallup*. June 3, 2005. https://news.gallup.com/poll/16582/about-half-americans-reading-book.aspx.

Moore, G. E. 1903. *Principia Ethica*. Cambridge: Cambridge University Press.

————. 1912. *Ethics*. London: Oxford University Press.

Nagel, Thomas. 1986. *The View from Nowhere*. London and New York: Oxford University Press.

Nagin, Daniel S., and John V. Pepper, eds. 2012. *Deterrence and the Death Penalty*. https://www.law.upenn.edu/live/files/1529-nagin-full-reportpdf.

Narveson, Jan. 1967. *Morality and Utility*. Baltimore: Johns Hopkins Press.

———. 1988. *The Libertarian Idea*. Philadelphia: Temple University Press.

Nozick, Robert. 1974. *Anarchy, State, and Utopia*. New York: Basic Books.

Paul, L. A. 2014. *Transformative Experience*. Oxford: Oxford University Press.

Perrin, Andrew. 2019. "Who doesn't read books in America?" *Pew Research Center*. September 26, 2019. https://www.pewresearch.org/fact-tank/2019/09/26/who-doesnt-read-books-in-america/.

Plato. 1974. *The Republic*, translated by G. M. A. Grube. Indianapolis: Hackett

———. 2002. *Euthypyro*, translated by G. M. A. Grube. Indianapolis: Hackett.

Pollack, Harold. 2013. "4.8 Million People Uninsured with Drug or Alcohol Problems." *The Incidental Economist: The Health Services Research Blog*, August 17.

Prillaman, Soledad Artiz, and Kenneth J. Meier. 2014. "Taxes, Incentives, and Economic Growth: Assessing the Impact of Pro-business Taxes on the U.S. State Economies." *The Journal of Politics* 76, no. 2: 364–379.

Prichard, H. A. 1912. "Does Moral Philosophy Rest on a Mistake?" *Mind* 21: 487–499.

Public Policy Research Portal. https://whatweknow.inequality.cornell.edu/topics/lgbt-equality/what-does-the-scholarly-research-say-about-the-wellbeing-of-children-with-gay-or-lesbian-parents/.

Rawls, John. 1955. "Two Concepts of Rules." *Philosophical Review* 64: 3–32.

———. 1964. "Legal Obligation and the Duty of Fair Play." In *Law and Philosophy*, edited by S. Hook. New York: New York University Press.

———. 2005. *Political Liberalism*, second edition. New York: Columbia University Press.

Reed, Elizabeth, Hortensia Amaro, Atsushi Matsumoto, and Debra Kaysen. 2009. "The Relation Between Impersonal Violence and Substance Use among a Sample of University Students: Examination of the Role of Victim and Perpetrator Substance Use." *Addictive Behaviors* 34, no. 3: 316–318.

Regan, Donald. 1980. *Utilitarianism and Co-operation*. Oxford: Clarendon Press.

Rhodes, Rosamond. 1992. "Hobbes's unReasonable Fool." *Southern Journal of Philosophy* 30, no. 2: 93–102.

———. 2002. "Obligation and Assent in Hobbes's Moral Philosophy." *Hobbes Studies* 15, no. 1: 45–67.

Rousseau, Jean-Jacques. 1967. *The Social Contract*, translated by Maurice Cranston. New York: Penguin. First published 1762.

Ross, W. D. 1988. *The Right and the Good*. Indianapolis, IN: Hackett. First published 1930.

Russell, Daniel C. (ed.). 2013. *The Cambridge Companion to Virtue Ethics*, Cambridge: Cambridge University Press.

Samuelson, Paul. 1954. "The Pure Theory of Public Expenditure." *Review of Economics and Statistics* 36: 387–389.

Schulzke, Marcus. 2016. "The Social Benefits of Protecting Hate Speech and Exposing Sources of Prejudice." *Res Publica* 22: 225–242.

Sher, George. 2003. "On the Decriminalization of Drugs." *Criminal Justice Ethics* 22, no. 1: 30–33.

Skinner, B. J. 2002. "Medicare, the Medical Brain Drain and Human Resource Shortages in Health Care." *Atlantic Institute for Market Studies*.

Sidgwick, Henry. 1981 *The Methods of Ethics*. Indianapolis: Hackett. First published 1874.

Smart, J. J. C. 1956. "Extreme and Restricted Utilitarianism." *Philosophical Quarterly* 6: 344–354.

Smith, Angela. 2015. "Responsibility as Answerability." *Inquiry* 58, no. 2: 99–126.

Singer, Peter. 1972. "Famine Affluence, and Morality." *Philosophy and Public Affairs* 1, no. 1: 229–243.

Sowell, Thomas. 2012. "'Trickle Down' Theory and 'Tax Cuts for the Rich'." Stanford, CA: Hoover Institution Press.

Steiker, Carol S. 1999. "Punishing Hateful Motives: Old Wine in a New Bottle Revives Calls for Prohibition." *Michigan Law Review* 97, no. 6: 1857–1873.

Stitch, Steven. 1990. *The Fragmentation of Reason*. Cambridge, MA: MIT Press.

Sue, Derald Wing. 2010. *Microaggressions in Everyday Life: Race, Gender and Sexual Orientation*. NJ: Wiley.

Tax Foundation, https://files.taxfoundation.org/legacy/docs/fed_individual_rate_history_nominal.pdf.

Taylor, A. E. 1938. "The Ethical Doctrine of Hobbes." *Philosophy* 13 (52): 406–424.

Thomson, Judy Jarvis. 1971. "A Defense of Abortion." *Philosophy and Public Affairs* 1, no. 1: 47–66.

U.S. Department of Treasury: Office of Public Relations. 2004. "Fact Sheet: Who Pays the Most Individual Income Taxes?" U.S. Department of Treasury: Office of Public Relations. April, https://www.treasury.gov/press-center/press-releases/pages/js1287.aspx.

U.S. Environmental Protection Agency. n.d. "EPA's Budget and Spending." Accessed November 12, 2020. https://www.epa.gov/planandbudget/budget.

U.S. General Accounting Office. 2004. "Defense of Marriage Act: Update to Prior Report." US GAO-04-353R Defense of Marriage Act. January 23, 2004. https://www.gao.gov/new.items/d04353r.pdf.

Vallentyne, Peter. 2007. "Libertarianism and the State." *Social Philosophy and Policy* 24: 187–205.

Van Den Haag, Ernest. 2010. "On Deterrence and the Death Penalty." In *Contemporary Moral Arguments*, edited by Lewis Vaughn. New York: Oxford University Press.

Van Zee, Art. 2009. "The Promotion and Marketing of OxyContin: Commercial Triumph, Public Health Tragedy." *American Journal of Public Health* 99, no. 2: 221–227.

Warrender, Howard. 1957. *The Political Philosophy of Hobbes: His Theory of Obligation*. London: Clarendon Press.

Waluchow, W. J. 2012. "Constitutional Interpretation." In *The Routledge Companion to Philosophy of Law* edited by Marmor Andrei, 417–433. New York: Routledge.

Weiss, Susan R. B., and Eric M. Wargo. 2017. "Commentary: Navigating the Complexities of Marijuana." *Preventive Medicine* 104 (November): 10–12.

Wyatt, Wendy. 2016. "The Ethics of Trigger Warnings." *Teaching Ethics* 16, no. 1: 17–35. doi:10.5840/tej201632427.

Zamir, Ewal and Barrak Medina. 2010. *Law, Economics and Morality*. Oxford: Oxford University Press.

Index

About the Author

Richard Fumerton is the F. Wendell Miller Professor of Philosophy at the University of Iowa. He has also published books and articles in metaphysics, philosophy of mind, philosophy of science, value theory, and philosophy of law. He is the author of *Metaphysical and Epistemological Problems of Perception* (1985), *Reason and Morality: A Defense of the Egocentric Perspective* (1990), *Metaepistemology and Skepticism* (1996), *Realism and the Correspondence Theory of Truth* (2002), *Epistemology* (2006), *Mill* (co-authored with Wendy Donner; 2009), and *Knowledge, Thought and the Case for Dualism* (2013). With Diane Jeske, he has also edited *Philosophy through Film* (2009) and *An Introduction to Political Philosophy* (2012).